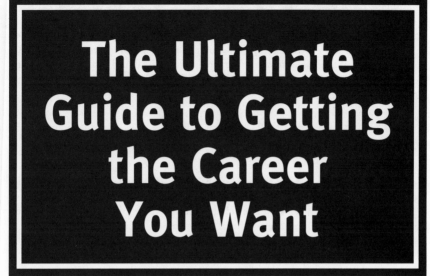

The Ultimate Guide to Getting the Career You Want

And What to Do Once You Have It

Karen O. Dowd, Ph.D.

Sherrie Gong Taguchi

McGraw-Hill

New York   Chicago   San Francisco
Lisbon   London   Madrid   Mexico City
Milan   New Delhi   San Juan   Seoul
Singapore   Sydney   Toronto

293280

The *McGraw·Hill* Companies

1 2 3 4 5 6 7 8 9 0   AGM/AGM   0 9 8 7 6 5 4 3

ISBN #0-07-140293-4

McGraw-Hill books are available at special quantity discounts to use as premiums and sales promotions, or for use in corporate training programs. For more information, please write to the Director of Special Sales, Professional Publishing, McGraw-Hill, Two Penn Plaza, New York, NY 10121-2298. Or contact your local bookstore.

This book is printed on recycled, acid-free paper containing a minimum of 50% recycled, de-inked fiber.

Library of Congress Cataloging-in-Publication Data

Dowd, Karen O.
    The ultimate guide to getting the career you want : and what to do once you have it / Karen O. Dowd and Sherrie Gong Taguchi.
        p. cm.
Includes bibliographical references and index.
    ISBN 0-07-140293-4 (pbk. : alk. paper)
    1. Career changes. 2. Vocational guidance. 3. Career development. 4. Self-realization. I. Taguchi, Sherrie Gong, 1961-II. Title.

HF5384.D69 2004
650.14—dc21   2003013299

Dedication

To my husband, Mark and Mom, Magen. My work and life are all the more joyful and fulfilling because of you.
—Sherrie Gong Taguchi

To Rosemary Doherty: teacher, mentor, role model, and friend. And to Tom, always.
—Karen O. Dowd

Table of Contents

Acknowledgments

Literally hundreds of people were involved in bringing this book to life, and we owe a debt of gratitude to every one of them. To Nancy Hancock, our editor at McGraw-Hill, whose wisdom, input, and shepherding of our project have been invaluable, and to Andy Winston, senior editor at McGraw-Hill/Irwin, and his staff for initially championing the book. Meg Leder, you have been wonderful, energizing, providing critical assistance for each milestone in our collaboration. Daina Penikas and Alice Manning, your expertise and copyediting suggestions have added so much to our book.

To the thousands of executives, managers, clients, students, and colleagues with whom we have worked, in industry and in academia, our work has been enriched because of you. To the remarkable individuals profiled in case studies and the numerous visionary executives who share their insights throughout the book, our gratitude for your generosity in sharing your lessons learned.

We acknowledge the organizations represented or contributing: Alameda County Social Services; Amazon.com; AOL—America Online; Andersen Consulting; Autodesk; Bank of America; Burger King; Carnation; Case Western, Chan CPA and Co.; Coca Cola, Inc.; Columbia Business School; Darden Graduate School of Business, University of Virginia; Dayton Hudson Corporation; Deloitte Consulting; Dole Packaged Foods; Dot Media Studios, Duke University, Fuqua School of Business; EDS; the Empower Group; Federated; General Electric; Field Glass; Greer & Co., LLC; Harvard University; Idea Works; Intel Corporation; International MBA Placement Directors Group; ITOCHU International Inc.; James Madison University; Jim C. Collins, Inc.; KPCB Venture Capital (Kleiner Perkins Caufield and Byers Venture Capital); London Business School; LVMH (Louis Vuitton Moet Hennessey); Marketocracy and the Masters 100 Mutual Fund; McGraw-Hill; McKinsey and Co.; Metro-Goldwyn-Mayer/United Artists; National Association of Colleges and Employers (NACE); New York City Partnership and Chamber of Commerce; NBA Asia, Nestle; NextPart; North Star; Northwestern University; Kellogg Graduate School

ix

of Management; Organic, Inc.; Russell Reynolds Executive Search; Saint Mary's College; SMU; Servidyne Systems; Society of Human Resource Management (SHRM); SixContinents Hotels/Latin America; Stanford University Graduate School of Business; Starwood Hotels and Resorts; Stauffacher Life Science, Inc.; Therapy Links, Inc.; Thunderbird; University of California; University of Chicago Graduate School of Business; University of Denver; University of Illinois; University of Nebraska; University of Pennsylvania—Wharton; Virginia Metalcrafters; WetFeet, Inc.; Xerox Corporation; and Yahoo!

Special thanks to Keith Wilson of Openwave Systems, Inc., for his creativity and expertise on our figures' design; to Agnes Le, Stanford MBA class of 2000, for her amazing research assistance and illustrations; to Jon Briscoe and Tim Hall for some of the questions used in our case interview protocol; to Dave Lazas for his research assistance; and to Bonnie Goebel for her help with our manuscript preparation across continents. Our appreciation to experts: John Celona, Diana Chan, and Ken Kam for their valuable contributions on values-based decision-making, budgeting tools and templates, and advice on developing a financial plan, respectively.

There are many colleagues who have helped us to clarify our thoughts and supported us actively in our own careers. It is impossible to name them all. Special thanks to A. Michael Spence for being an inspiring example on what it takes to be a great leader and manager, to Jim Collins who encourages his students to know our purpose and to follow our passion; and to Dick Bolles, and Howard Figler, who shaped our early views on how to best work with individuals who are exploring their lives and careers.

Part 1

Learn from Your Past

This book is based on the premise that in order to make life-affirming, career-enhancing, positive decisions we must learn from our past, identify what's important to us in the present, envision the future, and be ready to monitor how we are doing and what's next.

We begin Part One of gaining career clarity: learning from your past. In this section you will focus primarily on your previous experiences, both positive and negative, and on the learnings you have achieved through this experience. Like all good things, understanding your past and how it shapes your present and future takes time! But we guarantee that if you take the time to complete the self-assessment exercises presented in Principle 1, and to reflect on the ways in which you can learn from your experience in Principle 2, you will be in a stronger position to make important decisions about where your life and career are headed next.

Principle 1

Know Yourself

All serious daring starts from within.

—EUDORA WELTY[1]

Getting Clear about Your Career

Are you wondering about what's next for you? Are you contemplating making an important career or life change? Are you content with your present situation but wondering how to decide your future direction? Have your personal circumstances changed, so that whether you want to or not, you *have* to make a change? Regardless of your situation, the process of getting clear about the direction of your career and your life starts with some serious self-reflection—some foundational "inner work." Yes, it would be easier to simply pay a career consultant to tell you "what you should be when you grow up." But most, if not all, reputable career coaches won't tell you what to do with your life, even if they think they know what you should be doing with it. Instead, most of them will tell you how important it is for you to conduct a series of self-assessments, in order to uncover the answers you're seeking, on your own.

The reason for this is that no two people are alike. No two career situations or life decisions are the same. You are unique. You have a set of values, goals, interests, skills, abilities, and personal circumstances that differ from those of your colleagues, friends, coworkers, and relatives. Yes, it would be easier if someone simply told you what to do. But it's infinitely more gratifying to figure it out for yourself. Doing so does require help from oth-

3

ers, of course, but nonetheless, self-assessment is generally a process that starts from within.

In our work, our own careers, and our lives, we have found self-assessment to be immensely rewarding and illuminating. In this principle, we discuss what self-assessment is, why it's important, and the types of questions you need to explore through self-assessment. We provide a case example of two people who have benefited from ongoing self-assessment. We also give you a variety of original self-assessment exercises that you can use to understand yourself—your values, preferences, interests, and skills/competencies. This will serve as a strong foundation that you can use to clarify what's important to you as you consider your future career and life decisions.

What's Next in Your Life or Career?

Nearly everyone today is asking, "What's next for me—in my career and in my life?" There are many reasons for this: The up-and-down economy, the war, the aftershock of the tragic events of September 11, 2001, the demise of previously well-respected companies, and the recent turmoil of the dot-coms' rapid success and even more rapid failure have caused many people to sit up and think about what they're doing with their lives. Changing personal circumstances, heightened expectations in society in general, technology boom/bust cycles, and a roller-coaster stock market make it difficult for anyone to commit comfortably to a career or life direction without feeling at least somewhat anxious and uncertain.

The best and most enduring career decisions are those that are made after you have taken the time to consider your motivation, your resources, your challenges, your opportunities. Anyone can make a change impulsively, and a few lucky souls make spontaneous decisions that stick. However, most career and life decisions are important enough to be undertaken only after a thorough self-assessment has been conducted. Why are you contemplating a change now? What are you hoping to achieve? Who else will be affected by the change you're considering? What are the potential risks and rewards of making a change now? How can you evaluate the various options that are available to you? What resources (time, money, and emotional support) will be necessary as you make the decision and implement the change? These are just some of the questions that are best explored prior to making a commitment to a new career or life direction.

What Is Self-Assessment?

Self-assessment is a systematic process of evaluating your (and, if relevant, your significant other's) current and preferred situations, motives and objectives, opportunities and challenges, and obstacles and resources. It helps you to identify your strengths and limitations, your needs and preferences, your values and goals, your skills and competencies, and to link these to the future career and life decisions that you're considering. Self-assessment is a crucial first step in any personal change. Are you

- A recent college graduate who's wondering if "this is all there is"?
- Satisfied with your present job and interested in advancing within your organization?
- Concerned about sustaining a career during a difficult economy?
- Having or adopting a child and wondering how your career will fit with your new situation?
- Recently widowed or divorced and needing to start a new principle in your life?
- Burned out from your successful but all-consuming job and wondering if there's a way to continue making money but also gaining personal satisfaction, meaning, or balance in your life?
- Beginning to think about relocating or retiring?
- In mid-career and wondering whether you should "stay the course" or branch out now, while you still can?
- Newly coupled and wondering how to make life decisions with a significant other?
- Considering a change as a result of a significant change in your health?
- Caring for an aging parent and looking for a way to have more time for a personal life in addition to work?

- Succeeding in your chosen profession but wondering whether "I'm doing what I'm supposed to be doing with my life"?
- Still searching for your "dream"?

The Value of Self-Assessment

Regardless of your reason for contemplating a personal or career change, the process you should use and the questions you should ask are similar. It's worth taking the time to inventory your current situation and your desired outcomes before you begin to make and implement new plans. Self-assessment helps you to

- Identify what you're most drawn to at this time and why, and to define what's important to you now so that you can make a change that is reflective of your "true" self.
- Feel "centered" by understanding your past experiences and your current situation, and by identifying what you'd like to achieve by making a change.
- Discover your core strengths—the qualities you have to offer in any personal or work-related situation that benefit others and improve any group or organization of which you are a part.
- Discard old behaviors and principles that no longer work for you, and substitute new principles and behaviors that are more in line with your current objectives.
- Figure out options that you might not have otherwise uncovered or considered.
- Both dream and stay grounded in reality, being idealistic as well as realistic when setting new goals for yourself.
- Communicate positively and constructively with those who are important to you—your spouse, partner, friends, and family—about your preferences and about how a change that you're contemplating may affect these people.
- Do a reality check—give yourself feedback, and solicit feedback from others that will help you to develop a solid action plan.

- Think things through rather than acting too quickly.
- Develop a systematic process that can be used at any time in the future as you contemplate personal and career changes.

Identifying Your Dreams

What are you hoping to accomplish in the next phase of your life? Or if that's too forward-looking, what are you hoping to accomplish in the next 5 years? In the next 10 years? One of the best ways to uncover the answer is to complete a written assessment of your current and preferred situations. Writing down your thoughts makes them real. Even more important, the writing process itself helps you to think things through in a rational way. It helps you to bring to the surface issues that need to be taken into consideration and to identify patterns that can help you understand your motivations and your ways of behaving. Completing the exercises in this principle will take time. This is something you need to do if you're serious about evaluating your current situation and making action plans to help you get what you want. Before you conduct research, share your thoughts with your partner, network with colleagues, visit potential places, or apply for a job, you need to get a handle on where you're coming from.

Think of it as starting your own business, only *you're* the "business": YOU, Inc. Principle 9 introduces a marketing 5P framework for developing a job search or career change plan, with you as your "business." When one is starting a business, one usually conducts market research, develops a business plan, seeks out investors, and develops strategic and operational plans. Self-assessment is a way for you to understand your own attributes, the benefits of what you have to offer, and your positioning in the career marketplace; to take stock of your challenges and opportunities; and to create plans that can be acted upon. The exercises will make you think, are fun to answer, and will lay the groundwork for identifying what's next for you.

Making Personal Changes

Change is here to stay. Many of us are coming to realize that the only prediction one can make about one's life and career is that they will change.

This means that, like it or not, one of the major roles we play in our lives is that of *personal change agent.* To be an effective change agent, it is important for you to understand

- The current reality in which you find yourself
- Your preferred situation
- The factors that are driving you to make a change
- The obstacles you face in making the desired change
- The resources you have (or need) to make the change
- The impact the change will have on others in your life
- The best way to go about making the change

Principle 3 further discusses and offers strategies for dealing with change and uncertainty related to risk and decision making in career clarity and choices.

Like most good things in life, self-assessment takes time and commitment, but the outcome is almost always well worth it. For a look at how this works in "real life," consider the case of Doug and Brigitte Fletcher, a thirty-something couple who made a conscious move early in their marriage from the East Coast to Montana to start new careers and a new life with their growing family.

Case Study: Doug and Brigitte Fletcher—from East Coast Working Professionals to Montana Entrepreneurs Who Know Themselves and What's Important

"I can't remember who said this, but this quote is the motto of my life: 'You can have anything, but you can't have everything.' You've got to decide what is important to you—and be willing to accept the real trade-offs in life that come with your choices." Doug was reflecting on some of the career decisions that he and his wife, Brigitte, have made over the past 14 years. When they were in their late twenties, Doug, a management consultant for a prestigious strategy consulting firm, and Brigitte, who had worked in various art- and design-related jobs throughout their marriage, acted on their belief that there's more to life than just making money.

Doug had a degree in engineering, had worked at General Electric after college, had an MBA from the University of Virginia's Darden Graduate School of Business, and was doing well at EDS, the consulting firm at which he worked. "We thought a lot about the meaning and purpose of money. For us, we have to have work that we enjoy. We have to look forward to getting up in the morning. Yes, it's important to be financially successful. But not at the expense of other things in our life. We want to be remembered as successful businesspeople, caring and involved parents, contributors to the community, and good friends to others. We want to create a life that's worth living. This balance defines who we are."

That's a tall order. This young couple, who had a good but tradition-bound life going for them, decided to throw in the towel and start over. This wasn't an impulsive move: "Brigitte and I are constantly planning ahead—planning for our business, our family, our home, retirement, everything." Twice in their young marriage they took long breaks to travel the country. Both after college and after graduate school, they explored parts of the country with which they weren't familiar. They researched small college towns in certain locations, identified after starting with a blank sheet of paper that said on the top, "Potential Places to Live." They identified their criteria for the type of place in which they wanted to live—population, outdoor activities, economy, cultural opportunities, airports, and so on—and they visited literally dozens of locations before ultimately deciding on Montana.

During this time, Doug and Brigitte were living beneath their means—saving as much money as they could while contemplating where they wanted to settle and how they wanted to live their lives. They also had many, many discussions about where they were heading and how they would get there. "I'm a huge fan of writing down your dreams, aspirations, plans, goals, progress, and so on," Doug stated. "Writing things down makes them more real. For at least 10 years I've made it a habit to write down my 'big-picture' goals and what I want to accomplish. This process makes you think about what's important and helps you figure out how to get there. Every year now, around New Year's Day, I open up my journal and reflect on the previous year. Have I made progress toward our goals? If not, why not? Have our priorities changed? This journal is not just about work stuff. It also encompasses family and the personal, financial, community service, and spiritual areas of my life. This self-assessment process has been instrumental in getting us to where we are today."

These steps—the planning, traveling, research, saving money, and continuous self-assessment—gave Doug and Brigitte the experience, information, and financial resources they needed when they eventually set their sights on Montana as a place that they could move to, one where they could raise a family and begin a business venture. Doug and Brigitte now own and operate two successful business ventures in Montana. Their lifestyle affords Doug the opportunity to live a balanced life consisting of moderate work hours (rather than the 100+-hour workweeks of consulting), working out, spending time with his children, fishing, and contemplating new ways to improve their businesses. Even better, Doug and Brigitte chose a lifestyle that gives Brigitte the chance she wanted to be a stay-at-home mom until their two children are in grade school.

Did their move have consequences? Of course. You probably won't see the latest-model automobile in their driveway, and living far from family must be a sacrifice at times. But you'll hear no complaints from the Fletchers, who are living the life they envisioned for themselves years before they brought it to fruition. As Doug says, "Everything we do is a step toward our long-range plans. The short-term sacrifices don't really seem like sacrifices—they're simply choices. Most people would say that Brigitte and I took a big risk in leaving successful careers and moving to Montana. However, we don't see it that way. To us, a bigger risk would have been to not pursue our dreams, and one day wake up in a life that wasn't where we wanted to be. I would rather have pursued our dreams and failed than not to have pursued them."

As we said before, change is inevitable. The trick is reacting to unplanned changes in such a way that the change results in something positive, even if not in what was planned. The other trick is to try to create change before it creates you. As was made clear in Doug and Brigitte's story, it's all right to be spontaneous, and it's certainly all right to lead a life that one considers meaningful and even enjoyable. More times than not, this means identifying your goals, staying current with your changing personal and professional circumstances, and making plans for how you want to lead your life. It's rare for someone to lead a life that doesn't change endlessly. Plans that have been made can change in an instant. Anyone who has lost a loved one unexpectedly, who has been left by a mate, who has lost a job, or who has failed in a business venture knows the pain that can come when plans go awry. The key is to make plans and then to be ready emotionally and financially to withstand and overcome the inevitable variances that may come along.

A natural question might be, "But if plans can go wrong, why make them?" This is where the classic greeting-card line comes in handy: "If you don't know where you're going, you'll end up somewhere else." The fact is that just because plans can be interfered with doesn't mean that you shouldn't make them. In business, project managers know what happens to the best-laid plans. You know it too—the best-laid plans can go wrong. Seldom does a plan play out exactly as, well, planned. But project managers also know that the plans that they make in advance will hold about 80 percent of the time. That leaves them with the energy to deal with the other 20 percent, the part that was unexpected. The moral of the story here is to have plans, think them through, and write them down, as Doug and Brigitte do. There's one modification, though: Write them in pencil (or on a computer), so that changes can be made easily!

Self-Assessment Exercises

Assessing your career and life situation on an ongoing basis is the foundation for effective decision making. Whether you are trying to decide what job to take next, where to live, whether to seek a promotion, what career field to pursue, whether to retire, or whether to start all over, assessing your current and preferred situation is the place to start. Following are some exercises that help you do just that. Other exercises are interspersed throughout the principles in this book. These are exercises that we have used in our roles as professional career coaches to thousands of MBA students, undergraduate students, alumni, working managers, and corporate clients. They are grouped into three categories: learning from your past, defining what's important to you now, and envisioning your future (see Figure 1-1). You

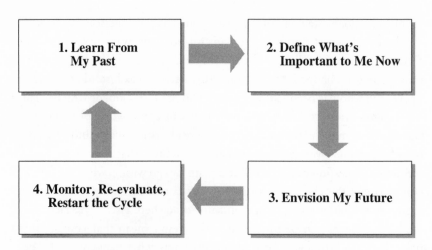

Figure 1-1   Self-Assessment Framework

can complete them in any order you wish, and you should complete only the ones that are relevant to you at this time. One suggestion: If you will be making a decision that affects a significant other, have him or her complete the exercises as well and discuss them. Doing so will provide an excellent framework for a joint discussion about identifying what's next for both of you.

We are not suggesting that you complete every exercise in this principle. Our purpose is to provide a variety of exercises for you to choose from and reflect on over time, whether in focused sessions or a little bit whenever you can.

I. Learning from Your Past[2]

In times of change, it's important for you to understand your current motivation and needs and how these may be affected by your past. An important step before making a significant life change is to review your life experiences to date, understanding your accomplishments and mis-steps thoroughly, analyzing your experience to discover patterns and trends, and bringing your learnings from the past to bear on the choices you have and the decisions you are making in the present.

Exercise: In-Depth Experience Review

1. List every job title (paid and unpaid), volunteer or leadership position, and/or significant life role you've ever held. Starting with the present, work your way in reverse chronological order all the way back as far as you can—to the first job you can remember, whether it be the lemonade stand you created in grade school or the baby-sitting or waitperson work you did in high school.

2. For each position, list the following (where relevant):
   a. Dates
   b. Type of organization
   c. How you obtained the position
   d. Why you accepted the position
   e. Name(s) of person(s) instrumental in your learning about or accepting the position (if relevant)
   f. Industry, function, and location
   g. Major tasks and responsibilities
   h. Beginning and ending salary, bonus, perks
   i. Reason(s) for leaving
   j. Other comments/thoughts about this position or role

3. Analyze your experience for patterns that may be relevant as you consider your next career or life direction. The following questions can aid you in this exploration:
   a. What are some recent life or career changes that you've made, and what motivated these changes (e.g., money, dissatisfaction, opportunity, or age)? How did you make these decisions (e.g., with help from others, impulsively, or after careful research)? What information/resources have you used when you have been faced with a change in your life or your career (friends, newspapers, professional associations, the Internet, or other sources)? In each case, how satisfied were you with the outcome, and why?
   b. Who are the two to three most significant people in your life? Who has influenced you (positively or negatively)? Who has served as a mentor or role model for you? Who has made an impact on the decisions you've made in life so far?

c. What are your two to three core strengths (e.g., optimism, follow-through, integrity)? What are the qualities that your friends or coworkers know they can always count on you to have or to demonstrate?

d. What are your core skills and attributes—things that you enjoy doing and do well (e.g., get along with others, sales, computers, business start-ups)?

e. What are two or three key behaviors (e.g., work ethic) and attitudes (e.g., helpful to others) that may have helped your career and your life progress over the years? What are two or three key behaviors (e.g., lack of emotional control) or attitudes (e.g., perceived arrogance) that may have hindered your career or life progress over the years?

f. In which experiences were you able to make a contribution or have some impact? In what ways did your presence make a difference?

g. Which situations were difficult for you? How did you handle them? What did you learn from them? What, if anything, did you change about yourself as a result of these experiences?

h. What were some of your major sources of satisfaction and some of your major frustrations?

i. What do you value most (for example, having money, wisdom, world peace, accomplishment, freedom, happiness, excitement)?

j. In which experiences was the perceived fit between what you needed from the situation (your values) and what it provided you with (rewards) the greatest, and why?

k. What have been some of your primary motivators (e.g., money, prestige, skill building)?

l. What are three to five things that you have accomplished and you feel good about? (These can be minor or major, personal or professional. Examples are becoming the best in your field, overcoming a personal problem, improving a relationship with a family member, getting your company out of financial peril, getting through a difficult childhood experience, or doing your best in a marathon.)

m. What have you learned so far about managing your life and career? What are some of the lessons learned that you would like to take into consideration as you explore your "what's next?" (Examples could be the importance of not overworking, the need to obtain honest feedback from others, and the need to be more planful.)

n. If you had it to do all over again, what would you do differently? (Don't spend too much time crying over spilt milk here, but reflecting a bit on changes that you've made and what you've learned from your experiences does help.)

o. What are some special issues you've had to face in your career to date (e.g., racial discrimination, glass ceiling, nonresident status, sexual orientation, religion, economic background, language, lack of education, physical challenge)? How have these issues hindered your advancement, your attainment of your goals, or the choices you have had available? How have they strengthened you as a person in terms of enhancing your ability to strive for and attain success in your life and/or your career?

p. What personal or family issues have affected your career and life decisions? How have you handled changing personal circumstances in your life (e.g., loss of a loved one, divorce, changing health, caring for an elderly relative or ill partner) to date? How has this affected your career choices and your success in the past?

Your Ideal Self

At your core, you have an understanding of who and what you are, of what's important to you, and of the person you are when you are at your most "natural," and that the best job or personal situation is the one that allows you to be most like your true self. This can be referred to as your ideal or "authentic" self.

Sometimes you may lose sight of who you really are, at work and/or in your personal life. You may be so plateaued or stuck in a situation that it becomes difficult for you to think about your career in a strategic and organized way. When this happens, it's best to stop the noise and activity of your day-to-day life and take the time to reflect on some of the highlights you've experienced in your life and career. By focusing on some of your best, or peak, moments, you can get in touch with those elements that represent who you truly are. Sometimes focusing more intuitively (using your gut instincts), rather than analytically, on your career and your life helps to crystallize your perception of your best qualities and how these might be applied in the future.

Reflecting on your past experiences, personal and professional, think of times when you felt, even briefly, that you were "at your best":

- Things were going well; you felt that you were on top of things or in control.
- You felt that you were making a connection, making things happen, or making an impact on those around you.
- You enjoyed the situation.
- You felt that you and your natural talents were valued, recognized, and appreciated.
- You didn't feel under pressure to perform—what you were doing well was coming to you naturally.

To help you find your "ideal self," answer the following questions:

1. What skills were you using and enjoying (e.g., persuading others, influencing others, helping people to look differently at a situation)?
2. What happened as a result of what you were doing (e.g., someone bought what you were selling, a policy was changed, a friend made a personal change as a result of your advice)?
3. What natural qualities (e.g., enthusiasm, optimism, interpersonal strength) were you exercising during these situations?
4. What was motivating you during these situations (e.g., a need to be recognized, autonomy, creating something new)?
5. Based on these "peak" experiences, what are:
   - Your core skills

- Your primary motivation
- Your natural abilities
- Your ideal work environment or life situation needs

Exercise: An Accomplishments Self-Review

In reflecting on your past experience, it is useful to focus less on your mistakes (you're human—everyone makes them!) and more on your accomplishments or achievements. Through looking at the positive events in your life, you can identify those qualities on which you'd like to focus in the future. What are some of your significant accomplishments or achievements? These do not have to be work-related, and they need not be significant to anyone but you. They do need to meet four criteria:

- You enjoyed both the results of the accomplishment and the process of making it happen.
- You did it well.
- You were directly responsible for it.
- You're proud of it.

To help you understand your achievements, list three to five personal or professional accomplishments (e.g., getting into school, helping a friend solve a personal problem, acquiring a start-up company; these can be taken from the previous exercises). Then answer the following questions:

- Which key skills did you use to attain your accomplishments?
- What did you enjoy most about these accomplishments?
- What enabled you to achieve these accomplishments—your skills, personality, drive, values, and interests?

Exercise: Defining Your Core and Developable Skills

Skill Identification[3]

In times of change, it is useful to reflect on the skills at which you've become proficient and on the skills you most enjoy using. As your life progresses, you will usually find that your skills fall into several categories (see Figure 1-2):

- Skills that you excel at and also enjoy using (your core skills)
- Skills that you excel at but *honestly* don't enjoy using (skills to avoid)
- Skills that you don't excel at currently but would like to improve (your "developable" skills)
- Skills that you don't and never will excel at, and that you aren't interested in enhancing (skills to avoid)

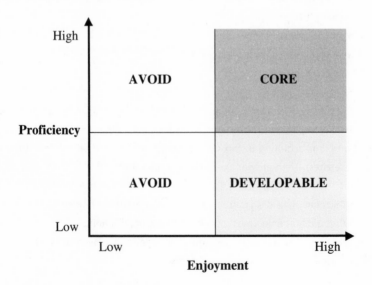

Figure 1-2   My Core and Developable Skills

To help you reflect on your skills, answer the following questions. Refer to the earlier exercises for inspiration.

- What are your core skills—the ones you want to exercise in your current or next situation?
- What are your developable skills—the skills you'd like to learn about and develop in your current or next situation?
- What are the skills you wish to avoid using in your next situation?

Exercise: Identifying Your Core Competencies

What are the characteristics of a good waiter or waitress?[4] He or she will take your order promptly, get the order right, and bring the bill at the end of the meal. What are the characteristics of an *outstanding* waiter or waitress? He or she will do all of these things, but in a way that is exemplary. He or she will listen attentively as you and your party order, make subtle suggestions that will enhance the dining experience, and anticipate your and your party's needs during the meal, being present, yet not interfering with the conversation. Can a waitperson be trained to be outstanding rather than merely good? There's an ongoing debate about this. Some experts believe that the answer is no. They believe that individuals have core characteristics that are natural and innate, and that consistently appear in whatever job or task the individual is engaged in. Others, such as David McClelland,[5] believe that some characteristics, particularly achievement motivation, can be taught, or at least encouraged in employees. Over the years, companies have used a concept based on this research called *competency modeling.* Widely used in industry today, competency modeling helps organizations to identify and develop top talent.

In competency modeling, an organization conducts research on its top performers in a variety of job categories and levels. Common patterns and themes are developed and tested, and these serve as the basis for identifying a set of characteristics that exemplify top performance within the organization. A framework or model is developed that describes and defines several core competencies valued by the organization. This model then serves as the starting point for attracting, recruiting, selecting, orienting, training, developing, promoting, and retaining top performers who can serve as a leadership pipeline for the organization. Some common core competencies found in "exemplars"—top performers in organizations—are listed here. Space is left for you to add a few of your own that relate to your profession.

Sample Core Competencies

Intellectual curiosity	Optimism
Ability to handle ambiguity	Emotional control
Strong customer focus	Competitive instinct
Driver of change	Business acumen
Judgment about people and situations	Stewardship/quality standards
Independent thinker	Organizational savvy
Strategic mindset	Active listener
Conceptual thinker	_____
_____	_____

Using this concept can help you to identify the core qualities and strengths that you bring to any job or task. Are you generally known for exercising good judgment? For being the life of the party? For helping others when they are in crisis? For carrying a difficult project through to completion when others shy away from the same project?

1. To help you identify your own core competencies, answer the following questions. Use this information to help you sort out your natural strengths. Identifying your core competencies can help you to ensure that your next situation plays to these strengths.

2. Select five work-related situations in which you've been involved.

3. For each of the five, write a detailed description of the situation, focusing on the following topics:

- What was the main task involved?
- Who were the key players? What issues were involved?
- What was your role? What did you do, and why? What was motivating you to act in the way you did? (Be specific here, using action verbs to describe your involvement.)

- How did you assess the situation and what was needed in that situation? How did you make decisions?
- What were your thought processes during and immediately after the experience?
- What (if any) problems arose? How did you contribute to solving these problem(s)?
- What skills did you use in the situation?
- How did you react to others involved in the experience?

3. Reflect on these experiences and consider them from the perspective of a third party, such as an employer or a teammate. How would a third party describe you and your strengths? What kind of patterns can be identified? What characteristics surfaced naturally in a majority of the five experiences you described?

4. What positive qualities did you contribute in a majority of the cases you described?

5. What are your core competencies? What qualities come naturally to you in any personal or professional situation in which you find yourself?

Others' Perceptions of You—360-Degree Feedback

One of the best ways to grow and develop as a person is to recognize that you can benefit and learn from your past experiences. Doing this requires an ability to realistically appraise yourself, recognizing your strengths and your limitations. One way to ensure that you have a "reality check"—that you're reading yourself accurately—is to elicit feedback from those who have worked with you. What are some of the things that you do exceptionally well? What are some of the areas in which you can improve? We all have strengths and weaknesses. What's important is that each of us has a realistic handle on what her or his strengths are, and also has an honest appraisal of areas that can be enhanced. Unfortunately, most of us can't be objective enough to be sure just exactly what our key strengths and areas for improvement are. It is extremely important for anyone who wants to be effective in life and in business to be able to solicit and learn from feedback from others.

One way in which companies routinely help their employees obtain objective feedback about both personal strengths and potential areas for improvement is a process called *360-degree feedback.*[6] In 360-degree feedback, typically a survey is distributed to an employee's boss and a cross section of his or her coworkers and direct reports (the employee's staff). More informally, feedback may be solicited and turned in on email. The following list gives sample questions. Such a survey allows the individual respondents to offer their personal perspective on the areas in which the employee is doing well and the areas in which the employee could make changes. The survey data are collected and analyzed, and the employee receives written and/or in-person feedback about his or her strengths and areas for improvement. This methodology is generally used for developmental purposes, including succession planning and identifying employees with high potential. Used constructively, it can provide the individual with a customized plan for skill building and improvement.

Sample 360-Degree Questions

- What are some of this employee's key strengths?
- How does this employee tend to react under stress or pressure?
- How effective is this person in groups or teams?
- How does this employee collect information when involved in a problem-solving situation?
- What developmental seminars and resources would you suggest for this employee in the coming year?

What are your strengths, and what are your weaknesses? More important, what would *others* say are your strengths and weaknesses? While it's nice to have a formal 360-degree instrument to help answer this question for you, you can conduct your own version of a 360-degree process by following these steps.

Exercise: How Others Perceive You

To help you understand how others may perceive you, on a separate sheet of paper, list the name of a

- Current or former coworker, classmate, or teammate
- Current or former direct report
- Current or former superior
    1. For each person named, answer the question, "What would this person say about me?" List three to five qualities that each individual would cite about you as a person. If you wish, you can divide the list into two columns: positive comments and areas for improvement.
    2. How would each of the persons named describe you to a potential employer? What would this person say are your strongest assets? What limitations of yours would she or he mention?
    3. Analyze the list for commonalities. What are the trends? What, based on your perception of others' perceptions of you, are your strengths? What are your limitations? What assets do you bring to the table? What are some areas in which you can develop in the coming year?
    4. How do your assets and liabilities affect the career or life decision that you are facing now?

II. Assessing the Present—What is Important for You to Know Now

Motivation for Change

When you are making any career or life decision, it is important for you to understand the factors that are most meaningful to you and that therefore should be present in any decision you make. As your life changes and progresses, as your experience builds, and as you age, you may find your personal values—those things that are the most meaningful to you—changing as well. Things that were important to you 2 or 10 years ago may not be as important today. What are the factors that are the most important to you today? Table 1-1 gives a list of factors that are typically important to people who are making important career and life decisions. At the bottom, add factors that are particularly relevant to your situation. Then mark the top five factors that are motivating you in your *current* situation.

Table 1-1   Sample Change Factors

Location	Building new skills	Time for friends and family
Work environment	Utilizing expertise	Building network of colleagues
Compensation	Preparing for retirement	Community involvement
Travel	Quality of people with whom I associate	Working for a cause
Spouse/partner considerations	New learning, challenge, experience	Autonomy/independence
Family considerations	Prestige, status	Chance to innovate, create
Health considerations	Finding a new career field	Time for nonwork priorities, personal interests
Working with others; collaboration; teamwork	Work/life balance	Creating new knowledge/ transferring knowledge
Chance to make an impact	Authority, being in charge	Financial stability
Wish to mentor others	Building wealth	Upward mobility
Lateral move	Flexible hours	Casual-dress environment
Enjoyment	Change	Controlling my future
Following my dream	Personal growth	Supporting my family
Do what I want for a change	Building on my strengths	Involvement in decision making
Variety	Friendship	Stimulation
Working fewer hours	Less travel	Intellectual challenge
Benefits	Being an individual contributor	Loyalty
Smaller or larger organization	Achievement	Increased responsibility

---

Exercise: Motivation for Change

To help you process your motivation for change, answer the following questions:

1. Why are you reading this book? What are the personal and/or professional circumstances (e.g., desire for change, wish to advance, divorce, unexpected widowhood, aging, disillusionment, natural desire for change) that are causing you to evaluate your present situation and explore new career or life options?

2. What factors are important to you now? If you were to make a career or life change now, what factors would most influence you to choose one option over another (location, meaning, impact, money, balance, autonomy, family considerations, new challenge, and so on)? Are some of these values different from the ones that would have influenced you at earlier times in your career, and if so, in what way?

3. What are your short-term (e.g., go back to school, go to graduate school), mid-term (e.g., buy a house), long-term (e.g., become an acknowledged expert), and ultimate (e.g., have a strong network of friends and a comfortable retirement) career and life goals? What do you want to accomplish, and within what time spans (e.g., 1- to 3- or 3- to 5-year increments, depending on your present age and circumstances)?

4. How important to you is financial security? Has this changed recently or over the years, and if so, why and how? What role will this play in your future career or life decisions?

5. How important to you is work/life balance? Has this changed recently or over the years, and if so, why and how? What role will this play in your future career or life decisions?

6. What are the five values that are most important to you now?

Your Career Stage

Career theorists such as Donald Super,[7] Douglas T. Hall,[8] and others have found that most people move through a series of career and life stages (see

Table 1-2   Stages of a Career

Stage[†]	Need/Area of Emphasis
Exploration	Information about available career/life options, alternatives
Trial/getting on board	Integration into organization/situation
Establishment/ advancement	Training/coaching/mentoring
Mastery	Expansion of responsibilities; recognition (internal and/or external)
Maintenance/ plateaued	Job stability and/or enrichment; balance
Change/reentry	Start cycle over
Preparing for/ in retirement	New role identity and restart of cycle

†Adapted from Super and Hall

Table 1-2). In fact, as people are living longer and working with more than one employer and in multiple job functions, it is common for an individual to cycle in and out of these stages, repeating stages as she or he makes a change from one career or life situation to another.

- In what stage are you? Identifying the stage you are in helps you to understand your primary needs and the areas to emphasize as you move through that stage.
- Your current career stage:
- Your current need(s)/area(s) of emphasis:

What Success Means to You

Definitions of *success* are changing. Some people measure success by accumulated wealth; others measure it by job title, status, or scope of responsibility. Still others measure success by the quality of the friendships they have built over time, the quality of their work/life balance, or their freedom to pursue interests that are passions. What is your definition of success? The following exercise will help you to define success for yourself. The key point is to define success on your terms rather than on others' standards or expectations of you.

Exercise: Defining Success

On a separate sheet of paper, answer the following questions:

- Would you work if you didn't have to?
- Who are some people whose work and/or lifestyle you admire, and why (e.g., Jack Welch, Mother Teresa, Oprah Winfrey, a parent, a coworker, a professor)?
- In what kinds of situations would you be willing to work for less than normal pay or for the highest pay that you could earn? What would be the intangible rewards that would make this worthwhile for you personally?
- What is your definition of life/career success?
- What issues are involved for you in defining/reshaping your concept of success at this point in your life?

Alternative Career-Path Models

Gone are the days when it was expected that you would work for one employer for 30 years, striving the entire time for upward mobility in a hierarchical organization. Today, there are many ways to conduct a career and a life, and many types of paths that you can take. Two concepts that have been around for many years, which we advance the thinking on in several future principles, are those of a career mosaic and a portfolio career. A *mosaic* is defined as small pieces of colored glass or stone arranged to form an overall design.[9] A career mosaic is the collection of all of your work experiences over your lifetime to create the design in total. Work can be defined in terms of a specific job or more flexibly defined as using your talents productively, whether you are or are not paid for the output.

Portfolio, a term that is often used in finance, means the set or collection of a variety of investments or assets that an individual or an organization holds.[10] A portfolio career is one in which you draw upon different assets (skill sets or competencies) for your work, which may be for more than one client or organization at a time. Principle 3 discusses portfolio careers in more depth, particularly in relation to taking risks. Principle 4 discusses alternative work models further, including the concepts of the career mosaic and portfolio career.

Academic researchers Michael Driver and Ken Brousseau,[11] among others, have found that there are a number of alternative career-path styles. Which one or ones you choose depends on your personal work and decision-making style. *Your* personal preference determines which type of path you should follow and in which type of organization or situation you are more likely to be happy and productive. Here are some things to think about when you are considering career/life path options.

- Fast-track versus steady-state progression
- Upward mobility versus lateral growth
- One job at one firm for life versus many jobs at many firms
- Single career versus multiple careers
- Full-time commitment versus part-time involvement
- Professional aspirations versus personal interests
- Making money versus making a difference
- Helping oneself versus helping others
- Technical expertise versus functional breadth

Which of these styles appeal to you at this point in your career and your life? Some alternative career-path styles and their corresponding values are given in Table 1-3. We start with Driver and Brousseau's four career-path styles and add others based on our work with clients. Feel free to add your own, based on your own experience, at the end of the table.

- Of the styles listed here, which one (or ones) best applies to you at this point in your life and career?
- Your preferred style(s) at this stage in your career or your life:
- This style meets these core values:

Table 1-3   Alternative Career-Path Styles

Style	Value
Upwardly mobile*	Achievement
Lateral*	Functional breadth
Spiral*	Variety
Plateaued*	Job enhancement
Entrepreneurial	Innovation
Contract consultant, "free agent"	Autonomy, expertise
Purposely "downscaled"	Balance
Own boss	Control, autonomy
Organizational citizen	Loyalty, relationship
Young millionaire (work hard for 20 years and retire)	Freedom, prestige

*Michael J. Driver, Kenneth R. Brousseau, and Philip L. Hunsaker, *The Dynamic Decision Maker* (San Francisco: Jossey-Bass Publishers, 1993).

Your Primary Needs

Seldom do we hold a career consultation without psychologist Abraham Maslow's[12] concept of the "hierarchy of needs" coming up. Maslow theorized that human beings have a series of physical and psychological needs that are depicted in the form of a triangle of needs.

The bottom needs, such as survival (food and shelter) and security (regular paycheck), have to be satisfied before one can pay attention to the higher needs, such as belongingness (feeling part of a community or organization), satisfaction (being gratified by one's job or task), and self-actualization (reaching one's full potential at work and/or in one's life).

Identifying the level at which you're currently operating can help you identify your core motivators when you are making a career decision.

- On what level of Maslow's hierarchy are you currently (financially, physically, or psychologically) residing?
- What is your current level on Maslow's hierarchy of needs?
- In what ways is this affecting the career or life decision that you're facing now?

Your Core Motivators

Over time, we begin to realize that we are making life and career decisions based on a set of personal values and beliefs. Researcher Edgar Schein[13] labeled these factors *career anchors*. These anchors are given in the following list. You can add any additional anchors that pertain to your specific situation.

Career Anchors
- Autonomy
- Challenge
- Entrepreneurship
- General management
- Lifestyle
- Security
- Service
- Technical competence
- _____
- _____

In his work with thousands of professionals, Schein determined that most people are motivated (at any given time in life) by one or two primary anchors. These anchors inevitably change as our life circumstances change. Identifying your primary anchor(s) prior to making a career decision can help you to make a decision that is consistent with the person you are today, not the person you were yesterday.

To help you apply the career anchor concept in light of your specific career or life situation, answer the following questions:

- What are your primary career motivators (first, second, and third choices)?
- How are these affecting the career or life decision(s) you are facing today?

Are You a Protean?

With the changing employee-employee contract, company–employee loyalty is a thing of the past. Within the past three decades, companies have downsized, right-sized, outplaced, and "talent-balanced" their employees away from any notion of job security. Employees have responded by showing less and less loyalty to their employers, job-hopping whenever the spirit moves them or whenever the next best opportunity arises. Even academe has joined this bandwagon, with many institutions reevaluating or abandoning altogether the tenure system that guaranteed lifetime employment to young scholars who proved their excellence while on the tenure track.

Professor Douglas T. Hall has studied this phenomenon for three decades. His work has identified a career orientation that he refers to as *protean.*[14]

Based on Proteus, the mythological figure who was able to change his shape at whim, but had difficulty committing to any single form, those who view their careers as protean obtain their identity from within rather than from any one employer. They have a very strong self-identity, and they develop an experience base that is valued regardless of the organization for which they work.

These employees are mobile, willing to explore opportunities both within and outside the organization that is presently employing them. They are often entrepreneurial, either within an organization or by developing sideline activities of their own. They are often more motivated by personal fulfillment and satisfaction than by financial security. They are increasingly aware of the need for balance in their lives and less willing to work in jobs that are "all-consuming." They are not dependent on any one organization to manage their career or ensure that their career moves along a certain trajectory. They are their own career managers. Table 1-4 lists just some of the characteristics possessed by protean individuals.

Table 1-4 Protean Characteristics

Protean	Traditional
Identity within self	Identity from employer or organization
Manages own career	Career managed by others or by the organization
Entrepreneurial; involved in sideline activities	Focused on one primary activity
Often motivated by personal fulfillment	Often motivated by financial gain
Mobile; not loyal to any one employer	Not mobile; loyal to employer or organization

To help you apply the protean career concept in light of your current career or life situation, answer the following questions:

- Does this sound like you? Are you conducting your career in a way that is very self-directed?
- If so, what are the implications of this for your current career and life situation?
- If not, could you benefit by taking more control of your life and your career path and direction, incorporating more protean, or self-directed, principles into your career and life decision making?

Evaluating Your "Fit" Profile

For years researchers and career counselors have been aware of the importance of person/job fit. This means that people are more satisfied with their work when that work is consistent with their personal values and preferences. Jeffrey Edwards, a well-known human resources expert, has developed a concept of person/job fit based on the interplay between the rewards an employee seeks in his or her position and the ability of a specific job or organization to offer those rewards.[15] The theory is that the more your current job, task, or situation rewards you with a supply of what you value (recognition, for example), the more likely you are to be happy, to be productive, and to stay with your current situation, despite any obstacles that may come your way. Conversely, the *less* your current situation provides you with what you need (autonomy, for example), the more likely you are to be dissatisfied, to not perform well, and to want to leave your current situation, letting even minor things bother you more than would typically be the case. Some of Edwards's core person/job dimensions are shown in Figure 1-3.

What is crucial here is not just being able to identify the rewards we seek in situations, but also being able to evaluate the potential of situations to offer us these rewards. Unfortunately, it is usually easier for us to understand our own personal needs than to evaluate the ability of an organization or situation to meet those needs. It's important that we *identify* our needs—that is, that we identify what we need to obtain from a situation in order to make being in that situation worthwhile. It's equally important that we be able to *articulate* those needs in such a way that we can evaluate the organization or

Figure 1-3 Edwards's Work-Values Framework

situation that we're considering objectively against our own personal selection criteria.

Exercise: Work-Values Framework

To help you process this work-values framework, answer the following questions:

- Which factors (from the work-values framework in Figure 1-3) are most important to you as you consider various career options?
- On what dimensions is there a fit between you and your present situation?
- In what ways is the fit not as strong?
- In what ways are these factors causing you to rethink your situation?

- In what type of organization are you likely to find the factors that are most important to you?

If you have identified some potential options, evaluate each of them against the work values you have listed here as being most important to you.

If you understand what you're seeking from a situation or job and are able to evaluate the potential of the new situation or job to meet these needs, you'll be in a position to make a better, longer-lasting decision about the next change you want to make in your career. Principle 9 provides insights into dimensions of potential industries, jobs, and organizations and questions concerning them that you should research before you decide on a career change in order to ensure that the change will lead to a fit with your values.

III. Envision Your Future

Transitions

Renowned British change management teachers and consultants Barrie Hopson and Mike Scully,[16] along with others, have found in their work with career changers that when people experience any transition, especially one that is involuntary or difficult, they go through phases similar to those experienced by people who have lost a loved one. Transition theory states that it is normal for people to move through these phases when they experience a significant life change, such as taking on a new role, losing a job, or making a decision that significantly changes their career or lifestyle. Even when the change is of a voluntary nature, the more dramatic it is, the more you can expect to experience both positive emotions such as excitement and difficult emotions such as apprehension and nervousness about the change. Table 1-5 gives some typical transition phases, plus space to add others that may be relevant to your situation.

In which of the transition phases are you? Knowing which phase you're in helps you to acknowledge reality and to know what steps to take as you move through the cycle.

Table 1-5 Transition Cycle

Transition Phase	Step(s) Needed
Change event	Ask questions; take time to understand the situation from your and others' perspectives
Surprise/disbelief	Try not to overgeneralize, blame (yourself or others), or react emotionally
Shock/denial	Protect yourself; don't make quick decisions
Anxiety/indecision	Channel your energy into collecting information about your options
Acceptance	Look at the positive implications of the change
Taking action/control	Generate and evaluate creative alternatives; collect the information necessary to make an informed decision; develop action plans
Decision	Make the decision and monitor progress toward new goals
Reassessment	Be prepared for the cycle to start over when the next change event inevitably occurs

Exercise: What Is Your Transition Stage?

- What is the career or life transition that you're currently facing?
- What is your current transition phase?
- What emotions are you currently experiencing?
- What action(s) can you take during this phase?

Your Support System

During any major life or career change or transition, it is essential that you have several individuals in your life on whom you can rely for support and encouragement. No one person can perform all of the roles you need; hav-

Table 1-6   Sources of Support

Role[†]	Name(s) of People Who Can Fill This Role
Supporter/advocate	
Challenger	
Motivator/encourager:	
Confidante	
Idea generator	
Problem solver	
Source of fun	
Other	

[†]Adapted from Doug Mosel, Consulting Resources, South Bend, IN.

ing a combination of people in your life is best. These people can help you articulate and meet your goals, advise you on alternatives and their pluses and minuses, and give you an honest reality check on the fit between various scenarios and your strengths and abilities. Think of your group as a personal "board of advisers." Each person in this group needs to think highly of you, but also needs to be able to be objective about both your strengths and your limitations. These people need to have good judgment so that you can rely on them when you're seeking an outside perspective. And they need to be positive role models/mentors, exhibiting in their own life the qualities you seek to emulate in yours.

Table 1-6 gives a list of roles that can be provided for you by others. Add any additional roles that may pertain to your situation. As you contemplate your current phase in life, which person or persons in your life can perform each of the roles listed? Write their names in the table. It is unlikely that you'll be able to identify people for all of the roles listed. Two or three is all you need in order to get started.

Your Personal Goals

It's one thing to set goals. It's another to accomplish them. One handy way to establish short- and long-term goals that you can act upon is to complete a personal goal-setting activity that is based on standard goal-setting theory and adapted by the authors for use with students and managers who wish to improve their and their employees' goal-setting abilities. Personal goal setting[17] has several underlying principles.

First, you should focus only on goals over which you have control. For example, if you wish to convince your spouse to move to a different part of the country, your objective should state, "To be persuasive with (*name of spouse*) and convince her or him to move," *not,* "To move to another part of the country," as that is a goal that is not totally within your control. You can succeed in convincing someone to make a decision that concurs with yours, being as persuasive as possible, but in the end, you can't be responsible for making the decision for another person. Set only goals over which you have some control.

Second, focus on just a few goals at a time. This personal goal-setting activity encourages you to dream and to identify as many long-term goals as you wish, regardless of whether they are practical. But it also offers a way to narrow a long list of goals to a short list of items on which to focus in the short term. If you focus on just two or three goals at a time, you will be less overwhelmed and more apt to experience success, and thus to have the opportunity to replace the goals you've met with new goals from your original list.

Third, this personal goal-setting activity helps you to integrate personal and professional goals. In pursuing goals, it's sometimes easy to get caught up in either personal or professional activities, to the exclusion of the other. We're better off leading lives that integrate the two realms. Personal goal setting helps you to focus on both.

Finally, expect to have setbacks. Don't worry if you deviate somewhat from your plans. Put the difficulty behind you, get back on track, and move on.

Exercise: Personal Goal Setting

- Brainstorm your current (<1 year), mid-term (3 to 5 years), and long-term (children's college, real estate, retirement) goals in the following categories or other categories that are relevant to your situation. Write down as many goals per category as you wish. Be creative and have some fun with this.

- Career, job
- Financial
- Family, friends
- Community, public service
- Health, fitness, sports
- Academic, intellectual
- Leisure
- Spiritual
- Other
- Of the goals you have listed, select from each of the categories the two most important goals that you would like to pursue in the short term (the next 6 to 12 months).
- From this list of short-term goals, choose the three that are most important to you at this time, regardless of their category. These are the three goals that you are committing to working on in the next few months. Write a goal statement for each one, using the following guidelines:
  - Each goal statement should begin with the word "to."
  - Each goal statement should be specific.
  - Each goal should be realistic, measurable, attainable, and within your control.
  - Each goal should reflect your aspirations—it should be "owned" by you, not by others such as your boss, your colleagues, or your significant other.
- Develop an action plan for each goal statement. This should include
  - Steps you will take to accomplish the goal
  - Dates (by when) and initials (who's responsible) for each step
  - Potential barriers you might experience in attaining the goal (problem-solve around these obstacles and convert them into steps in your action plan).
  - The information, feedback, and resources you will need in order to accomplish these goals
- Transfer the date of each step in the action plan for each goal to a daily calendar.
- Keep an ongoing daily or weekly record of the positive steps that you take toward meeting each goal.

- Review your goals on a regular basis, sometimes enlisting a friend, family member, or coworker to review them with you.
- Monitor your progress, celebrating as you accomplish even small steps, and deleting and adding goals as your circumstances change.

Putting It All Together[18]

Survey your responses to the exercises in this principle. Now that you've had a chance to reflect on yourself and your interests, on a separate sheet of paper, make a list of the things that are important for you to have in your next job. List as many features as you can think of, in no particular order. Don't censor yourself. List everything that comes to mind. For example, you might list close to family, opportunity to travel, access to cutting-edge technology, casual dress, enough money to live on and pay my debts, chances to use my strongest skills (list what they are), chances to learn new skills and increase marketability. Now rank the items on the list from the first in importance to the last in importance. If it's difficult to choose, ask yourself, "If I could have only one important thing from this job, what would that one thing be?" then go on to the second, the third, and so on.

This list defines the things that, based on who you are and what's important to you, you want to have in your next position. Naturally it's unlikely that you'll get everything you're seeking, but this list can serve as your blueprint for evaluating jobs, organizations, locations, and lifestyle options as you consider your next step. Refer to this list as you learn of openings, are contacted by prospective employers, or see position descriptions on the Web. It will help you to assess each opportunity in terms of your own needs, and it also will be a source for questions you can ask in job interviews with recruiters.

Where Do You See Yourself in 5 Years?[19]

Close your eyes and relax. It is 5 years from today. Where are you living? What are you doing? Whom are you with? What do you look like? What are you thinking? How are you feeling?

You are at the breakfast table. Is it early or late? Is anyone else there? Are you pressured or relaxed? How are you dressed? What are you thinking? How do you feel?

You are getting up from the table. Are you leaving? If so, where are you going? If not, what will you be doing? For what purpose? What are you thinking? How do you feel?

Principle 2

Bounce Back from Setbacks

The more I practice, the luckier I get.

—Arnold Palmer

Continuous Learning

The second principle in gaining career clarity involves bouncing back from setbacks by learning from your mistakes and accelerating your future learning curve. No review and analysis of your experience is complete if it does not address the disappointments, failures, mistakes, and misjudgments that inevitably occur in a career and a life. An example of this is Bob Kerrey, the former senator from Nebraska, who was interviewed by NPR (National Public Radio) on June 6, 2002, about some serious missteps in which he had been involved while serving in Vietnam. Kerrey remarked that it's easy to accept and learn from the good decisions we've made in life; what's difficult is accepting the fact that we've also made some bad choices in life. We have to acknowledge this, learn from our mistakes, and then move on.

Kerrey's comments demonstrate a capacity to learn from his mistakes: to be able to adapt to change, to listen to feedback, and to learn new behaviors and attitudes. These qualities are essential for anyone desiring career clarity. To be clear about where you're headed, you need to understand your past but not be hampered by it. This is part of what is referred to today as *continuous learning*.

41

Acquisition of New Skills and Experiences

Continuous learning is defined as the ongoing acquisition of new skills, experiences, and insights to help improve work and life. Continuous learning is self-directed. It is not something that is done for you by others. Your managers are not responsible for your learning initiatives; you are. Continuous learning is an ongoing process. The best is experiential, or —hands-on.

Learning can take place through both formal and informal activities. Formal activities include but aren't limited to development workshops, company- or industry-sponsored seminars, executive programs, coaching and mentoring programs, individual development plans, skill-based workshops and materials, feedback instruments, and training sessions and materials.

Generally it's advisable to be involved in at least one formal learning activity, such as a workshop or course, at least once each year. One can be involved in informal continuous learning through a variety of means. These can include but aren't limited to self-review of your own experiences, both positive and negative; learning from your mistakes, focusing on your accomplishments as well as your failures; reading books; informal mentoring and coaching programs; networking; and soliciting and responding to feedback. Continuous learning helps you meet your organization's objectives (if you are employed or own your own business), helps you set new objectives if you're in between jobs, and can also help you set ongoing personal development objectives.

Stretching beyond the Comfort Zone

Ken Kam is a great example of someone who has been successful as a result of acquiring new skills and experience. He moved smoothly from finance after college to strategy consulting after graduate school. He then started up a medical device company in Puerto Rico and later sold it. Next, he founded what grew into a multi-billion-dollar mutual fund and became a top mutual fund manager and CEO of an investment-related company. In addition to his dedication, integrity, and hard work, the reason Ken has achieved so much is that he has a solid set of core strengths that he constantly builds onto. Ken continues to learn by trying new experiences, taking on different challenging responsibilities, and stretching himself beyond his comfort zone. For each of his new roles, Ken uses roughly 65 to 75 percent of his core strengths. The remaining 25 to 35 percent requires him to adapt, experiment, and develop new competencies. This iterative process brings him powerful learning and new capabilities.

Advantages of Continuous Learning

Continuous learning is important for a number of reasons. Used consciously, it can be a resource for lifelong development and improvement.

The experiences you have and the learnings you acquire through each experience define who you are and shape how you are perceived by others.

Continuous learning, in which you constantly search for guidance, information, and feedback, permits you to obtain insights into yourself that would otherwise be impossible.

The inventor of the pacemaker, Wilson Greatbatch, has said, "I can't do anything about what happened [in the past]. But I can do something about the future."[1] Continuous learning is a way to acknowledge what has happened in the past, then move beyond it by learning from it and focusing on the future. Continuous learning responds to your need to keep stimulation in your job and your life. It is a quality that is attractive to employers. The ability—and motivation—to learn continuously is cited by experts such as EQ guru Daniel Goleman,[2] Carnegie Mellon professor Robert Kelley,[3] and others as one of the most important qualities one can possess today.

Another benefit of continuous learning is that it adds to one's sense of job satisfaction. Having the opportunity to gain experience and derive learning from that experience appears to be even more important at a time when lateral job moves are more common than upward moves. As organizational structures have flattened, there are fewer opportunities for people to advance in the traditional, upwardly mobile way. Learning new skills and having new experiences can be a source of renewal and rejuvenation for someone who is not going to change jobs or who doesn't want to do so.[4]

Becoming able to learn from your experience takes time. It seldom happens overnight. As a married thirty-something health-care worker, Ann Galloway, explains, "I have found that it takes at least 5 years to know what you're doing as an art versus a science; that any meaningful career takes time and effort out of your personal time, at least at the beginning. I am constantly learning, growing, and improving, and this process will probably occur all throughout my life and career."

How-to Strategies
Start Small

While this is a positive message, it can also be a bit daunting. Certainly we can't spend all of our time in a learning mode; we would be exhausted if we tried to do so. As a rule, we have just enough time to move from one experience to the next. There is often little time to process or to debrief the "lessons learned" from an experience, either alone or with others who were involved (team or family members, for example). To be a continuous learner, you need to focus on just a few key experiences that you've had recently and analyze them for patterns that exist, patterns that could be changed in the future. The following list provides several questions you can ask yourself as you assess your own experience.

Your Experience as a Source of Learning
1. Recall two to three recent experiences that have been a source of disappointment for you.
2. Analyze them in terms of what you were trying to achieve and how that compares with what you actually achieved.
3. Think about your role in the situation: what you did, what worked, and what didn't work.
4. What did you learn about yourself and how you handled the situation?
5. What were the take-aways (the "lessons learned") for you? What could you do differently in the future?
6. What behavior or attitudinal changes may be required for change to occur?

This type of review can aid you greatly in learning from your experiences and using them as a strategic aid in your own development.

Set Aside Time

One problem posed by the need for continuous learning is a lack of time for new learning. For many people today, the work environment is *not* conducive to learning. Work proceeds at such a frenetic pace that taking time for learning is frowned upon. Many workspaces afford so little privacy that thinking creatively is out of the question. These problems are only exacerbated once people are at home, where family commitments and community obligations can consume the little free time that remains after work. All of this can result in a feeling of being overloaded, with responsibilities becoming so all-consuming that little time remains for oneself. Role overload can prevent you from being open to new learning. "No new input" or "enough is enough" is a battle cry to which you may be able to relate. Conversely, you may be energized by the constant buzz of activity around you, and actually be better able to learn when many demands are pressing on you.

It is important for you to understand your personal learning needs. You can assess on an ongoing basis the degree to which you are encumbered by the needs of others and the degree to which this makes you embrace new learning opportunities or shy away from them. It's not realistic, for example, to take on a significant new learning activity, such as going to graduate school, in the same month that you're having or adopting a baby. To what degree do you feel encumbered by the needs of others, or by difficult life circumstances or incessant time demands? And how does this affect the amount of time and energy you have available for new learning activities? Figure 2-1 helps to chart this.

On the vertical axis of Figure 2-1 is "Time Available," meaning the amount of time and energy you have available for new learning. On the horizontal axis is "Level of Responsibility," meaning the degree to which you're encumbered with work and nonwork responsibilities.

- Those who are highly encumbered by others' needs or by work responsibilities and have little time to devote to new learning are depicted in quadrant 1.
- Those who are highly encumbered but feel energized by their responsibilities and have time available for new learning are in quadrant 2.

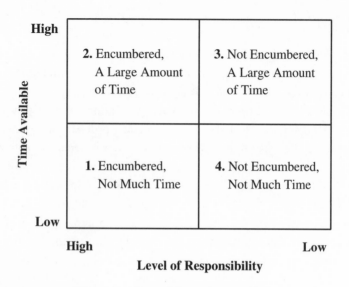

Figure 2-1   Personal Encumberment Scale

- Those who are not encumbered by others' needs or by work responsibilities and who have a larger amount of time available for new learning activities are in quadrant 3.
- Those who are less encumbered but who feel that they lack the time for new learning are in quadrant 4.

As Figure 2-1 demonstrates, the less encumbered you are, the more time and energy you have available for learning activities. The more encumbered you are, the less time and energy you have available for learning activities. To be a continuous learner, you need to adjust your schedule periodically to make time available for learning, either in small or in large doses, depending on the extent of your other activities. A good rule of thumb is to try to devote at least 5 percent of your work time to learning activities (defined broadly to include training programs, technology updates, team debriefing meetings, journaling, Internet research, and so on). This might jump to as much as 10 percent at times when you're less overloaded with other commitments.

An unencumbered crepe cook.   In the village of Hampstead, in North London, where one of the authors and her husband live, there's a woman named Anna who comes from an aristocratic family. Anna works as a cook in a small sidewalk crepe stand on High Street. The author and her husband have gotten to know Anna through their visits for dessert crepes. They have been impressed by her because she can remember perfectly about eight orders at one time, prepare three crepes at once, and engage in colorful small talk about the latest museum exhibit, the weather, or life.

What stands out about Anna is that she seems genuinely happy and takes immense pride in her excellent work—creating, cooking, and customer service. In brief, Anna left a well-paying office job in a travel company, worked in retail for a while, and then decided to pursue her dream of cooking, a love she inherited from her mum. Anna takes her craft seriously. She actively learns new spice combinations, cooking techniques, and recipes from her friends from North Africa, India, and Brazil. She continuously puts effort into honing her skills—her art.

Learn from Mistakes and Failures

What if you've made some mistakes from which you want to learn? Perhaps you quit a job prematurely, made a decision that proved to be wrong, found that the grass *isn't* always greener, or made a judgment that ended up causing pain to others. Even worse, what if you realize, through self-assessment, that you're making the same mistake over and over—for example, you're letting poor self-esteem get in the way of good decisions, or you're letting concern about financial security prevent you from taking some healthy risks? As they say, it's all right to make a mistake once, or maybe even twice. But making the same mistake repeatedly is stupid. It's important that you debrief yourself (and possibly those involved) after you've made a mistake or once you've identified a pattern of mistakes.

Learning from one's mistakes can occur through assessing the situation, viewing it from multiple perspectives, gaining some insight into how it could have been handled differently, being honest about one's role in the situation, and developing an action plan for the behavior or attitudinal changes necessary for improvement and development. Perhaps most important, learning from one's mistakes also requires the ability to forgive oneself for the honest mistakes and poor judgment calls that one inevitably makes in life.

As can be seen in Kerrey's experience, described earlier in the principle, this step is probably the hardest, especially if you're typically hard on yourself or are prone to feeling guilt over your role in situations as they arise. Of course it is important to be accountable when you've been wrong, and you can certainly apologize and try to correct the problem if possible. But once you have acknowledged your role in the situation, it's generally best to move on if you can, learning from the event but not overly dwelling on it. This requires an ability to be objective, to separate your personal self from the problem, and to remember the whole—the positives that were part of the picture as well.

Diminishing Returns

Continuous learning becomes particularly difficult when one has been employed in the same position or has been performing the same role for an extended period of time. In general, after about 3 years in a job or role, most people need a change of routine or a different position altogether. What about you? Where are you on the learning curve in your present situation, and where would you like to be? The longer you remain in a role or position, the greater the likelihood that your learning will decrease or even stop altogether. Sometimes this happens because a person is considered so valuable that her or his employer doesn't want her or him spending time learning new areas of the organization. Other times it happens because a person has become comfortable operating at a certain level. The "doom loop"[5] concept (see Figure 2-2) demonstrates the correlation between time on a job and ability to continue learning.

On the vertical axis of Figure 2-2 is "Competence Enjoyment," meaning the degree to which one is learning and using skills that he or she enjoys. On the horizontal axis is the length of time on the job.

- Those who are new on the job and are just starting the learning curve are depicted in quadrant 1.
- Those who have slightly more time on the job and who are learning and using a variety of skills appear in quadrant 2.

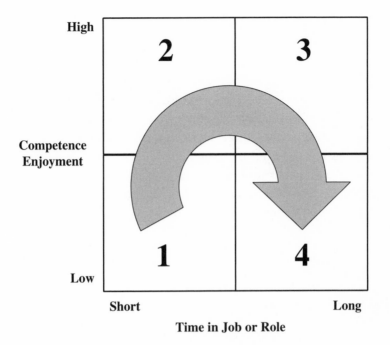

Figure 2-2 The Doom Loop

- Those who have been on the job awhile and are starting to experience a decrease in skills used or learned are depicted in quadrant 3.
- Those who have remained on the job long enough to stop learning new skills or being able to use skills that they enjoy are depicted in quadrant 4.

The point of the doom loop is that it is important to keep learning on the job. The longer someone stays in a particular job, the more vulnerable that person is to job dissatisfaction should his or her learning decrease or drop off altogether. Where are you on the doom loop?

- If you're in quadrant 1, you need to focus on learning your new role and doing it well.

- The point of peak performance is somewhere between quadrants 2 and 3. If you're in quadrant 2, you're starting to become expert in some elements of your job or role, and you're enjoying new learnings.
- If you're in quadrant 3, you've probably mastered many elements of your role, but you're slowing down on the learning curve. You'll want to find new ways to enhance your existing situation, and perhaps you will want to devote some time to mentoring others.
- If you're in quadrant 4, you'll want to engage in some activities, on or off the job, that can help you to recharge and to seek out new learning opportunities. If this isn't possible, you'll want to consider a role or job change.

Schedule Annual Career Check-Ups

Many people find that it helps if they assess their experience on a regular basis, say once a year, around New Year's or a time that is particularly meaningful to them. This helps them to identify what's working and what's not, and to put together a learning plan for the coming year. The following list gives some questions that you can ask yourself as a way of assessing the quality of the learning you're currently experiencing.

Annual Learning Assessment
1. What new skills have I acquired recently? What developmental experiences did I have in the past year? What opportunities did I have (or could I create) to practice my existing skills?
2. What are some new skills that I'd like to focus on learning in the coming year?
3. Will staying in my present situation allow me to develop and use these new skills? If yes, what avenues (if any) to acquire these new skills are available to me within my organization (mentor, technology, training program, course, and so on)? How can I find out more about the resources that are available to me? What specific activities can I engage in during the coming year? How can I obtain my manager's support for my involvement in specific activities?

4. If no, what avenues (if any) to acquire these skills are available to me outside of my current organization (professional association, local college or university, book, personal contact, the Internet, and so on)? What specific activities can I commit to in the coming year?

5. If no, would I be better off in a different organization, one that would allow me to develop and use new skills? If so, what is my plan for making a change?

A Competency-Based Career

As a framework for accelerating the quality of your own learning curve, consider the "intelligent career" model proposed by career experts Michael Arthur et al.[6] They postulate that just as organizations are pursuing a competency-based orientation, in terms of arming their core employees with the skills and personal characteristics that they need if they are to succeed in their environment, so too can individuals pursue a career that is competency-based. One of your primary responsibilities is to understand and acquire the skills and characteristics that are needed for success in your field and in your organization. In this model, you supervise or are a partner in your own learning, concentrating on creating and taking advantage of any and all learning opportunities that are available. Focusing your career on learning acknowledges that as your career progresses, you develop a set of skills and talents that is portable. In this age of "the new employment contract," where you're probably not guaranteed a job for life with one employer, the "portable skills" concept helps you to be ready to pursue a career with your current employer or with another organization should things not work out.

According to Arthur, et al, in the competency-based career, you're responsible for increasing your knowledge in three areas, as given in Table 2-1: (1) knowing why, (2) knowing how, and (3) knowing who. Focusing your organizational learning agenda on understanding an organization's mission and where you fit, the qualities needed to succeed in that environment, and the people whom it is instrumental to know makes sense. This can help you to become effective within an organization in the short term, and to equip yourself with skills that will be useful in subsequent work environments. You can craft a learning program based on your own career stage.

Table 2-1　Competency-Based Career Knowledge

Knowing why	Understanding the organization's culture, why it's in business, and what makes people successful in it
Knowing how	Understanding and possessing the skills and capabilities that one can bring to the organization (your "value added")
Knowing who	Understanding the players within an organization and developing collegial relationships in order to be more effective within the organization

Michael B. Arthur, Priscilla H. Claman, Robert J. DeFillippi, and Jerome Adams, "Intelligent Enterprise, Intelligent Careers," *The Academy of Management Executive*, November 1995.

What's Your Career Learning Stage?

In what stage of career learning are you? As we discussed in Principle 1, the career stage that you're in has implications for your primary needs and your action planning activities. It also has implications for your continuous learning agenda. Throughout your career, your learning agenda has two dimensions, personal and organizational. The Table 2-2 gives appropriate learning dimensions for people in various stages of their careers. Note that the stage model of careers is not age-based or chronological; as we progress through our careers and our lives, we cycle through these stages and repeat them as we move into new or changed circumstances.[7]

Are you in the trial or getting-on-board stage of your career (either entering the workforce for the first time or entering a new field later in your career)? Your organizational learning emphasis can be on gaining information about your employer or business—how it functions, your role, your employer's expectations of you, and so on. Some of the activities in which you may be involved are orientation, skill building, learning technology, understanding the organization's culture, and networking. Personally, you'll also want to acquire or improve self-management (stress, time, and so on) and intrapersonal skills (understanding oneself).

Is your career in the establishment/advancement phase? Your organizational learning objective will be to increase your knowledge base—to move from novice to expert in a particular aspect of your work. Some of the activities in which you may be involved are coaching and mentoring. Person-

Table 2-2   Organizational and Personal Learning Focus by Stage of Career*

Career Stage	Organizational Learning Focus	Personal Learning Focus
Trial/getting on board	Acclimation to the organization	Self-management and intrapersonal skills
Establishment/ advancement	Receiving training, mentoring	Supervisory and interpersonal skills
Mastery	Mentoring others; broader role within the organization and/or outside of the organization	General management and leadership skills
Maintenance/plateaued	Renewed commitment	Balance and perspective
Career change/reentry	Learning a new organization—restart of cycle	Learning new skills or applying skills in a new area within the organization or in a new organization
Preparing for/in retirement	Transfer of learning	Applying skills in nonwork settings; learning new skills; developing new interests

* Table adapted from two sources, Donald E. Super, *The Psychology of Careers* (New York: Harper & Row, 1957) and Douglas T. Hall, *Careers in Organizations* (Glenview, Ill.: Scott, Foresman, 1976), p. 201. For an excellent discussion of acclimating to a work environment, see E. H. Schein, *Career Dynamics* (Reading, Mass.: Addison-Wesley, 1978).

ally, you'll want to focus on developing your supervisory and interpersonal (working with others) skills.

Is your present position in the mastery phase, where you've learned all or most of what you need to know and are exemplary in your role? If so, some of the activities in which you may be involved are cross-discipline task forces and project teams, mentoring and coaching of others, professional associations, and continuous learning programs. Personally, you can broaden your general management skills rather than simply relying on your expertise in a specialized technical arena.

Are you currently in the maintenance phase of your career, or even plateaued? When the learning curve in your role or position is decreasing or has stopped altogether, you can let your organization know how committed you are to its objectives and initiate discussions about how you can continue to contribute to these objectives. Some of the activities in which you may be involved are annual reassessment, short courses, and volunteer experiences within or outside of the organization. You also may wish to explore potential new opportunities within your existing organization or, if that fails, in other organizations. Personally, you can engage in a balance of nonwork activities to give you a broader perspective from which to view the organization's inevitable problems.

In career change or reentry, the learning cycle begins again. Your focus shifts to your new situation, and the learning cycle begins anew. If you are preparing for retirement, your organizational focus shifts to knowledge transfer: ensuring that others in your organization have the knowledge they need in order to carry on. Your primary efforts shift to preparing for the transition, learning new skills, and adapting to change.

Are you preparing for retirement? Your organizational focus shifts to ensuring that others in your organization have the knowledge they need to carry on. Your primary efforts shift to preparing for the transition, developing new interests, disassociating from your former situation, learning new skills for this transition, and adapting to change.

Evaluate Yourself as a Learner

Are you a continuous learner? A continuous learner is characterized by qualities such as the ones listed here. Feel free to add others that pertain to your situation.

Intellectual curiosity

Willingness to look at all angles
before making a judgment

Willingness to admit mistakes

Adept at understanding self and understanding how to work with others

Adept at mastering the internal workings of organizations

Willing to find and use tools, frameworks, and methodologies to aid in decision making and problem solving

Willingness to seek and use external resources

Interest in learning about and using internal resources to competitive advantage

Lack of age bias (willing to take seriously ideas from both younger and older workers)

Positive attitude

Willingness to solicit—and listen to—feedback from others

Willingness to devote time to learning new things

Commitment to learning about a subject before making a decision

Adaptability and flexibility

_____   _____

_____   _____

Not everyone is a continuous learner. Some people lack the time to deal with anything more than what's immediately in front of them. Others like the comfort of knowing certain things and not having to go beyond a certain level. Still others consider themselves experts in a particular field and see no need to learn anything new.

- What about you?
- On the list just given, place a check next to those qualities that are generally descriptive of your behavior and attitude when you are in the workplace.
- Put a double check next to two or three items on which you're particularly strong.
- As a way of doing a reality check, for each of the two or three marked items, briefly describe in paragraph or bullet form on a separate sheet of paper some examples from your own experience

base that demonstrate the characteristic. Then place an X next to two or three items on which you think you can improve.

- On a separate sheet of paper, write some goal statements indicating changes that you can make in the near future to increase your level of continuous learning.

Identify Your Sources

Identify your sources of past and future learning. Where is the wellspring? Remember the teacher who was tough on you when you were a student, but who you later realized was the best teacher you had ever had? Remember some of the lessons you learned from a parent, lessons that you weren't particularly interested in at the time? Earlier in this book we discussed the impact that others can have on our lives and careers. Nowhere is this more evident than in our ability to learn from others. Others in our lives have a chance to make a huge impact on us, thereby speeding up the learning process. Sometimes this happens without their or our even realizing it until later, if we realize it at all.

Role Models and Influential People

As you reflect on your life and career, can you identify a person who has served as a role model for you? As a mentor? A coach? A guide? A supporter? Someone who has given you good advice? Who has helped you make a major career or life decision? Who has been instrumental in helping you to make the particular choices you've made in your life and career? On a separate sheet of paper, list the names of individuals in your life who have been instrumental in your personal and career growth, and describe the advice they gave you or the lesson(s) you learned from them. You can start with the names of the people you mentioned or thought about as you were completing the self-assessment exercises in Principle 1, and add others as relevant. Reviewing the names of people who mean something to you, and reflecting on what they taught you and how that has shaped who you are today, can be a gratifying experience. It's also a way to identify the source of some of your core values and operating principles today.

Case Study: Alana Baylor Invests in Herself through Lifelong Learning

It has been said that we can't learn if our only role model is ourselves. It is through interacting with others that we gain some perspective on both our abilities and our needs for improvement. This is evident in one of our case study subjects, Alana Baylor. Alana has been a proactive, continuous learner throughout her career. A successful businesswoman who has worked for major companies on the West Coast, in the Southwest, and in the Midwest, Alana describes herself as a continuous learner—"always looking to what's next, looking to see what it is I need to master in order to keep growing and doing well." Alana is her own career manager. She writes, "For the good and bad of it, I've completely managed my career. I feel strongly that everyone should manage their career, and I try to practice what I preach."

One of the core elements in her career management has been a constant focus on learning. Alana continues, "I have found that in order to remain competitive in the marketplace, I need to keep learning. Security can be found only within, so I need to invest in myself, keep myself current, and keep my skills up to date." Alana finds that while she's emphasizing learning in order to remain marketable, there's an intrinsic satisfaction that comes from learning something new. "I really like learning new things, and I have put myself into positions to do so." Alana has utilized numerous learning techniques over the years. Some of these have included 360-degree feedback (see Principle 1), career assessments and workshops, reading books, personal coaching, journaling, and talking with others. She says, "Experience is a great teacher. Using 360-degree feedback helps me to stay in touch with my strengths and to be aware of areas where I can improve. I know that journaling is supposed to be useful, but since I'm an extrovert, talking with others is much more helpful."

She also asks a lot of questions. "I try to be willing to ask lots of questions—even ones that seem dumb and persistent." Alana has found that her intellectual curiosity has been an asset to her over the years. "I'm constantly looking for ways to learn, ways to improve myself based on my experiences. This has helped me to be more effective as a manager, a coach of others, and a team member. I've completed numerous skill assessments—inventorying what I have and what I need. Self-assessment, paper-and-pencil tests, and career counseling have all been helpful to me over the years." Alana also realizes the role that others can play in her ongoing learning. She often teams with others on projects as a way of sharing or transferring knowledge. She writes, "Also, I'm a big fan of the concept of information interviewing, to fill in the blanks and build a network. While technology has spread the availability of career tools and information, they can't substitute for talking with people."

Alana has found that continuous learning is a way of investing in herself. It enables her to remain marketable, build new skills, enhance her network, and improve herself, both personally and professionally. Through continuous learning, Alana has been able to maximize her experience, learning from her successes as well as her failures and constantly improving as her experience base deepens.

Part 2 Ahead: Assessing the Present

In the first two principles of this book, we have looked thoroughly at your past and at what can be learned from your experiences, both positive and negative. We have discussed the importance of learning continuously, particularly what you can learn from your mistakes and setbacks. These principles have laid the groundwork for the next phase of gaining career clarity: assessing your present situation and identifying what's important to you now. It's not always easy to look at your past, but it's always useful. In the next section we build on that foundation and begin to think creatively about your present and your future.

Part 2

Assess the Present

In Part 1 we focused on our previous experience, covering the importance of self-assessment, learning from mistakes, and continuous learning. Now, in Part 2, we move into the present, focusing on what's important to you today. In this section we cover several principles that can help you take an actively different look at your life and your career. We will focus on:

- The importance of taking measured risk and ways to analyze this risk
- Ways to make your dreams possible through careful and creative financial planning
- The need to make people a priority as you make career decisions
- The steps you can take now to start planning for the future

We will provide frameworks that you can use as you make decisions about your next work/life direction, practical strategies and how-tos, and real case examples of people who are taking new approaches and making inspired decisions.

Principle 3

Take Measured Risk

A ship in port is safe but that's not what ships are built for.
—Rear Admiral Grace
Murray Hopper

A World Interrupted

The third principle required for gaining clarity about your life and your career is the need to take risks. In this principle, we create an awareness that there is risk involved in both taking an action and doing nothing. We give you useful tools, techniques, and frameworks for identifying, evaluating, and managing risk. And we share lessons learned by some people who have been there and done it, learning from their successes, and from their setbacks as well.

Professor Yoram "Jerry" Wind of the University of Pennsylvania's Wharton School says, "Everything bad that has happened during the past few years—the dot-com implosion, the recession, terror, the war—destroyed the illusion that we operate in a world that is continuous and continuously prosperous. As it turns out, our world is nothing like that. Our lives are routinely disrupted, our work dislocated."[1]

In this world of uncertainty, every decision is made within a decision environment that is composed of the information, alternatives, and preferences that are available at the time of the decision. In an ideal decision environment, all possible information would be available, all of it accurate, and every possible alternative would be known. The decision maker would then be able to calculate the payoff from every possible alternative and to choose the alternative that optimizes the variable(s) that best fit his or her personal preferences. In this environment, decision making would be done with complete certainty.

Imperfect Information and Decision Making

Most decisions are made under some degree of uncertainty because not all information is available and not all alternatives are known. Thus, decisions involve an undeniable amount of risk. For example, Ted Smith is considering whether he should accept a transfer to his firm's business unit in Frankfurt. Will he like his new boss? Will he enjoy being in Germany? Will the international experience resulting from the move be valuable for a career progression? Ted may expect that the transfer will be a beneficial career move; however, he knows that this decision involves uncertainty and risk.

What Is Risk?[2]

In his 1921 classic *Risk, Uncertainty, and Profit*,[3] Frank H. Knight postulated that risk was a randomness—as in a game of roulette—whose probability could be determined. George G. C. Parker, Dean Witter Professor of Finance at Stanford Business School and coauthor of *Risk Management*,[4] provides the current view on risk and uncertainty:

> Risk and uncertainty are different words for the same thing. With uncertainty comes the possibility of a variety of outcomes. Some are positive; some are not. That's also the definition of risk. Around business schools, we think of uncertainty and risk as the same thing. That approach to the words means that risk is not all bad. Indeed the possibility of an uncertain positive outcome is the positive side of risk. Without some risk (uncertainty), some of the best things in life are not possible. I am a big believer that it is essential to take some prudent, measured risk in life to experience the best there is to experience.

Risk Involves Both Gains and Losses

Risk is often misunderstood, skewed to the negative, or shied away from because it is too amorphous, yet risk *can* be identified, estimated, evaluated, and managed. The more common perceptions of risk tend to be negative, emphasizing loss. For example, the Merriam-Webster's dictionary[5] defines risk as "hazard, chance, or the possibility of bad consequences, exposure to mischance, to expose oneself or be exposed to loss." In other words, risk is the chance that something bad will happen. However, a broader understanding of risk takes into account both gains and losses. For example, in our everyday actions and decisions, whether we are buying a stock, taking a new job, or learning to ski, there is the chance for both negative and positive outcomes.

Why Take Risk?

Lee Iacocca has said, "Everything worthwhile carries risk of failure." In short, we take risks in order to achieve personal and professional growth, to try to gain more than we lose, and to improve our situation and our life. We can't make things better or different—our job, our career, how happy we are, a relationship, our financial situation, our knowledge—if we don't take action, that is, make a move or make a change. Taking risk can be uniquely powerful learning. As we experiment or try new things, we can learn from our setbacks and build our confidence with our successes.

Dr. Wind advances the idea that in turbulent times, there is no optimal strategy. His insights include the idea of adaptive experimentation. Suggesting that we create an environment of continuous experimentation for ourselves, Wind says essentially that bolder action gets bigger results and that experimentation allows us to learn really fast because we continually have to reexamine our strategy.

Finance Theories, Tools, and Terminology

Risk in decision making has been the focus of an enormous amount of innovative work by academics and practitioners, particularly in the area of finance. These theories, tools, and models provide a wealth of knowledge on which we can draw and which we can apply creatively to career and life decision making.

We promise not to give you eye-glazing mathematical formulas on certainty equivalents, net present value, and the like. And we won't use a lot of technical jargon about risk. We will, however, provide some background information that help you to take away the most from this principle so that you can apply it in your own career or life. Here are the definitions of some relevant terms.

Financial Terms Relevant to Career Decision Making[6]

Risk/return trade-off	The tendency for potential risk to vary directly with potential return. The more risk there is involved in a particular situation, the greater the potential return, and vice versa. In general, if you want a higher (better) return, you have to accept more risk.
Portfolio	A collection of assets (investments) held by an investor, for example, stocks, bonds, and real estate holdings. To minimize risk, an investor should not hold too much of any one kind of asset. Ideally, a portfolio is managed in a way that increases its overall value.
Diversification	A risk management technique that involves mixing a wide variety of investments within a portfolio.
Expected value (EV)	The traditional formula/tool used for evaluating risk. The EV of a risk is the value of the possible outcome discounted by the probability of its occurring. The formula for EV is $EV = PR$, or expected value equals prize times risk (or chance). Many risks have multiple possible outcomes, with each

outcome having its own probability of occurrence and its own value. The EV of a given decision in such cases is the sum of the expected values of all the outcomes. Each outcome is discounted by its individual probability. EV = summation of $(P_n \times R_n)$. This is complicated, so don't worry about it. We'll show some practical examples of EV later on.

Certainty equivalent	A technical term in data and decision analysis meaning the amount that would be accepted in lieu of a chance to receive a possibly higher, but uncertain amount.
Option	A right but not an obligation to take action in the future.
Risk propensity	A person's desire to either avoid or take risk.
Risk preference	The perceived level of risk and uncertainty that a person is willing to accept in a given situation.
Risk perception	The subjective view of the perceived risk associated with a hazard.
Risk tolerance	A person's attitude toward risk. The greater your risk tolerance, the closer the certain equivalent of a gamble will be to its expected value.

Career Risks

Making career decisions and taking action usually involves three different kinds of risks: physical, emotional, and financial.

- *Physical risk.* Just about any type of work has physical risks. There could be asbestos in the ceiling, you could get carpal tunnel syndrome from typing on your PC, or construction during the remodeling of your office building may inadvertently cause an injury. Some occupations are more hazardous than others. For example, being a firefighter is usually riskier than being an investment banker. Work that involves business travel to certain countries may expose you to physical risks. Extremely long working hours, sleep deprivation, or a stressful work environment can negatively affect your health.

- *Emotional risk.* These are the risks involved in interacting with people, both on and off the job. For example, your role may require you to speak to large audiences, even though it terrifies you. Or you may have to use selling skills and feel very uncomfortable about it. On the one hand, the risk may create internal tension. On the other hand, it can be an opportunity for growth and confidence building. Other examples of emotional risk are dealing with difficult coworkers or a bad boss.

- *Financial risk.* These include risks to both your financial well-being and that of your organization. There are financial risks associated with quitting a job, taking an extended period of time off, investing in your future by going back to school, or starting your own business. Your organization has its own set of financial risks that affect you. For example, a telecommunications start-up would have more financial risk than an established *Fortune* 100 high-technology company.

To illustrate these three kinds of career risks, look at Mary Yukawa, who is considering quitting her job as a brand manager for a food company to start her own business making and distributing healthy meals to busy professionals. Some of her risks include:

- *Physical risk.* Long working hours; tired arms, hands, back, and feet from lifting, chopping, mixing, and standing most of the day
- *Emotional risk.* Loneliness as a sole entrepreneur; tension from having to ask for money from investors
- *Financial risk.* Not raising enough capital; not breaking even in the first year

For Mary, starting her business involves risk. Not doing it also involves risk. If she maintains her status quo, she runs the risk of never fulfilling her dream of starting her food business. She may have regrets in the future, or she may have given up on a potentially lucrative, dizzyingly successful, and fulfilling career direction.

Common Career Risks[7]

Among the people we have coached over the years, we have observed some common risks that they have taken or had to consider in their careers. Here are some of these risks:

- Going back to graduate school—an MBA, law, Ph.D., or other degree program
- Getting too comfortable or set in a job
- Staying put after a merger
- Jumping ship after a merger or an acquisition
- Turning down a great job to hold out for the dream one
- Reducing a work schedule for a new baby or a sick parent
- Taking a break/a sabbatical/time off
- Taking on a high-profile new project that doesn't play to one's strengths
- Agreeing to a stretch role, one that is outside one's comfort zone
- Generalizing or specializing in a career or next job—what to do when
- Changing industries or jobs—making some kind of transition
- Taking early retirement
- Starting over after a significant loss or a change in health
- Being too closely aligned with a new or old CEO or senior executives
- Blind loyalty to an organization or its flip side, total lack of commitment

Don't Be an Ostrich

Some people are unaware that there are risks in the decisions they are contemplating or the actions they are taking. They do not realize that there are risks associated with almost everything. They haven't learned how to identify and evaluate the potential risks and rewards associated with their decisions. However, everyone has the ability to learn how to deal with risk and how to use risk to her or his advantage.

You have to realize and accept the fact that risk is out there. There's no need to be paralyzed by the fear of it, instead you can put it in your frame of reference. Actively seek to find out what the risks are for a decision or action that you are considering. Understand that inaction—not doing anything—also involves risk. In our current business environment, the status quo model is one of loss. You have probably heard the phrases "if you snooze, you lose" and "staying in place is losing ground."

Risks won't go away just because you ignore them, but you can analyze and manage them effectively. We're not talking, of course, about acting without thinking. That would be reckless. We are recommending taking measured risks, then doing what is in your control to manage them. As General George S. Patton said, "Take calculated risks. That is quite different from being rash." The following model will help you to take calculated risks.

A Five-Step Approach to Risk[8]

There is a five-step approach that can help you to think about risk, make decisions, and manage the risks you take.

Step 1: Know Your Risk Preference

Refer to your self-assessment work from Principle 1. What is important in your career and life choices? In particular, what are you motivated by? Is it money, status, quality of life, learning, not being bored, helping or serving others, or being happy? Ask yourself some further questions related to your risk-taking nature.

- Are you risk-seeking (you seek out risk), risk-averse (you avoid it like the plague), or risk-neutral (somewhere in between)?
- How much risk can you cope with at this stage in your career or your life, given your personal and professional circumstances?

- What is your risk tolerance? Someone with low risk tolerance would choose to work in a stable company, a familiar environment, or a job that utilizes skills and experiences with which she or he feels comfortable. In contrast, someone with high risk tolerance would opt for a role that stretches him or her, taking on unaccustomed challenges, seeking out new responsibilities and environments, and using and learning new skills.

Note that the amount of risk that someone is willing to take is very subjective. It is very personal and can change based on factors like age, financial situation, responsibility to others, and self-esteem.

The fear factor. Another essential element of knowing yourself is understanding that there can be fear and anxiety about loss, rejection, failure, or other difficulties before, during, and after making a decision. This is a natural human reaction. Think about how you can offset some of that. For example, become as familiar as you can with a potential new job or industry. Can you try it out beforehand—perhaps work on a project or do an internship for a company in the new industry or job you are considering? Can you research thoughtfully all of the questions that need to be answered before you make a decision? Can you ask others for their opinion before jumping in? After you have made a decision, managing the risk and developing contingency plans is the best way to mitigate some of the fear or anxiety.

Step 2: Analyze and Evaluate the Risks

Identify and evaluate the risks. What are your options—your alternatives? What are the possible outcomes for each option? Assign a probability or likelihood of occurrence to each possible outcome. Assess or rate the consequences for each possible outcome.

Given your analysis of the possible scenarios and their probabilities, figure out the option that maximizes your return in terms of the variables that are important to you.

A quantitative approach using expected value. Here's an example of how to use a simple flow diagram to think about a career decision. Anne Baxter

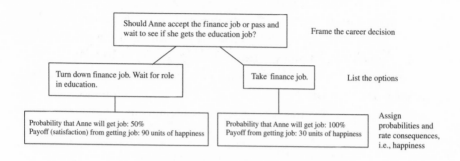

Using the expected value calculation that we referred to in the finance definitions, the EV for turning down the finance job and waiting for the role in education is 50% × 90 = 45. The EV for taking the finance job is 100% × 30 = 30.

If Anne is using EV as a guide, she should wait and take the education job.

Figure 3-1   Using Expected Value Calculations for Risk Taking

has just been offered a job as manager of business development for a bank. She has banking experience, and this is a good job. However, she really wants to switch careers. Her dream job is to apply her skills to the education sector. She is interviewing with a couple of educational nonprofits for business development positions, but she does not know whether she will get a job in education without previous educational experience. She estimates that she has a 50 percent probability of landing a job in education. Figure 3-1 shows the procedure for using EV to evaluate her options.

Many risks have multiple possible outcomes, each with its own probability of occurring and its own value. In these cases, the expected value of a given decision is the sum of the values of all the outcomes, each diminished by its individual probability. The formula is

$$EV = \sum (P_n \times R_n)$$

where p is the probability and r is the reward/value of the risk.

Here's an example of a situation in which you have multiple possible outcomes. Joe Lundgren is wondering whether he should take job A or job B. Compensation is the most important factor to him. If he takes job A, there are three possibilities this year: a 25 percent probability that he will do very well and earn $100,000 in total compensation, a 50 percent probability that

Scenarios for Job A	Probability	Payoff
Great performance	25%	$100K
Solid performance	50%	$90K
Below average performance	25%	$80K
EV	100%	$90K

EV = 100K*25%+90K*50%+80K*.25 = 90K

Scenarios for Job B	Probability	Payoff
Great performance - $150,000 total compensation	50%	$150K
Below average performance $50,000 total compensation	50%	$50K
	100%	$100K

EV = 150K*50%+50K*.50=100K

The EV calculations would indicate that Scenario B is better.

Figure 3-2   Sample Scenarios Using EV

he will be a solid performer and earn $90,000, and a 25 percent probability that his performance will be below average and he will earn $80,000 and no bonus. If he decides to take job B in a smaller company, he has a 50 percent chance of doing very well and earning $150,000 in compensation. However, he has an equal chance of doing poorly and earning $50,000 and no bonus.

Based on compensation, should Joe choose job A or job B? See Figure 3-2 for the answer.

A qualitative approach using a problem-structuring framework.   John Celona, a leading decision analysis expert, an executive with Litigation Risk Management Institute in Palo Alto, California, and the author of numerous books and publications such as *Decision Analysis for the Professional*,[9] formulated a problem-structuring framework for considering risk in career decisions. This framework is shown in Figure 3-3.

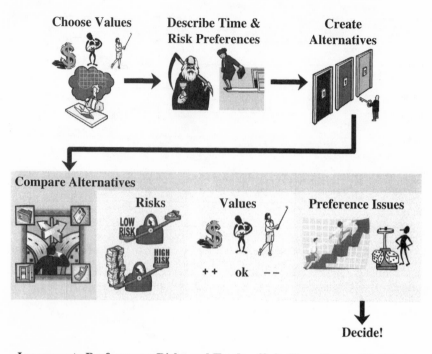

Incorporate Preferences, Risks and Trade-offs in Your Career Decisions

Figure 3-3 A Problem-Structuring Framework to Incorporate Preferences, Risks, and Trade-offs into Your Career Decisions

Celona walks us through the framework:

1. Start by thinking about and listing your values (refer to the exercises in Principle 1). What's important to you? Money? Industry? Job area? Career development? Time with family? Free time on evenings and weekends? List all the things that are important to you and that will be affected by your career or life decision.

2. Consider and describe your time and risk preferences. Your time preference is how soon you want things: Do you want them now, or are you able to wait for your ship to come in? This is equivalent to how much interest you would be willing to pay to get your hands

on a sum sooner. If you could get a $100,000 loan, would you be willing to pay 12 percent interest on it? Would you be willing to pay 5 percent? In economic terms, this is how you feel about the trade-off between present and future consumption. Risk preference, in contrast, is how much risk you'd be willing to take on. Would you be willing to take a big salary cut if a variable component came along with it? This could be stock options, for example, or a bonus plan. How big a risk could you tolerate and still get by? This probably depends on what your assets and monthly expenses are.

3. List your alternatives. Alternatives should be things you would actually consider doing—not just a laundry list.

4. Eliminate alternatives that are unacceptable because they would have a severe negative impact on one or more of your values. In other words, eliminate alternatives that you could not live with.

5. Think about risks as things that are not under your control. Decisions are things that you can control. Depending on the outcome, you obtain either more or less of a particular value from a particular alternative. List the risks for each alternative. Some risks may affect more than one alternative. Your risk preference comes into play here as you consider how much risk you would be willing to take on.

6. Compare your values to your alternatives. Which alternatives score better or worse on a particular value? Look at the risks. How do the risks affect how much of a particular value you get from a given alternative? This can all be done fairly simply by putting together a little worksheet.

The following discussion uses the example of Liliane Taylor Baxter. She has clarified for herself and her significant other the six values that are most important to her and to them. Liliane uses the framework to decide between two choices for her next career move: accepting a job in telecom marketing or teaching marketing.

- Choose values.
  - I have to make at least $80,000 per year to support our minimum standard of living. (V1)

- We want to have one or two children, and I'd like to be able to spend time with them while they're small. (V2)
- I would like to make enough to retire with my present standard of living, to pay off my house within the next 15 years, and to save for my children's college education. (V3)
- I'm willing to work 50 hours per week consistently and 80 on occasion, but I don't want to work 80 hours per week all the time. (V4)
- I want to have time to exercise three times a week, one of which can be on weekends. (V5)
- I want my job to be interesting and professionally and intellectually challenging, and I want to work with good people. (V6)
- Describe risk and time preferences.
  - I'm willing to take a job with a significantly lower salary (at the low end of my range) if there's a chance to make it up in bonuses or equity.
  - I'm not willing to work for a minimal salary in order to get a chance at a larger equity participation, or to invest my personal financial assets.
  - I'd like a company that seems to have a promising strategy and that is producing consistent results.
  - I'm willing to hold off on getting a new car and to delay paying off the mortgage if the eventual reward is there and I can be saving for my kid(s)' college education.
- Create alternatives.
  - Telecom marketing
  - Teaching marketing at local state university
- Compare the alternatives.
- Now, decide among the alternatives.

In the following table, each row presents a particular alternative. The first column lists the alternative, the second gives risks bearing on that alternative, and the third gives values. Rate each alternative for each value, using one or more pluses or minuses. Think about how uncertain the yield on each value is depending on how one or more risks turn out.

Comparing Alternatives—An Example

		Values						Preference Issues	Risk Preference
	Risks	V1	V2	V3	V4	V5	V6		
Telecom marketing	Industry takes a long time to recover, so little wage growth and no bonuses	+	–	+	OK	OK	+	Will take a while to get going with the present state of the industry	Certain initial advantage from higher starting salary
	Downstream opportunity if company emerges as one of the winners	+						Better long-term potential, but risky	Greater variability in eventual income, including possibly little gain from starting salary Greater overall chance of reaching financial goals

(continued)

Comparing Alternatives—An Example (Continued)

	Risks	Values						Preference Issues	Risk Preference
		V1	V2	V3	V4	V5	V6		
Teaching marketing	Might not get the tenure and course load to get the salary up	–	+	–	+	+	+	Good for quality of life	Significant risk of not getting tenure, but otherwise less risky than other alternative
	Consulting opportunities on the side might not be enough to make up for low income potential	–						Highly problematic in terms of income-earning potential	Less uncertainty in potential income, but less income potential
								Very secure once tenured	Little chance of reaching financial goals without permanent change in lifestyle or change in goals

Next, think about your preferences for time value of money and risk. Regarding the first, are you, for instance, willing to trade off fairly certain short-term returns (e.g., salary) for uncertain future rewards (e.g., equity)? This is the classic start-up company trade-off. How much do you need in order to pay the bills each month? What would it take in terms of lifestyle and so on to lower your minimum required monthly cash flow, and are you willing to do that? The fourth column could be maybe just a note or two on timing and the riskiness of potential financial returns for each alternative.

The fifth and last column could deal with risk preference. How much uncertainty are you willing to take on? Would you be willing to take a big risk if the returns on your values are highly uncertain? For example, would you take a job that will take a ton of hours and negatively affect your non-work-time values if the financial return were uncertain? And how much risk are you willing to take? Is a zero outcome for an equity package an acceptable outcome? Is taking a lower-level job an acceptable risk when you might not ever be promoted into the position you really want?

In this example, there is no clear-cut best option that you can determine. It's purposely ambiguous. People looking at this example would have different opinions about which job is better depending on which values are most important to them. Liliane will have to decide based on her values and those of her significant other, which are unique to them. The point is that different people will have different values and weigh them differently in coming up with their unique decisions.

The main idea here is that there's a lot you can learn about which choice would be best and that it is useful to spend time on risk assessment questions *before* you decide to act and make your plans.

Step 3: Manage the Risks

Once you know which option or action you will take and you have identified the risks associated with it, you will want to manage the risks that you know about. Managing risks relies on the ability to reduce either the probability of the event's (the risk's) occurring or the severity of the consequences of the risk.

For example, you can manage your risk of rejection in a job interview by preparing for it. There are a whole host of actions you can take before, during, and after your interviews. Principle 9, on developing and implementing a job search strategy and plan, discusses this in depth.

Minimize the chance of failure in your pitch to potential investors by studying them and their investment decisions and criteria, talking to their portfolio companies, and having a killer business plan.

Decrease the severity of the consequences of quitting your job by exploring options while you are still in your job, saving up a buffer, and perhaps lining up some project work that you can do part-time if you need to.

Develop a plan outlining the steps you need to take and by when as a way of reducing risk and thinking about contingencies.

Step 4: Implement, Learn From, and Adjust Your Plan

Keep these lessons learned and caveats in mind as you go forward with your plan. As we said in Principle 2, if you have setbacks or you fail, assess what you can learn. Make midcourse corrections and adapt accordingly and quickly.

- Decide whether the risk is truly needed or wanted. Don't take unnecessary risk.
- Don't fail to see the forest for the trees. Think about best- and worst-case scenarios for possible decisions. If the worst is not "bad" to you, but the best would make you incredibly happy, then what are you waiting for? (As Peter Drucker said, "People who don't take risks generally make two big mistakes a year. People who do take risks generally make two big mistakes a year!")
- Watch out for analysis paralysis—use tools and techniques, models, and frameworks (ours or others), but listen with your gut too. Listen to your instincts. Go with your educated hunches.
- Once you decide what you will do, go for it. Giving it your all will make a difference. Build the momentum and keep on going, adjusting as you need to. For example:
  - Could you have done more homework, particularly in terms of researching further the trouble that you sensed? Could you have talked to more insiders to gain insight into the problem? Could you have asked more probing questions in your interviews? Could you have set aside more time to analyze and evaluate?

- Could you have hedged your bets—not put all your eggs in one basket, but spread the risk by pursuing multiple options at one time? Hedging is a means of taking action to reduce risk that involves betting on the opposite in order to cut your potential losses. For instance, you may develop a business plan and line up your financing while waiting for the job you really want to come through. You may keep your day job, which calls on strengths that you are familiar with, while trying a completely new, competitive field by night part-time. For example, you may stay in an office job while trying stand-up comedy at night.

Case Study: The Spirit of Adventure in Life and Work . . .

Lance Hill and his wife, Janet, are examples of people who bring their spirit of adventure to their work and their life, taking thoughtful risks. They push the envelope with thoughtful mutual decision making and regular reality checks. Whether they are climbing in the Peruvian Andes, taking a trek through the jungle to a small town on the Yucatan coast, or sharing a mountaineering expedition in Nepal, they work supportively to understand what matters to them. Their work and life choices reflect this. Motivated by their core values of learning and growth, making a contribution, and honesty and integrity, they set off this year on another adventure: moving to New Zealand. They had always wanted to live abroad together. Also, Lance's father's died of a heart attack at age 52, and his mother had encouraged Lance to see the world, follow his dreams, and don't wait. Lance and Janet have factored these ideas into designing a work life that is bold, dynamic, and meaningful.

In a reversal of roles, "Janet accepted a job as a staff midwife at one of the major hospitals in New Zealand, which would satisfy her thirst for experiencing a different health system." Lance turned down the offer of several high-paying jobs in London and instead started his own consulting firm, which could draw on his considerable industry experience.

Janet and Lance identified the risks associated with the move and took thoughtful steps to manage them. For example, to deal with the emotional risk of leaving their families, they planned visits back and other ways to keep in touch. To deal with the financial risk associated with the starting up of Lance's practice, they set realistic expectations of no revenue the first year and took steps to live with that. Janet and Lance also developed a contingency plan, deciding that if nothing panned out for Lance and/or if their financial position were to become untenable, they would return to the United States, where they were confident of finding other opportunities. Lance doesn't see himself as managing his career perfectly, but he has managed the changes and risks by learning from his "mistakes and lapses in my resolve to pursue my interests which have added more clarity and personal growth."

To look at the bigger picture, the total of their life vision/career mosaic, in managing his career Lance has tried to be constantly moving in the right overall direction and building the skills and experiences in his portfolio. His lessons for others on managing careers are insightful:

- Set your own goals and standards, rather than living by those of others.
- Keep in mind that perfection is the enemy of the good—learn to let go.
- Hire people who will naturally step in when your energy gives out and you need help.
- Manage others' expectations instead of being their subject.
- Move on when things are going well, rather than after a failure.

Step 5: Diversify Now and for the Future

In the finance arena, diversification is a proven strategy for minimizing risk. This concept has numerous applications for career and life decision making. Here are some other examples of diversifying in order to reduce risk:

- Diversify your job and investment incomes. For example, it is preferable not to invest heavily in the industry in which you work. If you work for HBO, don't put a large chunk of your stocks in the entertainment industry. If you work for General Motors, you would not want to invest almost everything you have in the automotive industry.
- Diversify with your partner or significant other. If possible, one of you should be in a more stable job if the other is in a highly risky one. Working in different industries or in different types of roles also

minimizes your exposure to risk. If your industry takes a nosedive, your partner's may be stable or wildly successful. If your job is in less demand, your significant other's may be in higher demand.

- Diversity in your organization. The risk to your organization, which is passed onto you, will generally be less if the company operates in more than one industry, sector, business line, and/or market.
- Diversify your skills and competencies. Develop a variety of skills and competencies that are portable. Having skills and competencies that you can apply to different activities and different kinds of work allows you multiple options for generating income. If one set of skills is not in demand, you can use a different set, drawing from the portfolio of your "assets" as opportunities arise. Think about the core competencies discussed in Principle 1. In addition to your primary skills, there are also secondary ones that you can develop over time as contingencies. For example, you may have a passion or hobby such as event planning or teaching golf or French. Principle 10 discusses core skills that are recession-proof and valuable to build for your career over a lifetime.
- Diversify your clients. This involves having several clients rather than putting all your eggs in one basket and depending on only one company. This would mean working with clients from different industries/sectors, of different sizes, with different locations, or of different maturity. This also has implications for you if you are employed by an organization. For example, if you are an HR manager, you might try to work with multiple client groups internally or to spread your expertise among many managers. You might attempt to cultivate relationships with client groups outside your core responsibilities by serving on project teams—for example, on a companywide initiative such as a diversity task force.

The ultimate diversification—a portfolio career. In the year of her golden jubilee celebration, 2002, Queen Elizabeth II said, "*Change is a constant. The way we embrace it defines our future.*" In the past, changing jobs, moving back and forth from working to not working, and trying models other than traditional full-time employment (such as part-time employment, project-based employment, consulting, or contracting) was frowned upon. Often the perception was that people who were engaged in nontraditional work arrangements were unstable, less reliable, not committed to their employers, disloyal, or suffering from ADD (attention deficit disorder—a job could not hold their attention for long).

Times have changed. Now, moving freely among jobs is often considered a sign of versatility, adaptability, and confidence as long as it's not done too frequently. There is growing recognition of the need for and value of different career models for individuals, whatever you wish to call this—a career mosaic, a portfolio career, or a boundaryless career. (Refer back to the career path model exercise and discussion in Principle 1.) Principle 4 will discuss diverse career models in more depth. For now, consider the example of a "free agent." Think Hollywood. An individual develops a portfolio of skills that can be used within or outside of an organization. The person isn't tied to any one employer and, like an actor, may be involved in a variety of projects at the same time or over time.

The convergence of phenomena. The shift to nontraditional work arrangements is driven both by changing personal preferences and by shifting organizational needs. Two phenomena are responsible for the shift:

- The changing employee-employer contract. People seldom have the opportunity to remain with one company for life. Companies offer learning and skill-building opportunities, but they do not offer guaranteed employment—they can fire at will.
- The increased availability and use of sophisticated technology. New technologies are enabling people to work differently. They can work at home, work virtually, or work independently, taking their portable skills with them to anywhere they want or need to be.

Also affecting the changing views of work is the dramatic change in market cycles. The dot-com heyday (and then implosion), with its boom in hiring part-timers, contractors, and project-based consultants, coupled with sizable layoffs from established, old-economy companies, created a highly capable, but fluid workforce.[10]

Cash-flow lives—a portfolio career. The concept of a portfolio career was introduced in Principle 1. Creating a diversified career portfolio can minimize risk and also provide variety, stimulation, and satisfaction. First coined by Charles Handy in *Age of Unreason*,[11] the term *portfolio workers* refers to those who lead cash-flow lives, not salary lives. Money comes from different sources in fits and starts rather than coming consistently from one primary source.

Here's an example of someone who has a portfolio career. Gracia Hunter is a laid-off executive recruiter who now works part time in her own practice as a career coach for job searchers. She supplements her income by contract work through a career transition company that caters to large companies. She is also one of the founding team members of a new business coaching start-up. She is using her business skills to develop the business plan for this start-up. In her spare time, she volunteers to teach computing skills at a senior center.

A portfolio career encompasses the whole realm of work, both paid and unpaid. In addition to your "main" work, it includes the occasional supplemental project that brings in income or enriches your life. A portfolio career recognizes that work encompasses volunteering, lifelong learning, and managing your career. These bring you value and intangible compensation.

Learn from Setbacks and Develop Contingencies

No matter how much you can reduce risk, there will always be things that cannot be controlled or that lead to unpredictable events. For this reason, think about the worst thing that could happen—the worst-case scenario— and how you would handle the outcome. Make sure you have fallback plans and even an exit strategy. What will you do to extricate yourself from the situation if you need to? Refer back to Principle 2, which discussed learning from mistakes.

Factoring in Your Significant Others

Most career advice books are written as though the career needs of just one person—usually the primary breadwinner—mattered. In reality, though, spouses or partners, children, and other personal relationships affect career decisions significantly. In our research for this book, a former restaurant owner and parent of two children told us, "My priorities have changed. I can't think of only myself when I make career or life decisions. This is sometimes frustrating, but it's reality, and it has changed the way I make decisions."

Plan your career with both your needs and goals and those of your significant others in mind. The exercises in Principle 1 provided frameworks and inventories for considering your significant other in your decisions. Everyone has his or her own value system and set of work motivators. Find out what your profile is and how this both compares and contrasts with those of the people in your life who will be affected by your career and life decisions.

Our Top Risk-Taking Tips

- Don't take unnecessary risks. Be sure you have to or want to take them.
- Be thoughtful about risks. Give them the time and attention they deserve.
- Use all the tools and resources available to you, both those in this principle and others. Hone your risk-taking skills and instincts. With practice, and through both successes and learning from setbacks (refer back to Principle 2), you will become more skillful at risk taking.
- Allow yourself to feel your anxiety and fear.
- Make people a priority—get support from them, including your significant other.
- Enjoy your interests and hobbies, things that are familiar to you but that will also keep you in a positive mindset.
- Try not to magnify what will happen if you fail. Be as objective as possible about the consequences of a decision or action. Will you really lose your job if you fail at this new assignment? If you don't move to Asia to turn around that division, will your boss and colleagues not forgive you? If you don't start up your own business now, does it mean that you can never do so?
- Your nose knows. If you sense trouble, a problem, or underlying issues with something you are considering, talk to as many insiders as

possible. Do your research—due diligence—and honor your instincts.

- Take on only the amount of risk you can cope with at the point where you are (and where your significant other is) in your career and your life. For example, you might not move to another country, change industries and jobs, and get married all at the same time.
- Do make a plan and work your plan, including developing contingencies for managing your risks (see Principle 6).
- Aim higher but expect lower. Don't expect absolute success each and every time. Sometimes you will fail; other times you will succeed. That's just fine. Try to stay above water more often than not.
- When you are facing risk, ask the tough questions. The more information you have, the more able you are to make an intelligent decision—and to manage the risk of the actions you choose to take.
- Guard against inertia that keeps you from moving and changing. People can easily fall into inertia because of their training, education, and years of expertise. All these things are heavily invested in and deeply rooted. Also, being an integral part of a community (of colleagues, of an industry or profession, of a city or country) sometimes creates strong ties that can constrain your movement. The position or status that you have because of what you have achieved so far—your expertise and reputation—can be an anchor. That can be good or bad, depending on whether you want to make an active choice to stay put or whether you want to ride the waves.

Try to think about risks as opportunities. As Oprah Winfrey says, "Luck is a matter of preparation meeting opportunity."

Case Study: Skill and Client Diversification— A CPA Turned Entrepreneur Develops an Innovative Work Life[12]

Diana Chan has developed her risk-taking skills over time. The oldest daughter of a Mississippi cotton farmer/grocery store owner and a stay-at-home mom, she grew up especially fast after her dad's sudden death from cancer at the age of 35. She was a natural nurturer, and she became a second mom to her younger siblings and evolved into a compassionate leader. Says Chan, "Our family was incredibly close already, but my father's death could have made us either fall apart or pull together and move ahead. My mother was a remarkable role model for all of us. We watched her have to reinvent herself many times in her career, using different skill sets at different times to take care of the family financially. She taught me the value of a realistic optimism, hard work, and perseverance."

Chan chose to major in accounting at the University of Mississippi because she was good with numbers, she knew that an accounting major would be challenging, and accounting was practical. Upon graduation, she had her choice of opportunities, as she had excelled in both leadership and academics in school. As a double minority back in the 1970s (female and Asian), Chan was offered a position with Deloitte and Touche, one of the "Big 8" accounting firms (now the Big 5). Big 8 firms offered only two accounting positions to women at her university. Chan knew that she was both being given an opportunity and taking a risk by being part of the small group of women in what was at the time a mostly male profession. Later, Chan moved to Chevron Corporation to gain industry and finance experience, then she zigzagged back to another top Big 8 firm, KPMG, where she was on a fast track to tax partner.

When Chan became pregnant with her first child, the event nudged her and her husband to reflect on how their work should fit into their overall life vision. After discussions of their needs, their wants, what mattered to them, and possible trade-offs, they decided to make some changes. For them, the short- and medium-term priorities were a highly flexible work schedule, ample time for hands-on parenting, and making use of Chan's interest and experience in tax and accounting. She was willing to take a measured risk. She could rely on her strengths—her expertise—to start up a business and minimize financial risk by working from home and doing it solo at first.

Chan started up her tax practice, Chan CPA, working with high-net-worth individuals and a small group of companies. The business flourished, and soon she was hiring other accounting professionals who wanted to juggle parenthood with continuing to practice their craft. She managed the risk inherent in recruiting by bringing in only people whose work she knew or those who were referred by such people.

By the arrival of Chan's second child, her tax practice was thriving and she was still enjoying it, but she was ready for a new challenge. She wanted new responsibilities and to keep learning new skills. While still leading the practice, she developed other people who could stretch themselves and handle the day-to-day operations. Then, through her husband's windsurfing buddies, Chan networked her way into part-time consulting with Quantum Corporation. She was able to pursue her interest in high technology, a totally new field, while also keeping her tax practice going.

Over the 5 years she spent at Quantum, as her children needed less time, she took on more responsibility, moving to a senior manager role. She worked on a number of diverse projects, leading strategic project teams on a variety of business priorities such as an Oracle worldwide enterprise resource planning (ERP) implementation, developing and rolling out the first international systems application for strategic partners, and creating and implementing an integrated accounting and business system for materials costing. Her experience at Quantum gave her valuable new skills, colleagues and friends in a new industry, and more confidence as a leader and manager (the people and soft skills to complement her technical skills). The experience also deepened her knowledge of the high-tech industry.

When the dot-com frenzy hit, Chan was ready to create her next opportunity. Through her previous work with individuals and companies in her tax practice and through referrals found by networking with people at Quantum, she knew that small companies, particularly start-ups, often could not afford full-time talent for projects or professional services such as business strategy and planning, operations, finance, accounting, human resources, and purchasing. She expanded Chan CPA to offer these competencies on an interim and project basis, and she recruited an eclectic mix of people with a variety of skill sets who could grow with her as her business needs changed dynamically.

Now cut to the present—the dot-com implosion and its aftermath. Chan was able to keep her staff—there were no layoffs. The business has survived and thrived. Earlier on, she had managed risks by diversifying her client base beyond start-ups to financial services companies, old-line traditional companies, and other such areas. Chan also developed her people based on their interests and strengths. Her business was well positioned to offer competencies in the areas that were in high demand when others were slow. For example, when the interim professional services side of the business was bringing in less revenue, the tax and accounting services areas filled the gap. Chan's skill diversification (hers and her group's) insulated the business from the downturn because her group was versatile and adaptable.

Chan CPA and Company is still growing strong through continued innovation and diversification. Chan has started serving on selected boards, advising CEOs, and coaching female executives. The company recently began experimenting with a new service, an innovative "1040 to Go Program." This is an employee benefit that companies offer their employees; it provides in-house tax seminars, tax preparation, and financial planning. Chan embraces the adage, "no risk, no reward," but she takes risks by carefully considering all the possible consequences, including the missed opportunities if she decides not to take a chance.

Principle 4

Put Money in Perspective

You aren't wealthy until you have something money can't buy.
—Garth Brooks

Rich Rewards

The fourth principle in gaining career clarity involves understanding what money means to you and how much money is "enough." You've had a chance to think about what's important to you and what you want to achieve in the future, and you've been encouraged to take risks as you make new plans. All of this is made easier, of course, if money is not an obstacle. In this principle we explore how you might approach building a work life in which you make enough money but are not ruled by it. We offer you active frameworks and concepts that support your pursuit of being happy on your terms, and we show you how to create a solution set of options for doing purposeful work while being richly rewarded, either monetarily or through the fulfillment created by doing something meaningful with your life (or both!).

We offer you some exercises to help you define success for yourself, rather than using others' measures. We discuss the new paradigm of meaning over money, teach you how to develop a budget, and offer advice for being smart about your finances, including building a reserve for rainy days or to allow you to take a break. We also explore work options beyond the typical mode of full-time employment.

Meaning and Money

In our work with individuals and organizations, we encourage our clients to follow their heart, their bliss, their passion. However, we are also pragmatists, so we recognize the importance of having a secure base from which to operate and turn your dreams into reality. We offer strategies and how-tos that will work whether you measure success in terms of financial reward, nonmonetary rewards such as happiness, or a combination of the two. Our bias, based on our experience and based on the research that has been done on productivity, is that being engaged in activities you enjoy and do well renders your work life richer, more profound, and ultimately more satisfying than spending your life doing something just for money without being engaged in the endeavor.

The fact that money may not be all it's cracked up to be is borne out by numerous studies showing that compensation is not the main driver of job satisfaction. For example, a WetFeet Press survey of MBAs in 2002 showed that other factors, such as people, intellectual stimulation, career-broadening opportunities, and having responsibility, were more important than money. In this study and others like it, on lists of factors that are most important to job candidates, compensation is one of the top five or top ten factors, but it seldom shows up in the top three. Money is important, but it's not the only thing that's important. In this principle we take money into account while looking at the whole of what matters to you. We explore putting money into perspective—embracing the idea that while money isn't everything, it *is* something!

"Show Me the Money"

The well-known phrase found in the Tom Cruise movie *Jerry McGuire* represents a view that is held by many people today—that money is the be-all and the end-all. In this view, money is the *end,* not the means to the end. It is the primary driver or motivator for work. Grab the brass ring, strike it rich, go for the gold, make it big, get to the top, who wants to be a millionaire, lifestyles of the rich and famous. Most of us have grown up with these not-so-subtle messages concerning what society purportedly holds in high regard. Many people and many cultures equate being successful or being happy with having a lot of money or accumulated wealth. How much money somebody has or how much somebody makes is often the subject of awe or envy in many circles.

Think about the flood of media stories a few years ago heralding the 27-year-old dot-com millionaires. The lists of America's richest or most powerful people still grab our attention from the newsstands. Self-made billionaires are revered or singled out for their accomplishments or their transgressions. Our fascination with entertainers' and sports celebrities' pay packages is palpable.

Clearly, there is a lot of social conditioning around the whole topic of money and our pursuit of it. Conditioning isn't the only reason that money is important to us, however. The simple reality is that "money makes the world go 'round." It's a cold, hard fact that most of us need at least a foundation of financial security in order to feel secure enough to pursue our dreams. Of course money is a factor in many job choices and career decisions. If the truth be told, for some people, money is also the metric by which they value their self-worth or judge their success relative to that of others. Money does have value. But there's much more to the story than that. Within the larger context of our lives, there are other tangible and intangible factors that mean a lot to us. Having a purpose, making work and life choices that support our values, affecting people's lives positively—these are some of the intangibles that count. These *are* the big picture. Money is a part of the whole, but it is only one dimension, and for some people, it is not the most important part.

Measures of Success

If you are reading this book, you probably are already an enlightened soul. You know that living your life is important. You want to make your life meaningful, you care about the others in your life, and you're aiming for success on your terms. Maybe you have a long way to go, but you're on the road in that journey. Your self-assessment work in Principle 1 illuminated how you measure success as well as how you define your values, what matters to you, what you consider meaningful work, and what following your passion would look like.

You probably already embrace the idea that money isn't everything. You resonate with the beliefs that being happy, following your heart, and doing work that is purposeful are worthy work life objectives. You appreciate that attaining these intangible gifts can add much more to your personal wealth than hard dollars.

No One Size Fits All

Realistically, we all need a certain amount of money in order to live and to survive. We each have our individual needs, aspirations, and ideas concerning what we consider to be a "comfortable" lifestyle. There's no "one size fits all" perspective on money that works for everyone. We each develop our own perspective, which is shaped by our experiences and beliefs. On a rational level, most of us recognize that money alone cannot buy health or happiness. It cannot replace the indefinable wealth of true friends and real love. And we certainly know that we can't take our money with us when our time here on the planet is up. But what is the connection between money and career that will create a bold, dynamic, and meaningful career over a lifetime look like?

What Does Money Mean to You?

Vipasana is a form of meditation. It means seeing things as they really are. The emphasis is on clarity—on gaining deeper understanding and moving away from a narrow vision of life. We need to put money into perspective; we need to approach thinking about it not in terms of winning or competing to be the best, or even as merely a means of economic survival. Money is a means to an end; it is not the end itself. Money is the means by which we can achieve our life and career goals. It ultimately is a vehicle for enabling us to attain what psychologists call career actualization (self-fulfillment and reaching our potential) and career transcendence (helping *others* to find fulfillment and realize *their* potential). Vispasana helps us to clarify our attitude about money and its correlation with the life and career choices we make.

Post-September 11—Rethinking Priorities

As we've noted earlier, the tragedies of September 11, 2001 led to increased introspection and review of our priorities. That day, which has been etched forever in our minds and hearts, has led many of us to reconsider our deepest values and attitudes, to rethink what matters and what is meaningful. Many of us are reconsidering what we want, how we want to live, and what we want our lives to have looked like when our time on earth is up.

Creating an Inspired Life

Creating a life that is inspiring, or at least meaningful and purposeful, has become a central theme for many people. What is your central theme about money? Did September 11, 2001 affect your thinking about what you're doing with your life, and if so, how? Even before September 11, we had seen, in our work with career changers—from high school dropouts to CEOs— a shift over the past few years, and we have seen a sea change recently. To follow your heart in your work, to seek meaning in life, and to do what matters have become top priorities for many. How to combine these noble ideals with making a living and being successful is the million-dollar question.

In an investment class for a group of Stanford MBAs, the famed investor Warren Buffett told the students, "The most important things in life are love, health, and happiness . . . and money can't buy any of these." As one of our clients advises, "Find what you enjoy, and make that work. Don't do anything 'just for the money.' Every time I've taken on work just for the money, I haven't had any fun, and I haven't done good work."

Buying Freedom

It's true that money can't buy some of the more important intangible things in life. We are realistic, however, in recognizing that money can afford us a measure of freedom—more choices and greater flexibility in exercising our life options. Having enough money allows us to

- Take breaks for renewal
- Take more risk in our life and our career
- Hold out for jobs we really want

- Make a career change that requires a pay cut
- Free ourselves from jobs we don't really enjoy
- Contribute to worthwhile causes
- Support our spouses and partners in their search for their dreams
- Make sure that our children's needs are not ignored because of our work schedules

Baseline Needs

We recognize that for many people, money is essential for putting food on the table. If you're recently divorced or widowed, or if you have suffered a sizable financial setback, you're probably thinking that money is much more important than we're making it out to be. If you're starting a family after some years of living on your own, or if you're saving for your children's education, or if you're paying for your own health insurance, money is a necessity, and it will be higher on your priority list when you're making career and life decisions. Baseline economic needs must be met before we can even begin to think of more enlightened uses for money. As one of our clients notes, "Initially I worked for the passion of my work. As I progressed, our lifestyle improved, and eventually we needed my income to maintain that level." A colleague of ours, an African American single parent who had found the glass ceiling to be excessively low, was more blunt: "I used to want to save the world. Now I'm trying to save myself and make a secure life for my child. Reality 101 set in and demanded that the job 'show me the money!'"

We know that there are many people for whom these quotes ring true. If you're one of them, however, we encourage you to think outside this box and to think creatively about putting money into perspective, making it work for you and your objectives. The challenge is to determine your current state in life and the role that money is currently playing in your life. Then—and here comes the hard part—the next step is to determine the role that you want money to play in your life in the future, and make plans accordingly.

A Self-Inventory

In the exercises in Principle 1, you completed assessments that helped you to understand your values, what matters to you, what you mean by meaningful work, how you define success on your own terms, and so on. Revisit these exercises and, on your own or with a partner, reflect on these fundamental questions:

1. What do I value in life? How has this changed over the years? How might it change in the future?
2. What really matters to me (and to those who are important to me) right now? How has this changed over the years? How might it change in the future?
3. What would I really *like* to be doing with my life, if I could do anything I wanted? What do I *need* to be doing right now? Given my current realities, how can I incorporate what I'd like to be doing into what I need to be doing at this time in my life?
4. How do I define success for myself? How do others in my life define success for themselves? Where are the similarities and the differences? How are these similarities and differences affecting my decision making about my life and my career?
5. What makes me happy? How do I follow my bliss, either as a vocation (paid work) or as an avocation (unpaid work)?

Case Study: The Happiness Factor—Following Her Passion to the New York City Chamber of Commerce

Mary Jo Dunnington seems very comfortable with her perspective on money. She is an example of a person who is fulfilled and evolved. She was formerly a senior manager at the AMEX and a director at GOVWORKS, Inc., but her heartstrings and her higher calling have taken her back to her nonprofit roots. She's serving as vice president of corporate affairs for the New York City Partnership and Chamber of Commerce.

Mary Jo acknowledges that "for a lot of people, money and earning potential are important components of what they are seeking in a career. For others, like me, other things are more important drivers. For example, I've seen a lot of people in business who claimed that they would really like to work at a not-for-profit, but that they wanted to 'make it' (and make some money) in the business world first. That seemed like a reasonable approach, but I figured out that for me, doing something I really care about and believe in is always important as a core value. I need extra motivation, alongside my coffee, to want to get out of bed each morning. And since I do know that about myself, I also know that I have to prioritize jobs that provide me with personal satisfaction above those that pay well but that I would not find as rewarding."

For Mary Jo, following her passion led her to her most recent gratifying career move. She's in a job that she never could have described if you had asked her 10 (or even 2) years ago. Her role has allowed her to build new knowledge and competencies and to do work that really matters to her. She is running the corporate relations group of a major New York City business association, getting to know the city's business leaders, and looking for ways to both enable them to promote their interests with the public sector and engage them in helping to solve issues facing the city, such as the problems with the public education system, the need to rebuild downtown Manhattan after September 11, and the congestion and access issues associated with the city's airports. Mary Jo doesn't take her good fortune for granted, but she comfortably accepts her role in getting herself there. She says, "I ended up here because I paid attention to what makes me happy."

A Budget as a Planning Tool[1]

One is hard pressed to think about career clarity if one's basic needs are not met first. A budget is a fundamental baseline to help you plan how much you need in order to live, exactly what "enough" means to you (and, if relevant, to your partner), and how far you can push it if you choose to make a job or career change or to take a break.

Diana Chan, founding principal of Chan CPA and Company, an innovative Silicon Valley firm that provides business strategy and financial, accounting, tax, and other professional services, generously provided three budget planning tools to help you get started. The three figures that follow provide a template that can be used as a guide for developing a baseline budget (see Figure 4-1) and two more advanced tools for tracking expenses and assessing where your money is going.

	Monthly Budget	Actual												
		Jan	Feb	Mar	Apr	May	Jun	Jul	Aug	Sep	Oct	Nov	Dec	Annual
Income														
Total Earned Income (A)														
Total Unearned Income (B)														
Total Income														
Expenses														
Flexible:														
Clothing														
Dining														
Entertainment														
Household Furnishings & Improvement														
Miscellaneous (1)														
Recreation														
Savings and Investments (2)														
Vacations (3)														
Total Flexible Expenses														
Essential Expenses:														
Automobile (4)														
Childcare														
Education														
Financial Expense (5)														
Groceries														
Housing (6)														
Medical/Dental/Life (7)														
Payroll Taxes (8)														
Utilities (9)														
Total Essential Expenses														
Total Income														
Total Expenses														
Cash Savings/Deficit														

FOOTNOTES

(A) Earned Income includes: Bonuses, Salary, Spouse's Salary and Business Income
(B) Unearned Income includes: Dividend Inc, Gifts Rec'd, Interest Inc, Investment Inc, Other Income, Passive Bus Inc, Rental Inc, Tax Refund and Unemployment Income
(1) Miscellaneous includes: Cash, Charity, Gifts, Subscriptions and Sundries
(2) Savings and Investments includes: 401K Contributions, IRA, Employee Stock Purchase Plan, Rain Day Savings, Stocks, Mutual Funds, CD's
(3) Vacations includes: Lodging, Travel and Other
(4) Automobile includes: Fuel, Loan Payments, Service, Repair, Insurance and Registration
(5) Financial Expenses includes: Banking Fees, Interest Expense and Other
(6) Housing includes: Mortgage/Rent, Repairs, Association Dues, Insurance, Property Tax
(7) Medical/Dental/Life includes: Doctor, Medicine, Insurance, Other, Dentist, Dental Insurance and Life Insurance
(8) Payroll Tax includes: Fed, Medicare, Other, SDI, Social Security, State
(9) Utilities includes: Cable TV, Garbage, Gas & Electric, Telephone, Water, Other

This is a sample budget template you can use as a worksheet. Populate the spreadsheet with your own numbers, your inflows and outflows. Estimates are better than nothing.

Figure 4-1 A Budget Template

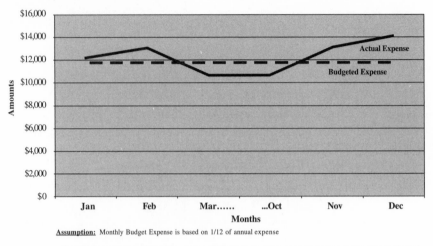

Assumption: Monthly Budget Expense is based on 1/12 of annual expense

Tracking Expenses is a useful exercise. Note especially variances where your actual expenses were way over planned.

Figure 4-2   Expense Tracking: Planned versus Actual

More Advanced Budgeting Techniques

After you have developed your budget, other more advanced tools for managing your money are tracking expenses (Figure 4-2) and charting how your money is being spent or allocated (Figure 4-3). The main ideas here are to understand your inflows and outflows, to refine your skill in forecasting them (looking ahead, which is crucial to planning), and to have a general awareness of where your money is going so that you can make adjustments based on your overall personal and financial objectives.

A Framework for Your Finances

A budget helps you understand your inflows, or sources of your income (how much you have coming in), and your outflows, or expenses (how much you have going out). Beyond your personal budget, however, thinking about your finances overall, on a macro level, is important.

Ken Kam, the CEO of Marketocracy, an Internet-based investment management firm and a top mutual fund manager, developed this framework

How You Are Allocating Your Money

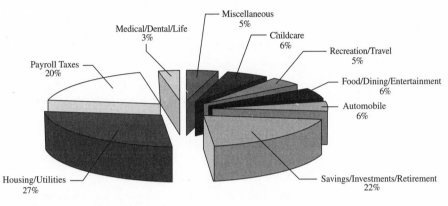

To be disciplined, know where your money is going - how your expenses are allocated as a percentage of your total.

Figure 4-3 Charting Where Your Money Is Going

and offers some advice for thinking about your financial planning and investment strategies. In June 2002, the *Wall Street Journal* named Kam's Marketocracy Masters 100 Fund the top performing multicap core fund for year-to-date performance. What is given here is not investment advice; rather, it is a framework for thinking about personal finances: how to approach financial planning, questions/issues to consider, and lessons that can be learned from an expert.

Basic Financial Planning

Kam provides his top ten tips for financial planning.

1. Have a plan. A sound financial plan is the best way for most people to achieve financial freedom.

2. Fund your plan by saving from each paycheck. Your financial plan should be the first thing you fund with each paycheck. Limit your expenses to what is left after you've provided for your financial plan instead of the other way around.

3. Don't be ashamed to start small. Small (but regular) savings add up quickly, especially if you start young, but it's never too late to start. When-

ever you get a raise, increase the amount you save. If you get a 10 percent raise next year, put half of the raise into your savings plan. Do this the next few times and soon you'll have a substantial amount of savings without ever cutting your spending.

4. Keep at least a 6-months' reserve of liquid assets so that you have enough to cover your expenses if you lose your job.

5. Broaden the definition of 'liquid assets.' In calculating 'liquid assets,' most people count only their cash and money market accounts. I would also include 50 percent of your nonretirement stock portfolio. I suggest only 50 percent of the stocks because you never know when you might need the money. I am confident that even if you needed the money typically, at the worst possible time in the market, you could get at least 50 percent of the stocks' value. If you are more risk-averse, you can choose to use a lower percentage of your stock portfolio's value when figuring your liquid assets.

6. Invest in stocks. Many people think investing in stocks is like gambling in a casino because you can lose money. The key difference is that in casinos the odds are always stacked against you, so the longer you play, the more certain you are of losing money. The stock market is different. The longer you play, the more certain you are to make money.

7. After building a safety buffer, start investing for the long term. For example, take all the money left over after the safety buffer is established and make a series of investments that is essentially a 5-year ladder (each year, one-fifth of the investments come to fruition and need to be reinvested). This allows you to make all of your investments with a 5-year investment horizon, but it also allows you to change the direction of 20 percent of your portfolio every year.

8. As your assets grow, invest more aggressively for longer time periods. Hardly anyone really invests with a 10-year investment horizon. This means that investments that won't come to fruition for 10 years tend to find few takers, thereby making for a very inefficient market where bargains and opportunities abound.

9. Set up trusts for various purposes. This is the best way to protect your assets from potential liability. Nowadays, people sue you *because* you have money. Putting the money in a trust makes you less likely to be sued.

10. Don't endow your children. Money can be a very destructive factor in a child's life. In order to mature, children need to learn how to value things properly. When money is not a concern, this lesson is not learned—

often with disastrous consequences. I suggest that wealthy parents set up a trust to hold their kids' college education money. The kids should not know that the parents own the trust. Then throughout the kids' lives, the trust can create 'scholarships' that the kids have to apply for. Winning these scholarship helps to teach children how to be self-reliant. The usual alternative is for the parents to pay for everything, thereby teaching their children that the way to get what they want is to kiss up to their parents. The 'trust' solution puts the parents and the children on the same side. The parents will be viewed as helping their children to apply for *all* the scholarship money they are eligible for.

In It Together

As we discussed in previous principles, if you have a partner, a close friend, or a family member who is affected by your financial decisions, it is important to involve this person in your plans. This may sound like singing to the choir, but what does taking others' needs into account when you are making financial plans to further your life and career goals actually mean? It means appreciating your differences and being open to a new way of making decisions. And sometimes it means making sacrifices for the good of the unit as a whole.

One of the main problems that couples face when making financial plans is fundamental differences regarding the value and purpose of money. Opposites do attract, so it's likely that, for example,

- One of you may be a spendthrift; the other, an impulse buyer.
- One of you may be long-term-oriented; the other, short-term.
- One of you may want to save for retirement; while the other wants to take expensive trips.
- One of you may be more risk-averse; the other, a risk taker.

What is your situation? Our feelings about money are fairly deeply rooted. It is difficult to make changes unless a significant event occurs in our lives that prompts a change. So what's important isn't to try to change your partner, but to have a dialogue with your partner and to develop financial plans that take into account both sets of needs and goals.

Negotiation, Not Compromise

What's important here is communication and dialogue about your needs, preferences, beliefs, and philosophy of money. This is especially important when your needs and wants and those of your partner are not in sync. We recommend that you and your partner *negotiate* with each other rather than *compromise* with each other. We say that you should negotiate rather than compromise because when you compromise, you most often meet somewhere in between, or even right in the middle. Neither person ends up getting what he or she wants. In negotiating, each person has the chance to lay out his or her core interests and issues. The goal is for each of you to understand where the other is coming from before you even attempt to evaluate your options and make decisions.

Understanding is central to being able to move forward with financial discussions. By negotiating, you are attempting to come up with "win-win" choices by agreeing to make intentional and mutual trade-offs at various decision points. In other words, consider an imaginary couple, Ben and Betty. Perhaps one time they do what's most important to Ben. The next two times, perhaps they go for what's most important to Betty, then they do what's important to Ben the next three times, and so on. They are not keeping score, however; each of them is accepting the idea that when they have different needs or preferences, they as a couple are mutually deciding to choose one set over another this time. There's reciprocal give-and-take over time.

Practical Matters

To understand what is important to each of you and to pinpoint areas where you may need to negotiate your differences, think about and discuss these practical matters and questions. Figure out what's important to each of you individually, determine collectively how you will help each other achieve your goals, and make it a habit to keep discussing this together. Here are some sample discussion questions for you and your significant other (if applicable).

On a separate sheet of paper or in discussion with your partner, use the following questions as a way of beginning your conversation about what money means to you.

1. What is your relationship with money? Do you see it as a necessary evil? Do you see it as a means to an end, such as retirement or the freedom to finally do what you love if it involves a big cut in pay?
2. What are your overall financial objectives?
3. What are you willing to trade off to get more of something else? For example, if one of you wants more time off and would like not to work for a year, what can you be flexible about and trade off to support that?
4. What do you need to make you happy? Do you need to have reached the top of your game and be pulling in six figures, or is a comfortable life that supports balance and provides enough to survive fine? There will be many variations in answers, and the answer you reach will be a work in progress.
5. Is one of you willing to be the "anchor"—holding a good job with good benefits—while the other pursues her or his dream? Are you willing to switch roles as you move through life's stages?
6. Will one or both of you want to take breaks? If so, then approximately when and for how long? How will you handle that together? What do you need to do now to support the breaks? Principle 8 discusses the idea of taking breaks in greater detail.
7. When do you want to retire? What does each of you mean by retiring? For some retirement may mean working, but without having to worry about making money. For others, it may mean finally enjoying all the activities that there was no time for before.
8. How will you work toward retiring, especially if you will not retire at the same time?
9. How can you plan for that now? Principle 6 will discuss planning ahead in depth.

Your Reserves—Saving for Breaks and Rainy Days

The old wisdom was that you should build a "buffer" of 6 months' expenses "in reserve." That is, you should have enough money/liquid assets to be able to live comfortably for 6 months if your source(s) of income—your job pay, investment income, or other inflows—were to stop today. This is one guideline that hasn't changed and is still good advice. Building a reserve can be achieved through a conscious effort to reduce spending and, where possible, supplement income.

Socking It Away

Saving money does not have to be painful. Principle 8 discusses ways of saving money to fund a break in your career. Formulating a savings initiative of any kind will get you to your reserve target faster. The more you save, the more you have for your reserve buffer. Saving entails being disciplined, thoughtful, and deliberate about how you spend your money. Some people have found that in addition to having a budget, tracking expenses in some form is useful. Knowing where you are spending your money is a beneficial step toward knowing where you can "afford" to save it. Try to categorize your discretionary spending (clothes, eating out, entertainment, travel, and so on). Rank-order the categories so that you know where you spend the most and where the least. Figure out what percentage of the whole each category represents. Then make some conscious decisions and set some goals for what you can cut back on realistically. The results of your saving will be apparent almost immediately, and will buoy you to continue on.

This involves setting a certain percentage, for example, 15 percent or 30 percent, that you want to save from each paycheck. Having it deducted automatically through your HR or payroll department is the least painful way of doing this. You don't even see the money, so you are not tempted to spend it. Over time, you will save up quite a nest egg. You can figure out where to hold the saved money or where to direct it. This may be in a low-interest savings account, a money market account, or another relatively safe alternative.

Making Money

There are a number of creative ways to build your reserve. You can make extra money "on the side" or take a higher-paying job. You can engage in work or projects that bring in supplemental income. For example, if you are a talented webmaster, you could help a friend develop a web site for her new company or offer your services via the Internet, such as through the FreeAgent.com site. You could work extra hours in your current organization if you are paid by the hour or paid for overtime. Another option is to take on an additional project leveraging your expertise, depending on how much "extra" time you have.

Depending on your core expertise, you might write a business plan, give advice on marketing strategy or the sale of a company, do some career coaching by the hour, edit annual reports and brochures, or prepare income tax returns during peak time. You might choose to give art, piano, or voice lessons in your home or to teach HR, finance, or computers at the local college. If going out and looking for this type of work is not your cup of tea, you might work with an "interim services" firm that matches you with a variety of projects that organizations need immediate help on. These firms work the way an agent does for an actor, taking either a fee from the company that hires you for the interim project or a percentage of your earnings. What are some ways in which you and/or your partner can bring in some additional income? Think about a specific time period (1 year, for example) and a specific goal (for example, building up a reserve) as a way of making the extra effort seem manageable.

Flexible Models for Work

After you have developed your budget, put your finances in order, and built your reserve, you will have more freedom to make more flexible choices about your work. As part of attaining career clarity, it is important that you periodically ask yourself what work pattern best suits you at this time. There used to be one primary style, full-time employment. Lisa and Dennis Monroe are an example of this. Dennis and Lisa have decided that it is important for Dennis to focus his efforts on making the most of his high-earning years. So they are doing whatever it takes to help him to focus full-time on his work.

While this used to be the pattern of choice for most working professionals, today there are many more options, including supplemental work, part-time work, delaying the start of your "real" career to pursue other priorities, contract consulting or project work, and episodic work. There are a variety of styles that are both possible and acceptable. It is more common now for individuals to craft a career portfolio or a pattern that is in sync with their personal circumstances and professional needs.

For example, you may begin your career working full-time, and over time move into part-time, flextime, or contract work as your need for independence or unscheduled time grows (to pursue other interests, to return to school, or to have a family, for example). Jane Meyer is an example of this. An expert occupational therapist, she had worked full-time for a hospital for 10 years: Now in her late thirties, she has moved into contract work: teaching part-time, speaking at occupational therapy conferences, and working on contract at a hospital. This model of working gives her more flexibility and less stress, enabling her and her husband to spend more quality time together and to think about starting a business helping baby boomers handle the specialized needs of their aging parents.

Or you may choose to travel the world when you are young and begin your "real" career later. Tim Danz is an example of this. After graduating from law school, he watched his grandfather retire at age 65, only to pass away shortly thereafter. Tim vowed to enjoy life while he could, and he opted to work at a job that enabled him to travel half the year, visiting friends and seeing new places. After 8 years of this, Tim chose to move into a more traditional situation. He is now a very successful university administrator, and he has no regrets about having started his "real" career later in life.

People who choose to remain at home while raising young children follow a similar path, either delaying their entry into full-time employment or slowing down their careers until the children are older. Jocelyn Miller is an example of this. She left a managerial role in finance for a defense company to be a full-time parent when her children were growing up, then returned to work when her two children started high school. Today, Jocelyn is very happy and is recognized in her field.

Or you may want to live in different places in the world, putting work on the back burner at least temporarily if not permanently. Susan Oliver is an example of this. She does project work, but only intermittently—enough to support her next life adventure, whether in Thailand, Australia, or Germany. Her travels and adventures, not a career to which she's devoted, are her life anchor.

Following are some models for you to consider. Each provides ways to make money while meeting your overarching life or career objectives. With each model, one can be either employed directly by an organization, employed by a third-party organization (an interim services firm or agency), or self-employed. Some of these models overlap. For example, it is possible to work part-time, do project-based work, and be a consultant. The models are divided into those based on amount of time and those based on type of work.

Work Models by Amount of Time

Full-time work: You essentially work 100 percent of the normal workweek. You may mix together various models of work into a portfolio career (having several jobs or roles at one time) or you may work off and on, but work 100 percent when you are working.
Episodic work: You work continuously for a while, then take time off; work again for a while, then don't again, and so on. Each work experience is different in duration—perhaps 3 years in one interval, 2 years in the next, followed by two 1-year jobs before a nice break.
Temporary work: You are paid by the hour for an indefinite amount of time.
Part-time work: You work fewer than 40 hours per week—for example, 36 hours or 20 hours. Companies are creating more part-time jobs than they did in the past.

Work Models by Type of Work

Contract work: Independent contractors are hired to work on projects in job functions that the company considers nonessential. For example, a computer firm may contract out the artwork for the packaging of its product or hire someone to do PR or to write its annual report. A staffing company may hire a computer specialist to set up its network.
Contingency work: This is often another name for contract work, but it is subtly different. Contingency workers are employed by a company full-time or part-time when the workload—the company's

business—demands. These workers are let go when the overflow work is completed and the company can handle the work with its existing workforce again. Examples are an HR in-house recruiter who is hired until three new divisions are fully staffed or lecturers who may supplement the full-time faculty for a university's executive education courses.

Project-based work: This is sometimes called freelancing. Companies hire people for a specific project. Perhaps they have one of their seasoned managers serve as the project lead, and that manager builds the team with talent that is already on tap, bringing in some core team members from the outside. When the project is over, the team is disbanded. An example is a film crew made up of freelance camera and production workers. When the film is finished, the members of the crew go on to other projects.

Consulting: This is similar to project-based work except that the consultant provides her or his expertise to a client (an individual or organization) on as as-needed basis during an engagement. For example, an executive coach may be brought in as a consultant to work with a senior management team that is ineffective and in conflict. A former chief technology officer who now consults may be asked by a company to help it figure out its technology strategy.

Career Mosaic

The concept of a career mosaic was introduced in Principle 1. Using the work models just discussed, you can create your own career mosaic design, melding together your different work experiences and models over your lifetime. Your work models can change as you age and move through your life and career. Your overall mosaic will represent your values, what is important to you at that time, your interests, and your goals. As we also discussed in Principle 1, careers today are much more fluid than they used to be. We have many more choices and many more ways of creating and living our life paths. Attaining career clarity isn't easy in this era of numerous choices! But sorting your finances and making them work for you—work to support your dreams—is one sure way of getting clear and getting results on your career.

Case Study: Right on the Money . . . A California Boy's Hard-Won Career Mosaic

Matt Roberts* is a good-looking, blue-eyed blond who is an engineer, a law school graduate, and a CEO/entrepreneur. He possesses a charming wit and lots of personality. He is also a triathlete, a good friend who goes out of his way to lend a hand, a humorous writer, and a gourmet cook. The perfect guy? No, but on the surface it would be easy to conclude that Roberts has lived a charmed life. That perception couldn't be farther from the truth.

Roberts possesses a remarkable amount of grit. He is a guy who has both succeeded and failed, who has struggled time and again with the trade-offs between the lure of money and "having a life." He has managed to put together a career mosaic of work-life choices that combine having "enough money" with having a life that supports what matters to him. Getting to this point, however, was a hard-fought journey.

Matt Roberts graduated from Stanford University in the 1980s with a degree in engineering and later went on to Hastings Law School, where he earned a prestigious Hawaii Supreme Court clerkship. He had stints as a senior manager in a top strategy consulting firm and as the CEO of an e-commerce start-up. With the money he earned, he was able to buy a house in San Francisco with views of the Golden Gate Bridge. Time and again, however, he would admit that he did not "have a life" and had to fight to regain it.

Roberts grew up in a dying factory town in the eastern United States. His primary goal after high school was to get out of town and get away permanently. He says that he "managed to get into Stanford University, and starting there was a shock that changed his life." Being a student there required Roberts to do more work in a month than he was used to doing in a whole year of high school. To cope with it, he developed a lifestyle that consisted almost entirely of studying and working, exercising to relieve the stress, sleeping, and eating—in that order of priority. Having no financial help from his parents, Roberts supported himself through part-time jobs. His lifestyle choice would come back to haunt him later.

---

*Matt Roberts is a pseudonym. All other details are actual.

Through a professor's recommendation, Roberts was able to land a good job as an analyst at a top management consulting firm. The money was great, and by then he was married. He soon had all the trappings of success—new cars, a house, vacations, and so on—and the pressures of maintaining them.

As a consultant, Roberts worked as much as he had at Stanford, if not more. For years, he would be one of the first in the office in the morning and one of the last to leave; he also worked every weekend and most holidays. His travel schedule was dizzying, and soon his home life began to suffer. To take a break from his work, and also to deal with the issue of his future's being limited if he did not have a graduate degree, Roberts went to law school. A J.D. seemed to provide the most future options, given his business and engineering background. Law school was a breeze compared to consulting. As graduation loomed, Roberts dreaded the prospect of plunging back into working such crazy hours, but he nonetheless returned to management consulting, both to build on his expertise and because the compensation was too good to pass up. In his senior role, he specialized in developing business strategies in areas with significant legal issues. His work included dealing with environmental liability, product liability, antitrust, shareholder litigation, and intellectual property experiences.

His travel schedule was intense, escalating from every other week to Monday through Friday every week. Quality home life was nonexistent, and deep down he was not satisfied with either his life or his work. Five years later, Roberts was divorced. As he sorted through the wreckage of his personal life, he reassessed his priorities. After 20 years of doing almost nothing but working and working out, he wanted a radical change. More than anything, he wanted the chance to make enough money so that he could do what he wanted to do. He was willing to make that one last trade-off so that in the future, he could choose work that he really liked rather than work that had the greatest income-earning potential. To achieve the "enough money" part, he wanted the leverage potential of an equity stake. And he figured that, since he was single again, now was the time to take that something on.

He began aggressively building his cash reserve, and when that was achieved, he moved from consulting into project work that would give him the additional experience that he needed in order to join a start-up. Eventually he became CEO, a position that drew heavily on his strategy experience. The company offered him an equity stake with a big potential upside. The start-up failed, but Roberts learned an immense amount.

Parlaying this experience, he mixed consulting gigs with working in start-up companies. One paid the bills, and the other helped him to learn what starting and running a company were really all about. As an entrepreneur-in-residence at a venture capital firm, he gained an understanding of how venture capitalists evaluated strategies, valued companies, and approached merger and acquisition negotiations. He then served as CEO of another start-up company. This time the company is still around and doing well, and along the way, Roberts was given the opportunity to invest in a company as part of a venture round of financing at the same valuation the venture capitalists were getting.

As he was starting a new relationship, a highly lucrative consulting opportunity came up, but it required a Monday through Friday travel schedule to Michigan from California. Although he knew that this would be a strain on his nascent relationship, Roberts decided to take it. He realized that he was falling into the money trap again, but he also recognized that he could use the opportunity to further build up what he considered to be "enough" money to buy him his future freedom. He's lived up to that promise to himself. When that project came to an end, Roberts took an extended break to spend time with his significant other, travel, and start writing a humorous book.

This time to reflect and renew allowed him to realize that the new relationship was "the one." He's made a value and a priority of "having a life," and he continues to take on project-based consulting and interim chief operating officer responsibilities that fit into his total work/life vision. It took him a long time to figure out how to balance having a great life and making money. Somehow you believe that this philosophy is going to stick.

Says Roberts, "I have learned that the people in your life, and the relationships you create with them, and what they mean to you and you to them, are all that really matters. Everything else you can work around. Love beats money any day."

And what about self-actualization? Roberts responded with a gleam in his eye. "I composed my own epitaph a few years back: 'I lived while I was alive.'" What a surprise.

Principle 5

Make People a Priority

Your wealth is where your friends are.

—PLAUTUS[1]

Cultivate Interdependence

The fifth principle in attaining career clarity is to both utilize and aid the people in your life. In this principle we discuss the importance of cultivating interdependence, of making people a priority in your career decisions. We discuss what interdependence is and why it's important, the role that others can play in enriching our lives, and ways to manage our careers as though others matter. There are many ways in which we can interact with others. We cover several of them here: collaborative decision making, networking, coaching, and mentoring.

The word *career* is derived from a French word that means "ladder." In the traditional view, a career consists of a number of steps that an individual takes, striving toward career success as measured by the extent of one's progress up through the ranks (see Figure 5-1). This metaphor is outdated in a number of ways. For many people today, moving up may not be their primary career driver or their measure of career success. Career growth can occur laterally, across jobs, by moving from one organization to another, and even by consciously downsizing your career. As we discussed in Principle 1, many people are now seeing meaning, fulfillment, job satisfaction, autonomy, opportunity for work/life balance, chance for travel and new experiences, the opportunity to be creative, or time for family and friends as being just as important as upward mobility, if not more important.

TRADITIONAL   **CONTEMPORARY**

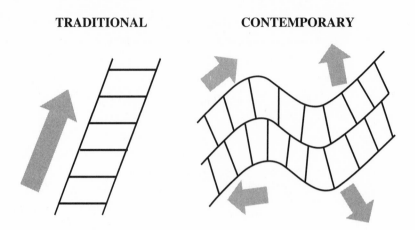

Figure 5-1   Traditional and Contemporary Career Ladders

Make Room for Others

The ladder metaphor is also outdated because it assumes that the ladder is narrow, with just enough space on its rungs for one person. It leaves out an extremely important component of anyone's career success: other people. It overlooks the role of others in helping one to be successful in life or in one's career. The steps on the ladder need to be widened to make room for the many people who help or influence an individual as he or she moves up, across, and even down the steps of the life and career ladders. To put it simply, interacting with others makes us better people, enriches our lives, and enhances our careers.

Managing Our Careers as though Others Mattered

Putting people first requires a conscious effort to develop a strategy and make time for others in one's life and work. One way to do this is to make a list of the people who are or could be important to you. List those people in your personal or work life with whom you are committed to spending time or with whom you want to spend more time. Examples include your spouse or partner, children and other family members, close friends, your boss, your coworkers and staff, professional contacts and colleagues, and members of your community. If you're currently looking for a new job or reassessing your existing position, you may wish to add individuals who can help you gain information about the options you're exploring.

Then list the approximate amount of time you're currently spending with each of these people during each month (or use another time period, if appropriate). What is working about the current arrangement, and what can be changed? Think of the ways in which you currently spend time with each person. Is the amount of time you're currently spending satisfactory? Does it allow you enough time to foster a strong, give-and-take relationship? Is there a better way (time, place, frequency) to spend time with the individuals on your list? How can you make time in your schedule to spend additional time with others? Examples of desired changes are spending more time with specific members of your family, making a commitment to take your staff out to lunch on a regular basis, and joining a professional organization and attending a meeting at least once per quarter. If you are dealing with a special situation, such as adopting a child or caring for an elderly relative or an ill friend or child, acknowledge this and be realistic about the amount of time you'll have to take to deal with those special needs. This may result in your spending less time with others for a certain period.

As you move through your career and make time for others, your recognition of the interdependence between your career and those of others grows, and your success is intertwined with the success of those around you. This is particularly true in three areas: collaborative decision making; "win-win" lifetime networking; and developing an "other" orientation.

Involving Others in Our Decisions

Other people are central in our lives and in the decisions we make. This concept may seem too basic to be mentioned in a book on careers. But a quick scan through many of the career books that are on the market today reveals the singular focus that many of them take. While most of the books acknowledge the role of others in networking and some recent books acknowledge the role of others in our learning and development, few of the commercially available "how-to" career books acknowledge the effect of others on our significant career decisions, or provide assistance in making decisions as though others mattered.

Most of these books are written as though people make career decisions independent of the needs and interests of others. In reality, the majority of people have to consider others when making life and career decisions. Few of us have the luxury of making career decisions, especially life-changing decisions, in a vacuum, without considering the needs of others. This is true regardless of our gender, age, or life circumstances. The "quarter-something" recent graduate whose parents have strong opinions about what he should do, the middle-ager with an aging relative or an ill companion, the dual-career couple, the single parent with children, the foreign national who needs to forego work and return to her home country every 2 years to fulfill family obligations, and the single person with community interests all have one thing in common: the need for collaborative decision making.

Naturally, involving others makes decision making more complicated, but for most people, the rewards are great. Many of the people we have coached identify these pluses of joint decision making: having multiple inputs, access to complementary skills and perspectives, and the sense of being in a partnership rather than being alone. One client explains it this way: "When I decided to return to work (after years of raising children and doing volunteer work), I found it very satisfying to add the dimension of business partner to my marriage." Another benefit of making decisions with others' needs in mind is balance. A male executive who has to make decisions about his son jointly with his ex-wife explains, "As we all know, the old work/life balance thing is not really about balance (which is impossible). It's about doing what you value." He found that when he made it a priority to spend more time with his son, he ended up being more productive than before. The challenges involved in being both independent and interdependent in career decision making can be seen in the following case study concerning Susan Higgins. below.

Case Study: Susan Higgins and Her Husband . . . Not Sleepless in Seattle

Susan has been career-minded all of her life. Early in her career she received a graduate degree in her area of specialty and began her career in the Midwest as an administrator. A desire to change her lifestyle, move to a different part of the country and meet someone to whom she could get married resulted in her seeking a change. After a search for new opportunities in her chosen field, Susan accepted a new position in Seattle. After several years she had met her goal of career enhancement, advancing to a senior administrative position with a local organization. She also met a man who would become her husband, a successful, independently employed lawyer. They began a life together, moved into a house and started a family. As their family grew (they have two children), Susan felt increasingly torn between the needs of her employer and the needs of her children. She commented that when she was at home she was thinking about work, and that when she was at work she was thinking about her duties at home.

After a careful self-assessment including in-depth discussions with her husband about their financial and family goals, she made the difficult decision to leave her comfortable, steady job with benefits to join the ranks of independent consultants. At the time her decision was motivated by the desire to put her family's interests first. Early on Susan felt she was taking a big risk, especially financially. Now, ten or more years after this move, she is ecstatic about the outcome. As an entrepreneur, her level of job satisfaction is higher than it ever was when she was employed full-time in a traditional job. And, she became so successful that her income is now higher than it would have been had she remained in administration. Susan made the initial decision to change jobs because of her family, but ended up benefiting personally and financially as a result.

Making Life-Altering Decisions with a Significant Other

How can you make a life-altering career decision in conjunction with a significant other? Much has been written about how difficult personal decision making is, even when it is not constrained by the needs of others. Putting others' needs into the equation further complicates matters. As the previous discussion illustrates, decision making with others' needs in mind can have positive benefits for all concerned, but significant risks are usually involved. Susan and her husband had several things going for them that aided them in making a good decision. First, Susan's husband was also an entrepreneur, so his level of risk-taking ability was probably higher than the norm. Had Susan been married to someone who was more risk-averse, she might not have received the support from her spouse that she needed to act on her decision to leave her employer (and its regular paycheck and health-care benefits).

Second, Susan took the time to carefully think things through. She made the decision over a lengthy period of time—a year or more—after thoroughly examining the factors that were of importance not only to her, but also to her husband. This gave her time to generate her options and weigh them completely—the pros and cons, risks and rewards of each. She and her husband also stepped up their savings program, giving them a bit of a cushion to rely on when she made her ultimate decision.

Throughout the decision process, Susan and her husband exercised superior communication skills. They listened to each other, solicited and offered feedback, and checked to make sure that each was being fully honest with the other. They each asserted their personal interests without being overly aggressive and ignoring the other's primary needs. Susan's spouse participated fully in the discussions with her, remaining as objective as he could so that the decision she would make would ultimately be hers. Had Susan's spouse been more dominant and less willing to allow her to act on her own needs, Susan's decision would have been more difficult to make.

Finally, Susan and her spouse were willing to be creative, bucking some traditional norms throughout the process. Unlike many married couples, who give precedence to one spouse's job needs, Susan and her spouse adopted a "partnership" approach to their situation, putting both of their career needs on an equal footing. Each of them was committed to the other's success, and each of them was willing to make sacrifices in order to ensure that both of them were able to develop their careers without having to place one or the other in the "first" position. Unlike many families, in which one spouse defers his or her career in favor of the spouse whose career has the greatest income potential, Susan and her spouse's primary decision driver was not financial needs. Early in their life together, they had both established fulfillment and work/life balance as priorities, even if this meant forgoing some income and financial security. Being willing to look at their situation nontraditionally helped Susan and her spouse to be open to new ways of making their decisions, as well as new ways of managing their careers and lives from that point on. Principle 3 gives further perspective on considering your significant others when making significant career decisions.

The following steps will help you to make decisions with others.

1. Determine the ultimate objectives you wish to accomplish—the factors that would make the decision or change successful for *all* parties concerned. (Each person can generate her or his own list, then a collective list of core factors can be developed that incorporates the two or three most important factors from each person's list. Include on this collective list only items that are agreed upon by all concerned.)
2. Prioritize this list. (Use the Expected Value exercises in Principle 3.)
3. Be creative in brainstorming a list of potential options that would satisfy the core factors thus established. If one option is already on the table—for example, a job offer or a location—generate other possibilities so that the offer can be compared and contrasted with other potential options.
4. Narrow the list of potential options to a manageable number. (Generally option lists should be restricted to no more than two or three options.)
5. Gather further information about each option. (This is to ensure that your assumptions are based on reality and that you are able to compare and contrast the options using accurate data.)
6. Evaluate the strengths and limitations of each option. (Weigh the degree to which each option best addresses each of the decision factors listed in step 2.)
7. Seek counsel and advice from trusted mentors, family, friends, and associates. (Generally, this should be done only after you have done all you can to identify your core decision factors and have researched each option.)
8. Mentally make the decision. The next day, do a "gut check": Ask yourself how you feel about the decision. If you don't feel sure, gather more information and, if possible, wait to make the decision.

9. Make the decision and act on it. If time permits, develop an implementation plan before you actually act on the decision.
10. Monitor your progress and reevaluate the decision if necessary.

Collaborative Decision Making

Our case study subject Susan was ultimately responsible for her decision. However, she made her significant other an active partner and collaborator in the decision process. As a result, Susan ended up with an enhanced situation both personally and career-wise, and her spouse felt that he had been a real player in the process, totally involved in the process, and a primary beneficiary of the outcome. Susan was able to make a decision that was ultimately both best for her and best for the others in her life. This was made possible by careful attention to her and her spouse's ability to handle risks, thorough assessment of each of their primary needs and motivators, preparing financially for a different lifestyle, continuous positive communication, collaborative decision making, and a willingness to be nontraditional in their approach to their lives and careers. This was not an easy task. But Susan and her spouse say today that the effort was well worth it.

Here are some tips for collaborative decision making:

- Consider yourself and the other person(s) involved as one unit. Do what's ultimately best for the unit (e.g., the team, the organization, the couple, or the family).
- Be open to new ways of looking at your career. Establish what's important to you beyond the traditional motivators of financial security and career growth. Many people are finding that over time, decisions made on the basis of fulfillment, meaning, balance, and connection with others are ultimately more satisfying than decisions based strictly on financial concerns.
- Sharpen your communication skills. Making decisions as though others mattered requires a shifting of focus from one's own interests to a set of joint interests—those of both oneself and others. Skills in self-disclosure, value clarification, assertiveness, sending verbal and nonverbal messages, active listening, persuasion, conflict manage-

ment, and interest-based negotiation are particularly helpful in collaborative decision making.

- Rely on your intuition. The analytical process described here is useful and important, but don't rely solely on a logical approach to decision making. Your feelings (and those of the others involved in the decision) are just as important as the pragmatic facts of the situation.
- Have a "veto" guideline. Some teams and couples rely on a veto guideline to prevent them from moving forward before everyone involved is on the same page. A veto guideline gives each party the freedom to "call time" and request that a decision not be made until all issues have been resolved.

Cultivating a Diversified Lifetime Network

Famed management expert and author Warren Bennis once showed us an article that he had drafted about his life and career. What struck us was the role that mentors and colleagues played in his career choices and career decisions. To be sure, Bennis has built a career over the years that is based on excellence and expertise. Even without mentors and colleagues, he would still enjoy profound success today because of the strength of his accomplishments and his contributions to his profession. However, it is clear that his career was helped along the way by others. In almost every job change he has experienced, Bennis can cite at least one person who was instrumental in helping him to either gain information about the position or actually obtain the position. This example highlights the significant role that your people networks can play in your career success.

Win-Win Networking

Networking increases your visibility within an organization, profession, locale, or industry and increases your understanding of a task you have at hand or a topic or concept in which you are interested. Your network consists of those personal and professional contacts with whom you have interacted, who have information that could be useful to you, and who might be able to benefit from information that you have. As you build a career, you're also building your personal contact network. Networking is a "win-win" activity: It has benefits for both you and those with whom you network. Your career benefits from your connection with others, and the careers of those with whom you interact benefit from their connection with you. Networking is not the narrow "help me get a job" concept that we knew in the 1980s and 1990s. It's a powerful, fluid, mutually beneficial interaction and information flow between you and others, and between your career and those of others, that enriches your life and opens you up to possibilities that otherwise might not have occurred.

Networking is a skill that can be developed and used over the course of your career, whether you are seeking a new position, seeking advancement within a current situation, or thinking about making a change. When job seekers approach us for career advice, we often say, "You already know your next employer." This means that it is far more likely that you will find a job through your contacts than that you will find a job through the classifieds or even through the Internet. In a survey by WetFeet Inc., a leading San Francisco–based company with expertise in providing services and resources to job seekers and employers,[2] personal contacts was listed as the number one source of referral to the responders' current jobs.

In a job search or job change, it is almost always essential, and always appropriate, that you utilize your personal contacts in your search for your next situation. In today's competitive job market, a personal contact can be considered anyone you know who has the power to hire you or to introduce you to someone who can hire you, or anyone who has information about a decision that you're considering (whether to accept a promotion, whether to relocate, whether to accept a job offer, and so on). Your contacts can be a source of information about potential opportunities and a source of advice concerning specific organizations or even specific people or departments within an organization. Personal contacts can include current and former coworkers, classmates, and teachers; alumni from your college or high school; friends of friends; relatives; members of your church, synagogue, or mosque; members of the community with whom you've served on volunteer committees; and colleagues met through professional associations.

One advantage of networking is its ability to help you expand your contacts. As you approach and meet with your contacts, they will begin to refer you to people whom they know who can be of further assistance to you.

Principle 9 discusses "new age networking" and tapping into valuable career connections for your specific job searches and career moves.[3]

Reciprocity

Many people are hesitant about asking others for help. This is why it helps to frame networking as a two-way exchange. It is possible for you to offer the people with whom you network something in return for their time. Following up with an article or a referral to their business is an exchange that is always appreciated by the recipient. Personal networking is a tried-and-true technique. It is a widely accepted business practice. The reason it works is that business relationships, like social ties, function on the basis of exchange of favors and information. Anyone in the work world, whether he or she is working for a nonprofit or a for-profit organization, understands the value of meeting new people, learning from them, and possibly even getting business from them. Exchanging information, resources, job leads, and customer leads is a way of helping both parties involved in a networking exchange.[4]

Diversify and Expand Your Network

Networking can lead to an exponential increase in the number of secondary contacts that you build from your primary contacts. The graphic in Figure 5-2 illustrates this. List the names of several personal contacts. Once you've met with them, list the names of people to whom these primary contacts directed you. As you continue to have meetings, keep adding to your list. Networking gives you the opportunity to meet an infinite number of people who can be helpful to you in your search for information.

Network for Life

Networking doesn't stop once you're employed; it has only just begun. Networking is a lifelong activity. Make a point of cultivating business relationships with colleagues, both internally within your organization and externally in your profession. Internally, networking can help you acclimate to a new environment, learn of new opportunities, keep you up to date on the

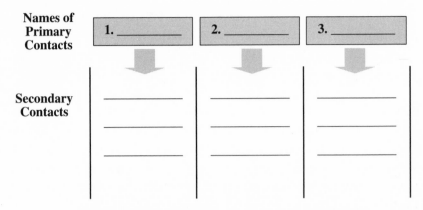

3 Contacts Can Produce Nine or More Additional Contacts

Figure 5-2 Expansion of Contacts *Source:* K. Dowd, J. Bierne, R. Muller, R. Scalise, and N. Schretter, Career Management Seminar, Cambridge Partners, 1993.

organization's activities and objectives, and give you the insights and information you need in order to perform well on the job. Externally, networking can help you to spot industry trends and issues, allow you to learn information about best practices, and arm you with the data you need in order to justify a new approach that you're proposing to your employer.

An Ideal Coach and Mentor

One of the author's former clients, the senior human resources executive for a global energy company, is an example of a person who takes developing others seriously. An African American who came from a disadvantaged background, he was all too aware of the obstacles that stood in the way of young people who were trying to succeed in business on their own merits. He made a point of meeting and staying in touch with numerous young people whom he hired or met at professional conferences. Whether they worked for him or not, these individuals knew that they had a lifelong friend, colleague, and mentor.

His example encouraged others in his organization to adopt a similar focus. Numerous programs were started under his watch that provided employees at all levels of the organization with access to informal and formal mentoring and coaching. Previously, this organization had made such development resources available only to those who were deemed to have "high potential." Widening the pool of employees who were eligible for these programs helped our client achieve one of his objectives: diversifying the candidate and promotion pools for his company. More important, it helped literally hundreds of people who otherwise wouldn't have gotten the chance to step up to the plate for development opportunities at the company. This would not have happened without the development example set by one trailblazer in this organization.[5]

Transcendence—Helping Others

In an expanded version of Maslow's hierarchy of needs, transcendence is the level beyond self-actualization. It leads to the ultimate experience of helping others achieve bold, meaningful, dynamic careers. Each of us has experience and wisdom to offer to others, regardless of our age, our experience level, our place in the organizational hierarchy, our tenure with an organization, or our background. What does it take to be a coach—not in the formal sense like the great football coach Vince Lombardi, but in the informal sense, where we each have skills and experience from which others can gain? Some of the factors that characterize good and ineffective coaching are listed in Table 5-1.

Formal and Informal Coaching

Coaching can be done either formally or informally. Organizations providing formal coaching resources are rapidly setting up shop in numerous communities (see Corporate Coaching University International, www.ccui.com, for example). As an informal coach, you want to make yourself available to others who may benefit from your gentle guidance and support. This point is brought home by the experience of Chris Gleason, who after a long career in industry made a career change to communications consulting. At sev-

Table 5-1 Good and Ineffective Coaching

Good Coaching	Ineffective Coaching
Supporting	Being critical
Encouraging	Discouraging
Role modeling preferred behaviors	Role modeling undesirable behaviors
Spending time to teach something new	Not spending time teaching something new
Helping someone learn from his or her mistakes	Blaming someone for mistakes

Adapted from Suzanne C. de Janasz, Karen O. Dowd, and Beth Z. Schneider, Interpersonal Skills in Organizations (Burr Ridge, Ill.: McGraw-Hill/Higher Education, 2002).

eral points in her career, Chris sought out her own coaches. She identified a particular expertise that she needed but lacked, identified someone within the organization who had the necessary expertise, and bargained with that person to obtain the knowledge. In return for acquiring the information she needed, she agreed to offer her own expertise to the "coach" as a way of ensuring that they both got something out of the arrangement. Chris recognized early in her career the important role that others could play in her success, and she returned the favor by coaching others in the knowledge they too needed in order to succeed. Here are some things you can do to be a supportive informal coach:

- Slow down. Be willing to take longer to do things, or to have things done by others. This affords others the opportunity to talk with you if they have concerns and to approach you with potential problems while there's still time to process the information.
- Be proactive. Initiate situations in which you can serve others in an informal coaching role. Be particularly available to people who are new to a situation. Offer your help; don't wait to be asked.
- Offer positive feedback. People typically respond favorably to constructive feedback.

- Foster a positive atmosphere and collegial relationships with people. This will go a long way toward letting people know that you're interested in their development, as well as your own.
- Incorporate informal coaching behaviors in your everyday interactions with people (for example, ask how you can help, offer resources, and reach out to others).

Giving Back through Mentoring

Study after study has demonstrated the impact that a mentor can have on one's career. The word *mentor* comes from Greek legend. Mentor was a guide, teacher, and facilitator. Both companies and community service organizations have realized the powerful impact that a mentor can have on one's development. People who have mentors report that they have a greater familiarity with the organization's goals and culture, receive information about opportunities for promotion more frequently than do employees without a mentor, and often have access to new job responsibilities and developmental opportunities more quickly and with more certainty than do those without mentors. This is particularly true of employees from underrepresented groups.

Mentoring has been shown to be invaluable to individuals who have few natural contacts among organizational employees from whom they can learn the ropes. Organizations are now realizing that the same mentoring programs that have been provided for members of underrepresented groups can be made available to all employees, with similar positive results. Like coaching, mentoring can be offered on a formal basis, although informal mentoring can be just as effective at helping people to grow their careers.

If you are firmly established and successful in an organization or profession, mentoring others is a way to "give back." Mentoring helps you to be a contributing member of your profession, not just a bystander, doing the minimum that is required to get by. By taking one or more less established people under your wing, you can help to improve your organization or profession by improving the capabilities of its talent resources. Mentoring also helps you to stay engaged at work. As you develop subject area expertise, you can become bored or disinterested. This can be diminished by helping someone else move up the learning curve in the same area. As you move up the "skill hierarchy,"[6] you move from learning to doing to improving and finally to excelling, thus progressing from novice to master.

Career Enhancement

At the point where you feel that you've mastered a certain job, competency, or task, your career can be enhanced if you have the opportunity to share your expertise with others. This point is documented in Kathy Kram's research on "relational career development."[7] Kram asserts that individuals can thrive in an environment in which the influence of others on their learning is recognized and supported. One of the ways in which this can be done is through mentoring. Mentoring typically involves the assignment of a junior staffer to a more senior employee. Traditionally, mentoring has been recognized primarily for its ability to convey information from one (senior) level to the next (junior) level. However, Kram's research is finding that mentoring provides two-way learning benefits for both the mentee and the mentor; as information is exchanged, both parties are able to learn from each other.

Reverse mentoring also demonstrates the importance of working with and learning from others. When Jack Welch headed General Electric, he recognized that many of his junior hires were more proficient with computers than most of his senior managers were. He immediately reversed the old age-based mentoring model and assigned his younger employees to be computer technology mentors to his senior employees. This program helped his senior managers become more proficient with computer technology and had the added benefit of fostering close ties between the two levels of workers, to everyone's benefit. As a related side note, we have observed the positive benefits for organizations that make people a priority, whether by supporting their employees' learning development (an effective retention strategy as well)[8] or by being socially responsible and caring about the planet and people in general.

Fostering relationships with others isn't as easy as it sounds. Making decisions as though others mattered takes time, energy, commitment, and, oftentimes, behavior changes. The rewards are well worth it. "Putting people first" is a good mantra to remember when you are trying to "get clear" about your priorities in your life and career.

Principle 6

Plan Ahead—Now!

It's an ill plan that cannot be changed.[1]

—LATIN PROVERB

Planned and Unplanned Change

The sixth principle in attaining career clarity is planning in advance. The importance of advance planning can't be overstated. In the board game "Monopoly," there is a card that reads, "Do not go any further. Do not pass Go." When you are considering "what's next?" for you, the same guideline applies, with some adaptation: "Do not go any further . . . until you have created a plan with which you can live for a while." This principle will tie together some of the earlier themes in this book and give you some planning tools that you can use when you are experiencing personal or career changes. We review the steps involved in the planning process, paying particular attention to the most important step, preparing for change. We offer some case examples of people who have experienced either unplanned or planned change. And we offer you some strategies and tips to use when making your own plans. Principle 9 will discuss in depth developing and implementing a specific job search/career change plan.

So, you've decided to make a change (or the decision has been made for you). Whether the change is voluntary or involuntary, it is time for you to put a plan in place. Figure 6-1 outlines the steps you can take to get the ball rolling.

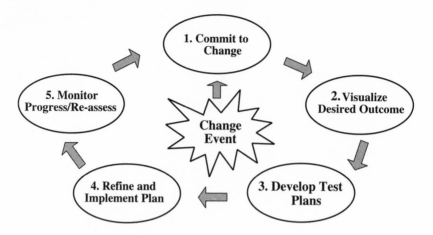

Figure 6-1   Steps in the Personal Change Planning Process

Step 1: Commit to the Idea of Change

The first step in your personal change plan is to prepare yourself—and those who are likely to be affected by your decision—for the change. This is an important step and one that many people who are making key life and career decisions leave out. The approach that you take has a lot to do with whether the change or decision you're considering is voluntary or involuntary. If the change is voluntary (you want a new job; you want to "downshift" your career; you want to relocate; you've just gotten married), you probably already have a degree of enthusiasm and a belief that the change is likely to benefit you in the long term, even if it may be difficult in the short term. You'll be able to jump more quickly into helpful activities, such as clarifying your values, generating and exploring options, and developing plans.

Case Study: George and Mary Trigiani—Mid-Fifties and Living Life to Its Fullest

George and Mary Trigiani (the names have been changed; all other details are real) are a married couple in their early to mid-fifties who have recently undergone a planned, voluntary change. The Trigianis began planning for early retirement when they were in their early forties. Lifelong career professionals, both in financial services, they decided at an early age that they would focus primarily on their careers while they were working in New York City, and then would focus on extended travel and other personal interests once they retired. George writes, "We were overcommitted to our work, and we decided that when we retired, the goal would be to strike a greater balance in our lives. We didn't focus only on work, of course—for example, we did take a big trip every year—but we wanted to shift our priorities substantially when we retired."

The Trigianis treated their retirement project like any other activity in which they were involved at the time. First, they developed their goals. Then they enlisted support from others who could help them, like a financial planner. Next, they began extensive research on places to live, visiting many communities before narrowing down their choices. Throughout this process, they had regular planning meetings, during which they would discuss their progress and exchange information about what they were learning from their research. They networked with others who had made similar decisions, and they communicated with each other (they called it "flexible negotiating") about their individual wants and needs. The Trigianis had several things going for them:

- First, they shared a set of values. Their move required much thought and discussion, but they were operating from the same perspective about what they wanted their life to be like.
- Second, they were very conservative fiscally. They had always overcompensated in their planning, so when the stock market fluctuated in recent months, their projections held and their basic plan didn't change.
- Third, they were both very organized and thoughtful, and they didn't need coaxing to stay with the process.
- Fourth, they made it a priority to have fun with the process, even naming the project after one of their favorite travel guide series.
- Last, and perhaps most important, they had a cardinal rule: "We agreed that the plan had to be fully acceptable to both of us. We engineered changes to ensure that the plan satisfied the needs of both of us."

If the change is involuntary (you've lost a loved one, you've been laid off, or you're caring for an ill relative, for example), you will need more time to deal with the "survival" needs we discussed in Principles 1 and 4. You'll need time to accept the new reality in which you find yourself, and you'll want to acknowledge the specifics of the situation, do a reality check on your options, and collect information. You'll also want to build up your financial resources and the physical and mental strength that you'll need in order to cope successfully with the transition. Some strategies and tips for handling personal change are as follows:

- Take a long-term perspective. Life is a marathon, not a sprint. Seldom do we get everything we want immediately. Don't expect instant gratification.
- Accept that there will be trade-offs. With every change, we're giving up some things in order to have other things. Keep things in balance and in perspective.
- If you are making a decision with others, take into account (and resolve) your differences in decision style *before* you are faced with a significant decision. Develop a strategy for working together, blending the best of each style represented. Develop decision criteria jointly.
- Think outside the box. Be creative and open to doing things differently.
- Hire a personal coach. This is an increasingly common personal change strategy. Personal coaches can help you develop and implement goals, and they are invaluable sources of support and counsel during times of personal transition.
- Minimize risk (both for you and for those involved with you). Understand the factors that are causing you or others concern. Take these concerns seriously, and brainstorm ways to make modifications designed to lessen those concerns.

Life After the Loss of a Loved One: A Marketing Executive Moves Ahead

An example of a person who faced an involuntary change is Donna Quist, who in her forties experienced the devastating loss of her husband to cancer. Donna had been very successful in marketing and strategic planning with a global consumer products firm, working her way up from trainee to vice president. Not only did she have to contend with the illness and passing of her spouse, but at about the same time the nature of her job changed, and she left the firm in order to reevaluate what she wanted to be doing with her life. As Donna writes, "So there I was, no job, no husband, and no responsibilities. The good news was that I could do anything I wanted to, and the bad news was that I didn't know what I wanted to do."

The need to recover. What Donna did know from reading books on grief was that she needed to focus on recovery. And as she says, "It was not something I could schedule in a planning book with a beginning and an end." Obviously Donna's situation is an example of how devastating and life-disrupting involuntary, unplanned change can be. She had excellent instincts, and she knew she couldn't take her usual task-oriented approach to her personal situation. She needed time to think, time to process what she had just gone through, time to come to grips with her new situation, time to develop some new skills and insights to help her once she was ready to move forward. Donna decided that what she needed was to be closer to her family. She had spent most of her career on the west coast, with a short stint in the Midwest, but her family was on the east coast. She rented out her house, stored her furniture in a trailer, and lived with her family for a year and a half before moving to a city nearby and setting up a small business.

Rediscovering what's important. In the 5 years since her husband died, Donna has learned new skills, such as working with the computer, and adopted new interests, such as biking. Most important, she has rediscovered the value of being with friends and family, so much so that she doubts that she could go back to "the corporate arena." Her new lifestyle affords her the flexibility she likes and the time she needs in order to deal with the reality of her unchosen and yet very real situation. She's hoping for a relationship and other things in life later, but for now she's taking it a day at a time, being grateful for what she has and looking somewhat optimistically to the future.

The Trigianis made a significant adjustment when they were in their early forties in order to be in a position to attain their goal of retirement by their mid-fifties. Donna Quist had to endure a life-changing loss unexpectedly. One choice was voluntary and planned, the other involuntary and unplanned. Yet both examples demonstrate the importance of taking the time to clarify your values, set some objectives, and slowly develop plans to meet those objectives. The Trigianis and Donna Quist had very different "change triggers." What is triggering the change that *you're* facing? The following list gives some common change triggers (feel free to add your own).

Bored	Values/lifestyle change	Spouse/partner transfer
Being fired or laid off	Spouse/partner career or other family considerations	Personal downshifting
Divorce or widowhood	Change in health	Corporate downsizing
Remarriage	Location	Want/need to take a break
Having a child	More or less travel	Plateaued in current situation
Reentry after taking a break	Sense of adventure/ need for variety	New boss or owner
Change in corporate structure, mission, or direction	Care of aging parent	Language barrier
Care of family in home country	Burnout	Death of a close friend or family member
A significant world event	Cost of living	Salary decrease
Retirement (or planning for future retirement)	Empty nest	Merger/acquisition

New business opportunity/ start own business		Discrimination
_____	_____	_____
_____	_____	_____

More about Change Triggers

If your change trigger, like Donna's, is a sudden, unwelcome life change such as a divorce or change in health, a flood of emotions, financial concerns, and a host of personal problems are likely to get in the way of good decision making. The flip side of this is that without a sudden change event, we may lack the incentive or sense of urgency that is sometimes needed to actually make a change. There's a difference between that dull, may-never-go-away feeling that something needs to change and the "hit over the head" knock of reality that one gets when something entirely unexpected happens in life (you meet "the one," you lose someone unexpectedly, you lose a job, you're offered a transfer/promotion, and so on). The law of physics dealing with *inertia* states that without an outside force, the tendency is to not make a change. An outside force generally requires a response. Without a major change event, it is difficult to devote the time and energy needed to assess a life situation and develop a new plan of action. Only a few people have the natural drive to create positive change for themselves without the "wake-up call" that an external life event provides.

A Twenty-Something Plans Ahead and Makes Changes for His Career: From Consulting to a Media Start-up in Hong Kong to Grad School

Rob Mannion is an example of someone who from an early age has taken control of his own life and career. Now in his late twenties, Rob knew when he graduated from college that he wanted to work for several years and then go to graduate school. Rob is very intelligent, self-motivated, and industrious, and he obtained an excellent first job after college with a consulting firm. This gave him the launch pad he needed to make a few changes on his own initiative.

Two and a half years later, craving line experience (rather than simply making recommendations to clients), Rob was able to parlay his consulting experience into a position with a media/Internet start-up firm (we all know what happened to the dot-coms, so you can guess where this story is heading!). This position took Rob to Asia, which actually met another of his earlier goals, which was to obtain international experience. About this move Rob writes, "All of these reasons added up to my taking the biggest risk of my life. Amid excitement, confusion, and disagreement between my friends and family, I quit a stable and lucrative consulting job, broke my apartment lease, and moved to Hong Kong." By the way, this move involved a substantial pay cut, but Rob felt that the experience was worth it. After one more job change, Rob is now planning on entering the Wharton Graduate School of Business in the fall.

Rob's story illustrates two major points. First, one doesn't need an external event to begin the change process. Rob initiated his changes as a means of furthering his goals and objectives. And second, we can't underestimate the role of serendipity, or chance, in the change process. As Rob himself states, "Much of career is luck, but you have to put yourself in a position to get lucky." Rob's early goal-setting behavior, his enthusiasm, his positive attitude, his strong work ethic, and his willingness to take risks helped him to obtain his first job after college and then to move on to two very different and interesting ventures before going on to graduate school.

Rob freely admits that later, when he has family responsibilities (and tuition debt to pay off), his priorities will certainly change. "I promised myself that I would not let years go by with my only memories those of being locked in a cubicle . . . in the future, as I have to put other people's interests ahead of my own, financial security will play a larger role in my decisions." Rob's story illustrates the importance of having a plan, but also being flexible and open to change as it happens. But for now, his goals of gaining terrific experience, traveling, and lifestyle balance have more than been met.

Planned and Unplanned Events

When a change event occurs, whether it is planned or unplanned, positive or negative, we move through a series of emotions that, while overwhelming at the time, may not be lasting. This is why we are often counseled not to make decisions and changes too hastily. If they are to have some staying power, the decisions we make need to be derived from our core, lasting values and needs, not from any temporary feelings that we may be experiencing at a time of upheaval. If you have the luxury of preparing for the change rather than just jumping right in, the likelihood of your decision's having staying power is increased. We will discuss this concept further in Principle 8, on taking breaks. Here are some tips that can be used to make effective decisions.

When you have the chance, always make the decision that

- Opens the most doors for you (look forward, not backward)
- Gives you the chance to build new skills (rather than simply using the ones you already have)
- Energizes you rather than drains you
- Is what *you* consider to be the best for you
- Contributes the most to your (and your significant other's) overall quality of life in the long term
- Is most likely to be long-lasting
- Brings a smile to your face

Laying the Foundation for Change

During this phase, it is helpful for you and those who will be affected by your decision (a spouse or partner, for example) to revisit the assessment exercises in the first principle of this book. This will help you to clarify your and your significant other's current values and set some new goals. The point is to build enthusiasm before moving ahead with any specific changes. During this time, you're laying the foundation for change. You're thinking of options, talking to those close to you, getting advice from colleagues, adjusting your ideas and emotions as you gain information, and beginning to commit to the idea of change, even if you haven't yet committed to a specific course of action.

Many people find journaling to be a useful activity to engage in during a major transition. Writing down your thoughts for a few weeks or months or longer can help you to process the emotions you experience during the change and to keep track of ideas as they occur to you. Communicating with a few trusted friends, colleagues, or family members on a regular basis can similarly help you to process your thoughts, obtain feedback, and develop plans that are grounded in reality.

Identifying Your Decision Style

Another important activity in the "preparing for change" phase of planning is identifying your personal decision style (and the styles of others in your life who are affected by the change or decision being considered). What kind of decision maker are you? You may be more methodical, pondering your situation and analyzing your options before deciding on one. You may be more impulsive, reacting quickly and intuitively. Or perhaps you are somewhere in the middle, acting based on your intuition after taking some time to explore the situation. Whatever your natural style, when you are considering a life or career decision or change, it is important to incorporate elements of both major approaches.

- If you are usually organized, analytical, and deliberate in making decisions, be somewhat creative and see what your intuition can contribute to your decision.
- If you are intuitive and tend to approach things in a roundabout way or to make decisions hastily based on your past experience, take the time to develop and implement a plan in consultation with others who can help keep you on track.

Whether we act intuitively, analytically, or a combination of the two, it is important that we take the time to make a decision with which we can live. Refer back to the discussion of risk taking in Principle 3 for additional insights into decision making. The following list offers pointers about steps to take before making a decision.

Don't make a decision until

- You've assessed your risk-taking ability, clarified your options, and generated creative options.
- You've communicated with and obtained full support from those in your life who are affected by the decision.
- You've gathered the information you need.
- You've predicted the best and worst outcomes and developed contingency plans.
- You're ready to follow through on and stick with your choice.
- You've "slept on it," and your intuition is telling you that it's the right thing to do.
- You have an exit strategy for "just in case."

Step 2: Visualize the Desired Outcome

The next step in the planning process is to visualize your future. Once you're ready to make a change, it's time to generate some creative alternatives and try them on for size. This is a pre-taking action, "no accountability" step in which you freely brainstorm ideas that might appeal to you and to those who are affected by the decision. It's a no-commitment way to generate the alternatives that may be available to you and to think about those alternatives. A question that consultants sometimes ask their clients is, "What would you like to see happen as a result of the change you're considering?" or "What would success look like to you?" Answering such a question can help you begin to envision some of the likely scenarios in which you may find yourself after you make the decision, as well as to identify some of the positive outcomes that could result from the change.

Vijay Toofan is an example of someone who was able to conceive of a different lifestyle for himself and his family while living in an existing situation. A native of India, Vijay obtained his undergraduate degree in his home country and after graduation worked in industry for a number of years. He then realized that he had come to a crossroads. He and his wife and children could either remain in India or move to another country and start a new life. Vijay realized that his and his wife's long-term goals of financial security and quality of life could best be realized by leaving India. They made the very difficult decision to leave their friends and family and moved to the United States, where Vijay obtained his professional degrees and began a new career.

Envision the Future

Vijay admits now that he could not have made such a significant change had he and his wife not been able to envision their future. "We had long-term goals that we wanted to achieve in life. We actually identified more than one way to achieve our goals, in case our first choice didn't work out. And we worked very, very hard to reach our goals. We made financial sacrifices and had no spare time to speak of while obtaining the education necessary to make our long-term goals possible. We were looking for a better life personally. We were also seeking professionally the chance to make an impact. I believe we have that chance now." They certainly do (Vijay is a professor and his wife is a dentist), because they were able to look ahead and make the sacrifice necessary to make a better life for themselves and their family.

Frame It

It also helps to frame a new situation before it takes shape. This means defining the characteristics that would make the situation attractive to you and to those who are affected by your decision. One time, one of the authors of this book was working on a project with a top entrepreneur in the Washington, D.C., area. The entrepreneur asked the author and her colleagues if they could "see" the product that they were thinking about creating. Entrepreneurs often have this ability to bring a new service or business to life before most "ordinary" people do.

What are the components that you'd like to have be a part of your "new reality"? What are some of the positive (and negative) outcomes that could result from the change? What are some of the potential costs and benefits of such a move? The ability to perceive a new reality that doesn't exist yet, and to define its features and qualities, can aid you enormously in the planning process. Sometimes it helps, when shaping potential courses of action, to engage in "scenario planning," in which several options are listed and an-

Table 6-1   Scenario Planning

For each option you're considering, answer the following questions.

1. What would you like to happen as a result of the change you're considering?

2. What would success look like to you [and if relevant, to your significant other(s)]?

3. What are the features you would like to have in your new reality?

4. What are the likely disadvantages or trade-offs of this option?

5. What are the likely advantages of or gains available through this option?

6. What are the likely outcomes (best and worst case)?

7. Based on your analysis of several options using the above questions, what is this option's priority ranking (compared with other options; 1 = most preferable)?

alyzed according to personal decision criteria. An example of this is given in Table 6-1.

Cross-comparing options can help bring to light choice factors that you may not have realized are important to you at this time. Once you've generated and considered a number of alternatives, you can adjust your priorities, adding to your list of desired features and changing the priority order of the options you're considering. That sets the stage for you to be able to identify your objectives—what you'd like to achieve through the change or decision. Remember that each of these steps is best done in coordination with the others in your life who will be affected by the change or decision being considered.

Step 3: Develop and Test Plans

When you are reacting to or initiating a significant life change, or when you are faced with making an important career decision, it is helpful to have a road map. This is a draft of a plan that can be used to help you (and those affected by the change) maneuver through the situation and emerge from it successfully. The plan (or plans, one for each option being considered) should start with a written description of your objective. Refer back to the exercise on personal goal setting in Principle 1 for additional detail on this step. This topic is also covered in Principle 9, on developing and implementing strategies.

Narrow Your Options

Include the values that need to be satisfied by the plan, the resources needed to implement the plan, a description of the barriers faced, and plans to overcome these barriers. Also list the steps that will be needed to implement the plan, with initials indicating who's responsible (if relevant). In this phase you narrow your options to those few that are realistic, possible, and able to be acted upon. Unlike the situation in the earlier steps, where your objective was to be creative and brainstorm numerous options, in this phase it's important to select a plan (or plans) that is substantive and based on facts. Up to about three alternative plans can be listed here. Any more than that makes planning decisions cumbersome.

Do Your Homework

At this stage, research is critical. This could include talking with others who have experienced a similar change, doing Internet research on specific organizations or locations, or collecting data on specific options you are considering. While reality wasn't a factor in the earlier stages, it is now a very important factor. Based on the data you have, is the option you're considering realistic? Is it one that you have the resources, the skills, and especially the patience to implement? A while ago one of the authors was experiencing an early midlife crisis, and she was discussing this with a good friend. She had recently moved to a new city for a new job, and she had seen a house that she liked. The friend reminded her that it was good to have a goal; she just needed to remember that it would probably take a good deal of time to accomplish that goal. The friend's reassurance was helpful to the author at a time when she needed both a little hope and a gentle reminder that good things generally take time. The friend was right. The author didn't get a house right away, but she slowly worked toward her goal and eventually achieved it.

This is a simple reminder of an important lesson: One can dream, and one can be realistic too. What about your goals? What kind of time frame is realistic? What barriers, if any, exist that would change the expected time frame? This approach may sound overly analytical; however, careful analysis at this stage can prevent a decision from being made on the basis of limited or inaccurate data. The plan (or plans) being considered also has to be possible. Is the plan supported by others in your life? Do you have the financial resources to move forward with the plan? The plan (or plans) also has to be able to be acted upon. What specific steps would be needed to implement the plan? Are you in a position to follow through with each of these steps in a timely fashion? What problem areas exist, and how can these be resolved or reduced? Last, at this stage, it is useful to test thoroughly any ideas you're still considering. For example, if you have narrowed your list of places to live down to three, visit each of these areas *before* making the big decision to physically move to a new location.

Countless individuals have made the mistake of moving somewhere because of a previous vacation or an article they read in a magazine. Once they arrive, they find that daily life is far different from what they thought it would be. Or if you have a job offer or offers from employers, try to obtain the name of the person who previously held the job or the names of some current or former clients.

Talking with these people can give you a richer picture of what the job is really like, increasing the likelihood that the ultimate decision you make will be based on facts rather than assumptions. Testing can prevent you from making costly mistakes and can ensure the ultimate success of your final decision, once it's made. Here are some questions to consider before accepting a job offer:[2]

- Have you developed a decision-making strategy, listing your alternatives and the criteria met by each alternative?
- Have you taken the time to generate more than one alternative?
- Have you weighed the costs and benefits of each alternative, and discussed these with your significant other (if relevant)?
- Have you thought about "plan B" should the offer you accept not work out?
- Have you researched fully the organizations that extended the offers? Do you understand their motivation for wanting you, what they want you to achieve, and the resources they'll give you to attain these objectives?

- Have you been fully honest with your prospective employers (e.g., not oversold or misrepresented your credentials and what you can do for them)?
- Have you collected data to help you negotiate effectively?

Principle 9 introduces three specific exercises for evaluating and deciding among offers: the McKinsey 7-S framework, using T accounts, and weighted averages.

Step 4: Refine and Implement a Specific Plan

It's no coincidence that the lion's share of the work involved in making a decision or change happens up front, before any action is ever taken. Preparing for a change or decision is complex work. Many factors, including the needs of others, need to be taken into account. Questions have to be explored, research conducted, and initial plans developed and tested. All of this takes a great deal of time. Once the prep work has been done (the steps described so far), implementing the plan is relatively easy.

At this point, your priority is developing a time line and specific action steps and staying with it or modifying it as needed. The time line can be relatively simple and should be incorporated into your regular day planner. It's helpful to list as many of the anticipated steps as possible (remembering that there will always be unanticipated steps). When possible, assign specific steps to actual days or weeks of the month to ensure that your planning objectives won't get lost as you go about your daily life. For example, if you are researching places to live, incorporate the steps needed (e.g., do library research, check web sites, talk to others who have moved there) into your regular schedule. Set up a regular time for your personal "decision" project, just as you would set aside time for an ongoing appointment such as working out with a personal trainer.

Exit Strategy and Fallback Plans

It's smart to have a backup plan. What is your exit strategy if things don't work out? For example, if you've accepted a new job, do you have associates whom you can contact quickly if things aren't working out? Do you have a financial cushion for this possibility? Jane Dunphey is an example of someone who needed a backup plan when she suddenly lost her job shortly after September 11, 2001. Jane, a twenty-something who is ambitious and intelligent, took advantage of her job loss to leave the business world and go to cooking school. It was something that she had always wanted to do, although she hadn't chosen the circumstances (being laid off) under which she was able to do it. Jane's strategy was to talk to as many people as she could, get their advice, and then write down a description of her ideal job. As she says, "I put out a call to the universe, and the universe delivered!" Being in cooking school is giving her the time she needs in order to decide what she wants to do next. Going to school, switching careers, and moving to a new city are all options for this Manhattanite. But for now, the creativity and camaraderie she's experiencing can only help her when she's finally ready to make a decision.

What is your backup plan? As the quotation at the beginning of this principle implies, plans can—and probably will—change. Your backup plan doesn't have to be as much fun or as unusual as Jane's, but it is important that you have one. Having a backup plan can reduce the risk that is involved in any change. You are also responsible for helping yourself and those involved cope with the transition. Any change, even positive, voluntary change, causes one some uncertainty. Exchanging the known for the unknown is seldom comfortable, and it almost always involves some change in the initial plan. For this reason, it is important that you remain flexible and be willing to adapt the plan (and your emotions) as new developments occur. As you obtain experience and information about the new situation, your confidence and your ability to handle the unknown will improve.

Step 5: Monitor Your Progress

The final step in the personal change planning process is to monitor your progress, fine-tuning the plan when necessary and being aware that you might need to start the process all over again. In business we often set up "checkpoints" throughout the duration of a task force or special project to ensure that we communicate with our staff regularly. This practice can be useful in a personal change process as well. Once the change or decision has been made, periodically set aside time to review the success of the change or decision in helping you move toward your goals.

Vive la Différence: A Parisian Takes on Tourism as Her Life's Priorities Change

Marie Fontainebleau, a tour guide in France, is an example of someone who reassessed her life and career after previously having made a substantial change. Marie and her husband had relocated from Paris to the countryside for his work and to raise their family. During this time, Marie had the opportunity to get involved in the tourism industry as a guide, lecturer, and tour creator. After a period of time, Marie felt that her career needs were being stifled, and she relocated herself back to the city. She writes, "For the first time in my life, I was putting my needs ahead of those of my family! But I believe it's important (in one's life and career) to never put on an act, to be who you are today."

Marie made a significant change after evaluating where her life was heading. Her and her husband's earlier goals had been achieved (they had raised their children before she returned to Paris to start her own business). Had she stayed in the countryside, she probably would have been happy, but she would have been living out yesterday's goals, not today's or tomorrow's.

A Nonlinear Planning Process

What about you? When you make a change, be sure you're getting the results that you thought you would get. If you're not, rejuggle your priorities, make the necessary changes, or talk to the persons involved to help you ensure that you're on track for meeting your personal goals. Here is a useful list of questions to consider when you are faced with an important decision.[3]

Think

1. What do you need to do? What is the problem that you are trying
   to solve? Or what are you trying to achieve? What values do you
   want to realize through the change? What do you want to happen?

2. What choices do you have? What alternatives are available to you?
3. What resources do you have available (e.g., time, money, ability, energy, support from others, information, or data)? What resources do you lack?
4. What results can you expect if everything goes as planned? What can you expect if it does not? What is your contingency plan?

Plan

5. What choice seems best? After thinking about all of your choices, the values addressed by each, the resources you have and need for each, and the possible consequences of each, which choice seems to be the best for you (and for others who may be involved) at this time?
6. What resources will you need? Identify all the things you'll need (see question 3) in order to accomplish your plan. What do you need to get? How will you do this?

Do

7. How will you carry out your plan? If things don't go exactly as you anticipate, how will you adjust your plan? Ask yourself, "How well am I doing?" "What about the others in my life who were affected by the change?" Do you need to make adjustments, and if so, how and when will you do this?

Seldom do things happen as planned. More likely you'll experience a constantly moving, fluid, ever-changing life. Planning ahead can usually help you to at least have some say as to where your life takes you!

Part 3

Envision the Future

You've reviewed your prior experience and assessed your present situation and your needs. Now it's time to look to your future life and to the career you want to be engaged in. In this section we discuss two important topics. In Principle 7, "Enjoy Your Life and Sustain Your Career," we discuss the concept of embracing change and introduce a concept called career sustainability—the features that you'll want to incorporate into your plans in order to have a lifelong career that is fulfilling and energizing. In Principle 8, "Give Yourself a Break," we encourage you to consider something new when planning your life and career—the concept of taking breaks periodically in order to recharge, renew, and rejuvenate your career. Together these principles will enable you to not only envision but implement a future that is both compelling and realistic.

Principle 7

Enjoy Your Life and Sustain Your Career

Nothing great was ever achieved without enthusiasm.
—RALPH WALDO EMERSON

Life Is Beautiful

The seventh principle in gaining career clarity is to enjoy life as you go by developing a life and a career that can be sustained over time. The career landscape is changing. Work is taking up more of our time. We are living longer, and we are working longer before retiring. And for many, it's difficult to lead a balanced life because their responsibilities at home are as significant and potentially overwhelming as their responsibilities at work. With downsizings, work/family overload, and an expected increase in the number of years we'll be spending in the workforce, the need to lead a balanced life has become even more important, yet this goal remains elusive for many of us.

The Need for a Sustainable Career and Life

In the architectural world, the concept of sustainability means building residential and commercial structures that can last over time, don't squander the earth's resources, are enduring, and are as energy-efficient as possible.[1] This concept can, with some adaptation, be applied to our careers. As we make personal and professional decisions, it is important that we craft a life

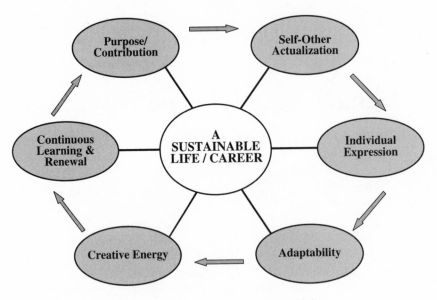

Figure 7-1   Features of Career Sustainability

and a career that meet our needs, are rewarding, and can hold our interest over a lifetime. The features that describe a career that is sustainable are listed in Figure 7-1.

Having a Sense of Purpose

Having a sense of purpose greatly enhances our ability to sustain our life or our career, especially when things are difficult. When Sherrie was working her way through college, she taught dance classes in the evenings and on weekends. She didn't get much sleep, and her time was often spent rushing among studying, friends, and activities. To get through what would otherwise have been a huge stressor, Sherrie reminded herself that she was lucky to be able to earn her tuition money by doing something she loved doing. She was motivated by helping her students to develop their jazz and tap skills (and often their self-esteem and confidence as well), have a creative outlet, and build new friendships with their classmates outside of work. Reminding herself of her ultimate goal of an education and learning also helped her to deal with the sacrifices and gave her a sense of purpose.

What Is Your Sense of Purpose?

When someone is writing a business plan, the first questions that are asked are, "What is the purpose of the business?" and "What is the market need that it serves?" The promising new business operator is wisely counseled to craft his or her "30-second elevator speech." What is *your* elevator speech? What are you about? Who are you? To answer this question, begin at the beginning: What is your goal? What are you all about? What gives your life meaning? What do you feel passionate about? Kevin McCarthy, in his insightful book entitled *The On-Purpose Person,*[2] speaks of purpose as not being "making sense of your life," but rather "making your life make sense."

This may be easier for some people than for others. The late famed musician Jerry Garcia, when asked about his choice of career, said that it wasn't a choice; from a young age he simply "wrote songs in his head." Music is what drove him, what gave his life meaning. Many people who are artistic—artists, writers, actors, musicians, stylists, composers—say that, like Garcia, they knew early on that they had a specific talent, in fact a passion, that came naturally to them, and that this talent later became their bread and butter. Others, like ministers and some teachers, say, when asked, that they feel "called" to their work. In fact, many of those who are called to a particular line of work think of their career not as work but as a vocation, something that they didn't specifically choose but are drawn to do and are meant to be doing.

What Does Your Life Mean?

Would that we were this lucky. More often than not, we lack the clarity to know (or to be able to act on) what we're "meant to be doing." A friend who was facing a career decision recently said to me, "How do I know if I'm doing what I'm supposed to be doing with my life?" This is a question that keeps many of us awake at night. In the hit Hugh Grant movie *About a Boy,* based on the novel of the same name by Nick Hornby, the lead character, played by Grant, comments that he was living the life he wanted, and he was living the way he wanted. But in the end, it just didn't mean anything to him. What does your life mean? What would make your life make sense?

Toward the end of the 2002 movie *Cat's Meow*, directed by Peter Bogdanovich, the narrator comments on the characters' propensity for lapsing into the Charleston (dance) whenever they got bored or there was an awkward lull in the conversation. She explained that of course they had to keep dancing, for if they stopped, they'd have nothing, and they would have only thinking to do. What do you think about when you stop dancing, when you stop overworking, when you stop the endless errands and parties and promotions, when you wake up at three in the morning with your own thoughts? What do you mean? What does your life mean?

Career Ambiguity

Several years ago a close friend and colleague of one of the author's, now president of a top liberal arts college, was part of a group that was discussing career plans over beers. After listening quietly for a few minutes, he said he didn't know about career planning—"What about *career ambiguity?*" His question stopped the conversation, if only for a minute. Who among us really was really clear about where she or he was headed?

About 75 percent of MBA students enter graduate school seeking to change careers. From anecdotal evidence gathered from speaking with our business school career management colleagues, we estimate that over half of graduating MBA students change jobs within 18 months of graduation from business school. About 90 percent of college first-year students enter without a major or change their major within the first year. Adults can expect to change jobs at least seven times over the course of a career (and that number is growing). The number of adults seeking second careers outside of their original profession is growing by leaps and bounds.

These realities illustrate that we will probably experience career ambiguity more frequently than moments of clarity (see Figure 7-2). It is difficult to throw yourself into a plan 100 percent when you're not all that certain that the plan is what you want. The adage "be careful what you wish for; you may get it" applies here. Ambiguity, or a lack of commitment to a spe-

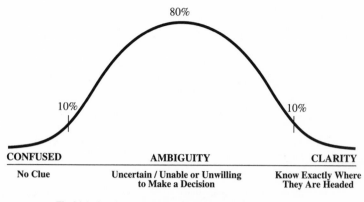

Figure 7-2 Career Ambiguity

cific course of action, results in much career indecision and procrastination. When this happens, crystallizing your sense of purpose can help you clarify your goals and point you in the necessary direction to attain them.

Finding Purpose in Life

So how do you get in touch with your purpose? Let's return to our example of the business plan developer. Generally a business plan starts with an idea. Often this idea is based on the person's expertise—what he or she knows. Or it is based on the person's interests—what he or she feels passionate about. Or it is based on the person's value system—what he or she believes in. The simplest way to understand your purpose or goal in life is to identify your primary expertise, passion, and values—those things that naturally motivate you to be your best. Some of these were identified in Principle 1 of this book. Acting on these can lead you to your life's purpose. Your purpose, or primary goal, can and most likely will change as you move through life. What's important is that you keep up with your changing skills, interests, and values; incorporate them into your current goals and objectives; and make changes when needed to stay current with yourself and with the needs of others in your life.

A Wake-Up Call

A life-changing event can help us to crystallize our purpose or give us the sense of urgency that we sometimes need in order to put our beliefs into action. Michel Benoit was a highly successful graphic artist who had risen to the presidency of his company. A single gay man with no family responsibilities to encumber him, Michel had been in his career long enough to be actively preparing for a second career based on his lifelong interest in aviation. Then, at the age of 47, less than a week after receiving his commercial pilot's license, Michel suffered two heart attacks. Not only was this a life-threatening situation, but he soon learned that because of his health, he was no longer eligible to fly commercial aircraft.

New realities.   Michel Benoit is now coping not just with the medical realities of his new lifestyle, but also with the problem of what to focus on now that his lifelong career dream isn't possible. Like many others who have faced a similar situation, Michel experienced a significant change in personal priorities as the result of his heart attacks. They have literally served as a wake-up call to him, leading him to change his priorities from a primary focus on his career to a focus on making the most of life. While no one would wish a heart attack on Michel or anyone else, life-threatening episodes quickly get us in touch with what's really important. Career counselors like to ask their clients, "If you had one year to live, what would you do?" or "What would you want people to say about you at your funeral?" Table 7-1 gives a brief set of questions to get you thinking about *your* life's purpose. You can also refer back to the exercises in Principle 1.

Table 7-1   Finding Your Purpose

My primary expertise:

Things I feel passionate about:

My core values:

Qualities I have to offer:

If I had one year left to live, I'd . . . :

What I would like said about me at my funeral (eulogy):

While it's not enjoyable to ponder some of these difficult questions, answering them may help you to focus on what your priorities are right now. In Michel's case, he's exploring other ways to be involved in aviation and revamping his freelance business model to make it more realistic financially. And in the meantime, he's enjoying traveling to favorite new and old places with close friends and family as frequently as he can.

Case Study: Changing Roles—From Lawyer to Broadway Producer

Sometimes our current primary role or situation in life helps to narrow our choices (sometimes temporarily) and focus us on what we're meant to be doing (or at least on what we have to be doing). Patricia Holden is a highly successful theatrical producer. But this wasn't always the case. After graduating from a small women's liberal arts college in the Midwest, Patricia went to law school and received a degree in law. She worked full-time for a period after receiving her degree, including holding a prestigious clerkship for a judge on New York's highest court.

Patricia stopped working full-time shortly before her first child, a son, was born. Five years later she had had two children. While she was doing some work, including legal research and pro bono work, her primary role was, by choice, that of a stay-at-home parent. Many parents will be able to relate to what happened next. She returned to school to obtain another graduate degree, planning to reenter the legal workforce. But her family had other ideas. They expressed their desire for her to be more available to them at home, and Patricia discarded her return-to-work ideas and continued working full-time as a parent. She enjoyed this period of her life, but she acknowledged that her choices certainly had drastic effects on her career. However, there is a silver lining to the story.

Reentry after raising children. When her children were on their own, Patricia, now divorced, once again entered the work world, but this time in a field that was dear to her heart, the theater. Being at home had helped her to get in touch with her creative side (rather than the analytical side that had led her to the legal field), and she found that theatrical producing appealed to both her creative and her analytical talents. Now able to devote full time to this pursuit, she has produced one Off-Off-Broadway play, two Off-Broadway plays, three plays on Broadway, and one play in London—all within the past decade! She says, "The producing business is cyclical, and this works very well for me now. When I'm engaged in producing a play, I work very hard and all hours. At other times, I simply read scripts, go to readings, go scouting for plays, and vote in the Tony awards. *It's not the type of job you need to retire from, and I don't intend to.*" Patricia's earlier primary life role of parent changed later in life, allowing her the freedom to choose her next career role. In both cases she was able to identify, and live out, her life's purpose.

Economic Constraints

Sometimes one's economic background either severely limits one's ability to determine one's purpose or dictates what that purpose should be. Vanessa Gray was a single parent with three children. It was a very difficult situation for all involved, and it resulted in Vanessa and the children living week to week with very few financial resources. Vanessa's husband had moved out of state to attend school and be near his aging parents, leaving Vanessa and the children to fend for themselves. Vanessa obtained a job in the only business she knew—the restaurant business. She worked full-time as a bar manager and took classes in restaurant management at a local community college. For a number of years they lived hand-to-mouth, focused almost exclusively on financial survival, the bottom levels of Maslow's hierarchy of needs (see Principle 1).

When her children were older, Vanessa received some advice from her boss, who became her mentor. He encouraged her to pursue her lifelong goal of becoming a professional in a helping profession. She changed career paths and slowly worked her way, after age 40, to an undergraduate degree in social work, and then to a master's degree. She is now working full-time in her field, has a private practice, and is pursuing a doctorate. She eventually was able to act on her life's purpose, after years of delaying it to focus on her family's financial needs. She would definitely say that she is now successfully functioning at the higher levels of Maslow's hierarchy. Her children admire her persistence and have learned from her excellent role modeling that one can find and act on one's purpose, even later in life.

Three-Peat Success

Michel, Patricia, and Vanessa each found and acted on their life's purpose, albeit in a roundabout fashion. They each embarked on a path that had changed from their earlier plans in a very significant way. They each used the change as a way to explore their options and look creatively at new ways of approaching their life. And they each ended up following a path that led to their pursuing a lifetime passion or interest. One of the authors once wrote the words "a *good* life crisis" on a note when she meant to say "a *mid*life crisis." But we know from the ancient Chinese proverb that crisis often does translate into opportunity.

Each of these examples demonstrates the positive outcome—the sense of purpose—that can arise from a personal crisis. Life—real life—isn't as linear as many of the career books depict it. It has twists and turns, most of which couldn't have been predicted; some of these are delightful, but many of them are not. Finding and acting upon one's life purpose isn't always easy, and it often doesn't play out as planned. But doing so is instrumental in living a life and career that can be sustained over time.

Shaping Our Identity—Actualizing Ourselves and Others

When one is beginning a career, starting over, or reentering after a period of absence, it is common to begin, as they say, at the bottom. The apprentice and testing years are invaluable in providing you with the experience and exposure to situations that will help you to perform well in later jobs. But eventually, moving up to the middle level and higher is essential for shaping one's professional identity, attaining long-term gratification, and reaching one's full potential. How can you reach your full potential? By staying with each work or life situation—e.g., job, personal circumstance, relationship, life role, or activity—long enough to cycle through a series of developmental or personal growth phases. A sense of well-being can develop from a career and a life that contain a number of these types of experiences.

Being Who You Are

Career sustainability requires locating, over time, career and life situations that allow you to be authentic—to be your "ideal self" as described in Principle 1. The more you're able to express your individuality in your personal and work life, the better you'll perform, both at work and in life. As you identify and take on roles that play to your natural strengths, your levels of both enjoyment and productivity increase. This requires an ability to evaluate your prospective "fit" with potential situations as they arise.

Typically, when you are considering a job or promotion offer, you develop a list of "fit" criteria such as the work environment, the compensation, the responsibilities, and the reporting relationship, and you evaluate your options with this list in mind. There are two problems with this approach. First, lack of job fit often won't surface until one is fully ensconced in a situation and has a chance to learn firsthand what the role and the climate are all about. Second, this method is very narrow, and usually takes into account only criteria that are specific to the person and the job.

Not an Island unto Ourselves

In reality, though, as we discussed in Principles 3 and 5, decisions are seldom made in a vacuum. More often than not, decisions involve both your criteria *and those of others in your life* (or others whom you want to have in your life). In addition, whenever a specific position is being considered, that role is performed in a *broader organizational context* and within a *competitive environment* that includes other organizations.

A more thorough "environmental scan" can be done by broadening the scope of your criteria list and the dimensions of the job or situation that you're considering. One strategy for doing this is to expand the notion of "person/job fit." As Figure 7-3 depicts, this involves, on the personal side of things, considering not only your own "fit" needs, but those of others who

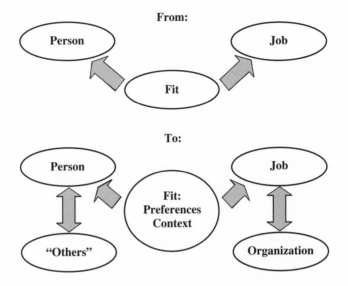

Figure 7-3   Context-Based Person/Job Fit

are involved in and affected by your decision. On the organizational side of the equation, this means broadening the context beyond the immediate job and evaluating the organization and the industry of which the organization is a part.[3]

Thus, the preferred job-fit method is context-based and expands the scope of the evaluation effort. The steps involved are as follows:

- First, list the criteria that are important for you to have in your next job or situation and prioritize those criteria. Look back at the exercises you completed in Principle 1 (specifically, see ideal self, 360-degree feedback, motivation for change, and work-values framework) for ideas.
- Add to this list the criteria that are important to others (a spouse, for example) who are involved in or affected by your decision. Be sure to include personal factors such as lifestyle preferences as well as factors that are specific to the job.
- Next, evaluate what the job involves and how it meets your and your others' fit criteria. Conduct additional research if necessary to enable you to adequately assess the ability of the job to meet your needs.

Table 7-2   Relevant Personal and Organizational "Fit" Questions

Personal (Self and Others)	Organizational (Job and Industry)
What are our primary needs at this time in our lives?	What does the financial picture for the department in which the job is located and for the organization overall look like?
What are the short-term advantages and disadvantages of this situation for us?	What are the responsibilities of the job? How is this job expected to contribute to the organization's overall objectives?
What, if any, are the long-term upside and downside potentials of this situation for us?	What is this organization's niche in the marketplace?
Is there a way in which we can satisfy our needs by staying with our current situation rather than changing at this time?	What about the state of the industry? Is it one that is experiencing growth, decline, or maintenance?
How can this job help or hinder us in attaining our goals?	How does the organization treat its employees (involvement in decision making, compensation, training and development, up/down/across communication, and so on)?

- Then, do the same with the organization and the industry in which it operates. Look beyond the narrow scope of the job function to the broader unit in which it operates. What about the organization's management style? Its standing in the industry? Its ability to be a market leader? Take into account the broader organizational situation, not simply the environment that surrounds the specific position you're considering.

Examples of relevant "fit" questions are given in Table 7-2.[4] Additional questions can be gleaned from the self-assessment exercises in Principle 1.

People who are in jobs or roles that offer them rewards that are in line with their personal values report higher levels of job satisfaction. Finding life work and roles that meet your personal and professional fit criteria increases the likelihood that you'll be able to sustain your career over a period of time.

Adaptability: Understanding and Embracing Change

Another strategy for achieving a sustainable career and life over a period of time is to be able to deal with continuous change. Those who are seen as managing well in change situations are able to tolerate ambiguity, react calmly and rationally when presented with unanticipated change, look forward rather than backward (accept reality and move on), have an organizational mindset (don't take things personally), and are able to be positive in the face of adversity (the glass is half full, not half empty). They also have a tendency to look at the big picture when solving problems or assessing issues (rather than getting lost in the details). Skill at managing change is one of the top qualities that employers seek in candidates today.[5] Many company competency modeling charts include the ability to understand and embrace change as a distinguishing factor of exemplary employees.

Counteracting Inertia

In the ad world, it is said that a television commercial needs to be seen 13 times before it "sinks in." Remember the earlier reference we made to the concept of inertia—it takes effort to counteract inertia, and it takes time to adapt to change. Yet the ability to overcome inertia and to adapt to change has become a hallmark of successful careers in the twenty-first century. The ability to be flexible and facile with change is no longer a luxury; like computer and interpersonal skills, it is a must-have for anyone who wants to cultivate long-term personal relationships and life/career satisfaction.

A Change Exercise

Take a break for a moment to reflect on how you handle change. Clasp your hands together. Note which hand you've placed over the other. Is the left hand over the right, or is the right hand over the left? Unclasp your hands. Now reclasp them, this time making a conscious effort to clasp them opposite to the way you clasped them the first time. How does the new arrangement, the one that is opposite to your natural tendency, feel? Does it feel awkward? Was it difficult for you to clasp your hands in a way that is different from your usual style? Unclasp your hands again, then reclasp them in any way you feel comfortable with. If you're like many of us, you reclasped them the way you clasped them the first time, in line with your natural style. This is how most of us deal with change. When we are involved in a change, or when we are trying to change a behavior, our human tendency is to revert to what we're used to, to what makes us comfortable. We can deal with the change if we have to, but it feels awkward, especially initially.[6]

Coping with Change

The more one is in control of one's actions, the greater one's ability to cope with change is.[7] For example, while the actor and director Christopher Reeve (*Superman*) has adapted masterfully to being confined to a wheelchair and having only limited capacity for movement, his situation is drastic and not one that fits the typical "welcome change" speech. Obviously there are many tragic situations in which change is not welcome and in which things are *not* going to be all right. How people cope with this type of stress is the subject for another book. In this book we are focused on the kinds of changes one can expect in one's career and one's life.

Change Management Capabilities

Cultivating a career that embraces change requires a number of qualities, including willingness to adapt, flexibility in considering varieties of options, the ability to develop and maintain a level of creative energy, and continuous learning. According to Karl Weick and Lisa Berlinger,[8] people in organizations need to focus on five career activities that build change management capabilities:

• Cultivate spiral career concepts (a complex career path that changes often and incorporates both work and nonwork activities).

- Decouple their identity from their work (view any job as temporary and shape their identity through other life roles).
- Preserve discretion (a need for personal autonomy and risk taking).
- Identify distinctive competencies (understand their "value added" to an organization).
- Synthesize complex information (understand what the organization needs in order to move ahead).

This scheme puts you in charge of your career and encourages you to focus on both work and nonwork roles. It views careers as fluid and organizations as constantly changing shape and form. In this view, a career is more of a mosaic, constantly shifting in shape and direction. If your career is a mosaic, you are a change artist, creating plans as you go and reacting to and initiating events as required. How skilled are you at coping with change? At managing your career as it moves through planned and unplanned change? Looking at some case examples can help you to think creatively about your own career. What follows are three compelling stories with three different strategies. They provide powerful lessons learned.

High Notes and Low Notes—A Musician Composes Her Life

Gwen Watson is a highly successful business owner, consultant, facilitator, and trainer who has experienced change—some of it voluntary and some of it not—all her life. Always ambitious and motivated to succeed, Gwen initially embarked on a musician's career path, majoring in piano in college and planning to be a concert pianist. At that time (three decades ago), there were no opportunities for an African American woman in that profession, even one as talented as Gwen. She married and had children, and later divorced. On the advice of her mother, Gwen returned to school. She made a career change to higher education administration, earning both master's and doctoral degrees and serving as a senior administrator of a university for a number of years. Throughout her life, Gwen compensated for her inability to work as a concert pianist by working in music education, becoming minister of music at her church, giving piano concerts, and being involved in colleges' musical arts series.

Up against the Color Ceiling

After an involuntary separation from her employer, Gwen opened her own business. She writes, "My personal priorities have changed over the years. I'm not sure I would have chosen earlier in my life to be a small business owner. Through my work, I am now able to look for ways to make a difference when dealing with issues of diversity and race. Racial discrimination and sexual discrimination have been the biggest challenges that I have had to face. Financial management and security are the next. It is often depressing to know you have all the skills needed, but you can't get your foot in the door because of either race, the glass ceiling, or lack of network opportunities." Obviously Gwen has had to deal with a lot of change over the years, most of it in areas outside her span of control.

Overcoming Obstacles

The problems Gwen has encountered are staggering. Even more staggering is the way she overcame these obstacles. Even when she was denied her choice of profession, she was creative and found other ways to continue learning and to be involved. Once she made a career change, she worked exceedingly hard and rose to the highest levels in her profession, becoming nationally recognized and the recipient of several awards for her commitment to her profession, to women, and to African Americans. Then, after a lifetime in one profession, she used her involuntary separation as a way to open her own business. This new, unplanned business venture is highly successful financially and has also given her a chance to have an impact on others and to make a difference in people's lives—a reward in itself.

A Book Editor's Career Shifting

Aaron Weinstein is a thirty-something textbook editor in the Midwest who weathered a different type of career challenge. After a number of years with one employer, Aaron took a risk and went to work for a competitor. He had "hit the ceiling" at the firm where he was working, and he left for a different position, hoping to be able to advance in an area that needed his expertise. Unfortunately, things didn't work out, and after 2 years he left his new firm, first for a stint with a not-for-profit organization and then to work on his own as a freelancer. After all of this, Aaron was offered a position by his former employer. Violating the adage that one "can't go home again," Aaron's move back to his former organization has been very successful. He has received one promotion and is in line for another. As the father of a new baby girl, he is ecstatic about the turn of events that led him back to his previous employer.

During his "time away," Aaron was very productive. Freelancing gave him the ability to allocate time to important nonrevenue projects, a luxury that was not available in corporate life. During that time he also continued to learn new skills and finished a novel that he had been struggling to complete while working full-time. Aaron used his time away from corporate life to recharge his creative batteries. He was also highly conscious of taking "the path less followed." Aaron writes, "I opted very early for security, modeling most of my decisions on my parents. While they are great role models in almost every sense, I did learn late that I stayed too close to the path I had seen them on as adults . . . not in their younger years. I trusted too little to chance in my youth, and I have grown to understand its role in my life only in recent years." Aaron refers to what he did as "career shifting," trying on a new role for size and focusing on what could be learned from the new situation, rather than concentrating on what he missed from the old.

Two Men and a Baby

Sean Christophoulos is a gay man, HIV positive, who with his partner, also a gay HIV-positive male, recently adopted a baby whom they are raising together—an unusual circumstance, although one that is becoming more common today. What is uncommon about Sean's situation is the complete turnaround that his life priorities took to enable him to accommodate this change. Anyone who knew Sean before knew him as a high-flyer, a classic Type A personality who was at the top of his profession when he had to retire to the area where he owned a summer home because of his health. His friends, colleagues, and family were worried that stepping down from his high-level, prestigious job in educational marketing would result in his literally falling apart.

A New Identity

Up until this time, Sean's whole identity had been derived from his work. As a single man without family responsibilities, he had been able to live, work, make decisions, and travel on his own. But he proved his naysayers wrong. Like Gwen and Aaron, over time, Sean was able to make peace with the life change that had been thrust upon him. He began to foster nonwork interests that he hadn't had time for before. Again like Gwen and Aaron, Sean also cultivated his creative side through several endeavors. He found several non-work-related things at which he excelled, and he began to do volunteer work in these areas.

In his mid-forties, Sean realized that his life priorities had changed drastically, and that family was more important to him than it had been previously. Sean writes, "Although the break [his retirement] came by health necessity, I had a sudden recognition of life's values and a need to quickly change my life in order to save it. 'Stress' is something I am very conscious of now, e.g., the need to monitor it and *try* to reduce it in my life. For years it was career, career, and more career! As a new parent at age 47, I find self-awareness is critical to being able to manage career/life decisions. Meaning, impact, and family are more important to me now than salary/advancement."

Successful Change Strategies

Gwen, Aaron, and Sean were each able to develop and exercise some useful change strategies. They maintained a positive attitude, spending less time on blaming others and more on figuring out what to do when their circumstances changed. They showed a willingness to learn new things and to take risks, even though all are relatively risk-averse, with financial security having been their primary career driver. They also focused on creative outlets both during and after their transitions, gaining a sense of accomplishment and fulfillment that had been lacking in their previous situations.

As a consultant with The Empower Group, a global management consultancy based in London, one of the authors used to fly weekly to the firm's New York office (formerly Brecker & Merryman, Inc.) from a college town in the southeast. The closest large airport was 2 hours or more away, outside of Washington, D.C., so she would fly back and forth on small commuter planes affectionately referred to as "puddle jumpers." These planes had a maximum cruising altitude of about 10,000 feet, and turbulence was routine. Initially the author was nervous during these flights, but eventually she was able to get used to the constant up, down, and around movements that the plane (and its passengers!) would experience throughout the flight. Rather than dreading these shifts, as she once had, she began to "roll" with them, actually letting herself move *with* the plane rather than resisting its movements. Over time she got so used to the movement that she would coach others who were taking the flight for the first time. "Move with the plane. Don't resist it. Go with it. Expect it. It'll be OK."

Change may not always be comfortable. But in most cases it can be managed.

Principle 8

Give Yourself a Break

What we call the beginning is often the end. And to make an end is to make a beginning. The end is where we start from.
—T. S. ELIOT

Beginnings and Endings

The eighth principle in getting the career you want is to plan ahead so that you are able to take one or more breaks during your career. This is an excellent strategy for maintaining the energy needed to sustain a career over a lifetime. It's also a way to build in time for continuous learning and creative renewal, activities that were identified in previous principles as essential to anyone who wants to gain clarity about his or her life or career and take appropriate action. More and more high-achieving, successful professionals of all ages—quarter-life, mid-life, or well into their eighties—are taking one or more breaks during their working life.

Perhaps you are a new parent, you have recently lost a loved one, or you need time to recover your health. Maybe you have been laid off or you realize that you are just not enjoying your work anymore. You decide that this is the year you will take some action to move in a new direction. It could be that you were one of the lucky ones who made lots of money in the dot-com frenzy, but you are now searching for your next big thing. You may have a gnawing feeling that there is something more meaningful out there for you—something more purposeful to fill up your life. Maybe you have dreamed about pursuing a passion (following your bliss), but your finances have not permitted what you or your significant other considers "an indulgence."

Perhaps you have been working 80+-hour weeks for many years and are burning your candle at both ends. You realize that life is too short, especially after the tragedy of September 11, 2001 which made many of us reappraise how precious our time and our loved ones are. You have enough money to support not working for a while, if you make some selective sacrifices. You want to take time now while you can enjoy it, with significant others, to pursue personal interests, or for renewal.

In our roles in industry and academia, we have advised many people who have either strategically planned and initiated time off from work or used transition time that resulted from something unplanned, like losing a job or changing personal circumstances, wisely. In this principle, we discuss the concept of taking breaks and the options available for taking breaks—all the way from a short creative break each day to an extended period of time off to build new skills or reconsider priorities or career direction. We discuss some interesting global practices of time off and the pros and cons of taking breaks. We offer strategies to consider when you are planning for a break, including communicating with your boss and your significant other about your desire to take a break. We review the relevant financial questions that were covered more in depth in Principle 4. We also identify some worst-case scenarios that you should be aware of as you plan for a break or breaks. We discuss how to make the transition both into and out of a break, and we close with a case study of someone who is successfully enjoying a career break to change directions from a fast-track high-tech career to being a pastry chef.

The concept of taking breaks is a relatively new one, but one that we think has lasting value for anyone who is planning a lifelong career. Those of you who are now in your twenties or thirties are in a particularly good position to develop a career plan that builds in time off from work for renewal and recharging. No matter what age you are, however, you can consider taking a break—for learning, to repot, to redirect, for creativity, for sanity, or for fun! Get ready to have some fun now as you sit back, read this principle, and think outside the box about possibilities that you might have only dreamed about before. Enjoy!

Global Perspective

In some countries, taking a break, a sabbatical, or a "gap year" is commonplace. Breaks, especially those for new parents, are either supported—and even paid for—by employers or legislated, and are accepted as a natural part of one's life and career. For example, in Sweden, new parents receive 19 months or 480 days off for leave; 13 months are paid at 80 percent. Dads are required to take 2 months or lose it, and parents have the option of working 75, 50, or 25 percent of their normal time and drawing benefits for the remainder. Austria has also always had generous parental leave regulations. Each family is entitled to full-time leave until a child reaches 24 months—18 months for one parent, but 2 years if the father takes at least 6 months. Norway has a compulsory 9-week maternity leave and allows for 52 weeks of parental leave at 80 percent pay or 42 weeks at 100 percent pay. Cuba recently increased its 6 months fully paid maternity leave to a year.

Effective January 1, 2002, Belgium replaced its career breaks policy with a system of time credit. Employees are entitled to take up to 1 year off during their working lives, and their employers are not required to replace them with an unemployed person (as was the case under the career break system). Under the new system, employees also are entitled to reduce their working week by one-fifth for a period of up to 5 years.

Several countries also offer paid educational leaves that are a form of structured or constrained sabbaticals. With paid educational leave, employees can take time off on a short-term or part-time basis to learn new skills; they continue to be paid and return to their job afterward. For example, in Austria, with the employer's permission, an employee can take 6 to 12 months off work every 3 years, with benefits equal to those paid during parental leave. Finland and Denmark have similar options.

Europeans typically receive 5 weeks vacation. Students around the world often take a gap year off before starting their university studies. The global picture, therefore, is quite different from that in the United States, where companies award a limited amount of time off for childbirth and few offer sabbaticals. Companies that are generous in this regard are an exception, not the rule.

The American Way

In the United States, taking breaks is not yet a mainstream idea. Whether it's because we are a younger country that is still striving, because of our ingrained work ethic, or for other reasons, in most circles, being busy and being in demand professionally are the most revered conditions. There is peer pressure as well. Some people regard taking time off from work as a luxury, a whim, or just plain silly given the cyclical nature of job markets, with booms being followed by tight markets. Read: "Hold onto your job because you're lucky to have one."

The concept of taking time off, however, is generating more interest—even allure—as more people take breaks and experience the many positive benefits firsthand. Teachers have always taken summer breaks. Academics have had the opportunity to go on sabbatical, typically every 7 years. Exemplary companies, such as Xerox, award core employees breaks to engage in not-for-profit service or to pursue further education. The media's fascination with some high-profile cases has also generated wider awareness and greater acceptance of the concept.

You are probably generally aware of some very public people who have stepped away from hard-charging careers to take sabbaticals or gap periods of time, downsize their careers, or retire for a while. Steve Jobs, cofounder of Apple Computer, took a few years off from Apple before returning to bring the company back and improve its lackluster performance. Singer Celine Dion stayed home with a new baby for 2 years before resuming her career with a less hectic and a more family-friendly schedule. Burt's Beeswax millionaire Roxanne Quimby took time off for family before launching her hugely successful company. Michael Jordan retired from basketball, took a break to play baseball (fulfilling a lifelong dream), and then came out of retirement and returned to his sport a few years later. The *San Jose Mercury News*, in its "about people" columns, periodically mentions elite venture capitalists, entrepreneurs, and other high achievers who are taking a break—going "around the world" on open-ended airline tickets or taking time off to pursue a passion like sailing or writing a book. The *Wall Street Journal, Washington Post,* and *New York Times* have all run articles in the past year (post–September 11, 2001) about people who are going "on the road again" in search of adventure, and of themselves.

Early Adopter Phase

Some early adopter types are already in on the "break" act. They have come to the conclusion that they want or need to take a break as a result of a watershed event, a planned happenstance, an incredible opportunity, or something good or bad that was unexpected. These people are generally very self-confident, have portable skills that will be in demand when they return from their break, or have a financial cushion to sustain them during the break and the subsequent transition.

Variations on a Theme

Sabbaticals were once the sole domain of academics, who recognized that they needed time off from the day-to-day demands of teaching and service activities to engage in research and the generation of new knowledge—creative activities that require a different pace from what is possible in everyday work life. Many companies in the high-technology industry have adopted this practice during the past 10 years, primarily to give people in fast-paced, intense environments time off to renew, recharge, and rejuvenate. Hollywood, with its hiatus concept, has also been on the cutting edge. Actors, directors, writers, and others routinely take time off in between projects to get ready for the next project and to recover from the last one!

Why Take Breaks?

What people do during their breaks is as unique as their interests, values, and personal situations; however, one thing is for sure: People of all ages, backgrounds, and levels of accomplishment are discovering that focused time off—taking breaks—is valuable for renewal, reevaluation, and retooling. For example, one of our clients, who owns his own business, says, "I consider it [taking a break] critical to focus on my personal self, as well as to bring 100 percent focus to the new [postbreak] opportunity. It's a practice I learned from participating in competitive athletic outdoor activities—cultivating the ability to focus on the action on hand as a matter of maximum performance."

During our career coaching and consulting over the years, our experience has shown that people take breaks for many reasons, some of which are planned and some of which are unplanned. Some of the reasons we've seen are

1. *Relationships:* To spend more time with family, a new baby, or a family member or friend who may be in need.
2. *Repotting and career exploration:* To renew, reevaluate, or retool; or to assess a career, consider what's next, including a change in direction, and work toward achieving it with a job search plan.
3. *Planned happenstance:* To take advantage of a once-in-a-lifetime opportunity or one that would cause serious regret if not accepted.
4. *Intellectual, physical, or emotional renewal:* To travel; write; research; go back to school or continue education; build new skills; or engage in inner work or outside activities that improve health or happiness, recharge creativity, improve focus, or increase motivation.
5. *Giving back:* To serve others formally or informally, with a group or individually.
6. *The happiness factor:* To enjoy life, pursue interests, follow a passion; to take time to *be* rather than to *do*.

Paradigm Shift

The old model of work dictated that people stayed with one company, worked until retirement age with perhaps 1 or 2 weeks of vacation per year, then moved into a less active phase in life, relaxing or enjoying the things they had not had time for during all the years they were working. Our parents and their parents lived this model, and it may have worked for some of them, for some of the time.

The world has changed. It has become more sophisticated, technology has enabled virtual and portable work, companies have changed the "contract" they have with their employees, people move and change jobs more frequently, and we are living and working longer. A new work paradigm is emerging. Our generation has greater work-life flexibility than ever before. We have the opportunity to have a career mosaic, a portfolio career, a boundaryless career.[1]

As you'll recall, in a boundaryless career, we direct and guide our own career rather than waiting for an employer or organization to do so. Our identity comes from within, from a set of skills and competencies that we develop over time and use in our work. A boundaryless career is not based in an organization; it is directed by us to accord with our core values.

The boundaryless career can include having several mini-careers over a lifetime or having many careers within an organization or profession. Melding together all of your work experiences creates your career mosaic, an overall design that evolves into a masterpiece that we define rather than our employer's doing so. In a boundaryless career, when one job or set of work experiences ends, a new one begins. You draw from your portfolio of skills and assets to do work that is meaningful to you.

One of the author's inspirations, who she met while serving on the Board of the Career Action Center, was the late John Gardner, former secretary of HEW and Stanford University professor. She'll always remember what he said to groups of students who were about to embark on their careers, their futures: "Life is the art of drawing without an eraser." The concepts of boundaryless careers and career mosaics allow us to draw our own work lives. As we assume more responsibility for managing our own careers, the opportunity for taking breaks—in between projects, in between jobs, in between careers—is more within our grasp than it was when we relied more on organizations to manage our careers. While taking breaks involves risks, as discussed in Principle 3, and change, as talked about in Principle 6, taking time off can allow you to get to know yourself, continue your learning, make people a priority, plan ahead for your future, or rejuvenate, rebound, or redirect.

The Principle—Give Yourself a Break

What we are encouraging in this principle is the idea of incorporating breaks into your lifelong career strategy and planning. When managing your career, give yourself strategic breaks throughout your lifetime. Plan financially to make this possible down the road. Schedule or make opportunistic use of time off for periods of renewal. This can be done in a variety of ways:

- Taking breaks in between jobs or careers
- Taking short breaks in between projects
- Taking mini-breaks during a job, e.g., giving yourself periodic "creativity" days (or longer!)

- Planning a series of mini-careers (a career portfolio or mosaic) within one's lifespan and/or alternating periods of working with planned breaks

Benefits of Taking Breaks

The concept of taking breaks underscores the value of thinking about your career as a fluid journey—one with many twists, turns, and roads less traveled, sometimes charting new ground and sometimes hitting dead ends that lead to new beginnings. For "career athletes," taking breaks is an acknowledgment that they are running a marathon as opposed to a sprint. By pacing, taking time to replenish and fortify, receiving support from those cheering on the sidelines, doing what we know we need to do for endurance and efficacy, and realizing that we have a long road ahead of us, we have a better chance of reaching the "finish line"—accomplishing what we set out to do, physically, mentally, and emotionally.

Anecdotally, for 95 percent of the people we have career coached or counseled, breaks have enriched their lives, enhanced their relationships with their significant others, reenergized them, and/or given them renewed creativity, energy, and focus for their next steps and their futures. Whether you take a sabbatical that you have strategically planned, a mini-break, or transition time after something out of your control occurs, allowing yourself a break or breaks at points throughout your career can be a powerful impetus for sustaining yourself and your career over a lifetime.

The Basics of Breaks[2]

Simply put, breaks can be

1. Planned or unplanned
2. Between jobs or careers, or within a job or career
3. Mini-, short, or long
4. Formal or informal

Planned Breaks

Maryland Eastwood took 4 months off before assuming her new position as president of a prestigious women's college in the Midwest. Prior to that, Dr. Eastwood, who was married and the parent of one child, had worked for over 20 years without a break other than normal vacations. She says, "My motivation was to have some downtime between two very intense and time-consuming positions. The nature of the break was pretty much relaxation and catching up on home projects that had been let go for years."

Planned breaks are those that you anticipate and plan for in advance. These types of breaks are usually within your span of control and are taken as part of your overall career management/career sustenance strategy. For example, perhaps you have been asked to take on an enormous challenge, such as turning around a group or a company. You might give yourself a period of time in which to accomplish that, then plan to take a break before your next role. Another example of a planned break may be taking family leave, pursuing a graduate or postgraduate degree, or moving to another location. With such a break, you have time to plan the break in advance and to communicate with those who will be affected by it (and those who may need to approve it). You also have time to plan financially for the break and to put into place transition activities that can minimize the potential negative ramifications of your taking a break.

Unplanned Breaks

Unplanned breaks occur because of unexpected events or changes. These breaks are usually outside of your control. For example, you may have to take a break because of your or a family member's ill health, being made redundant by your organization, or a move with your significant other for his or her job promotion. Unplanned breaks typically get off to a rough start, as there is seldom time to put your finances in order, communicate effectively with those who will be affected, or implement a transition plan, but you can do your best, and usually everything works out if you make the extra effort.

One of the authors moving to London with her husband last year is an example of making the most of an unplanned break. Although London had always been one of the couple's favorite cities and they knew that they wanted to live abroad at some point; her husband's being offered an exciting expanded role by his company was unexpected. After assessing the opportunity and checking in together on their larger life vision and priorities, they decided to embrace the change as a "joint adventure" and as a treasured move into the next phase in their careers and their lives. To ensure a smooth transition for her employer, Stanford Business School, where she had served for 7 years, the author delayed joining her husband for several months to help prepare her team, find a successor, hand off responsibilities, and finish up key projects. The move to London would bring a change, as the author had either worked or gone to school full-time as part of four very different but wonderful organizations since 1979.

The author adopted a positive attitude about the adjustments involved in taking an unplanned break. Some of these adjustments were difficult, like leaving their families and best friends behind in California and missing her colleagues. Following her own advice from coaching others on their careers, she gave herself transition time, taking a break of 2 months to set up their new home, immerse herself in learning the new city, travel, and establish her home office overlooking a new English garden. The author has used the time and circumstances as an opportunity to create a stimulating and meaningful portfolio career: writing, speaking, and keeping her passion for career coaching integrated into her work. The author and her husband are "drawing without an eraser" as they fulfill more of their life vision and priorities.

Shifting Gears Time

Whether an unplanned break is the result of a positive event or of a more negative event such as being laid off, taking time to make the transition and to regroup is valuable. In our work with reorganizations, advising managers about layoffs and counseling employees who have lost their jobs, we have observed that the natural tendency of recently laid-off employees is to want to jump into another job right away and forget about the layoff. Although the stigma of being laid off has diminished over the last 5 years, given that layoffs have become more common and happen even to high performers, the newly laid-off person has to deal with real or perceived issues such as a sudden loss of identity, income, and regular schedule; separation from colleagues; and figuring out what's next, often with little or no help. It's natural for the person to want to jump from the lost job to a new job without taking the time to process the unplanned change.

This is perhaps one of the worst mistakes such a person can make. Although the temptation is strong and at times others' expectations come into play, of those whom we have coached, the ones who have made it through the transition the best are those who have taken the time to acknowledge the loss and then given themselves time and space to regroup and redirect. Most individuals ultimately land on their feet, with healthy attitudes and resilience. We have seen that after the initial shock, giving yourself permission to take a break can be liberating, and you are in a better place to seize your next opportunity.

Between or Within Jobs or Careers

Perhaps the easiest time to plan for and take a break is when you are between jobs or careers. Leaving an existing situation is the perfect point for introspection, taking time to recharge and explore alternatives. When you take time off from a job, you can either return to your same position or move to a different position within your organization, or, alternatively, you may decide to make a change to another organization in the same industry or to make a leap to a totally new industry or function/field. Quitting one job before having another used to be frowned upon. There is no longer a negative connotation to this. It has become very common for people to take breaks in between jobs. Of course, it would be ideal to have a job lined up that would start after your break (for example, to leave one job in June and start a new job in October), but if that's not possible, taking a break and then looking for a job also can work.

Mini-, Short, or Long

The length of breaks varies enormously. We know of:

- A marketing vice president who moved back home and took almost 2 years off to recover from the loss of her long-term spouse

- A man who was the trailing spouse to his wife on her international assignment
- A business writer who takes 6 months off each year to sail with her partner
- A young married couple who decided to take a year-long break early in their lives together, before having children
- Children who accompanied their father when he was offered the chance to teach in a different state for 6 months
- Many clients and colleagues who have taken from 6 weeks to a few months in between jobs
- Many others who have learned that they can't "burn the candle at both ends" for too long and who now fit creativity "moments" into their daily work lives or take "creativity weekends" (no chores) once a quarter.

The breaks we're discussing here may be mini-, short-, or long. They may have an anticipated ending or be open-ended. There are no rules on the subject, but for the purpose of this book, let's say that a mini-break is a day or a weekend; a short break is between a week and 6 months; and a long break is 6 months or more.

Formal or Informal Leaves

Many organizations have formal leave policies that allow you to take up to a year off without pay. If you return within 1 year, your benefits will be bridged. In the most generous cases, you will be able to return to your job or a similar one. More often, especially if you are in a critical role, the company will need to replace you, but you will be able to return to a similar level of responsibility within an agreed-upon time frame. We recommend that you request a formal leave of absence only if you are positive that you will be returning to the organization at the end of your leave. Many individuals who think that they will return change their plans. Therefore, because you do not know how you will feel after the time off (whether you will want to return to the same organization or try something different), we suggest that you request an informal leave as a way of being fair to your employer, your colleagues, and your teammates.

Taking a formal leave during which you are not to be replaced puts an unfair burden on your organization. It cannot hire someone else and benefit from having a new leader in your role. Your absence can let down your team and colleagues, leaving them in limbo. If you are more than 75 percent sure that you will not want to come back into the role you are leaving, do not betray the goodwill of your organization by asking it to grant you a leave and hold your job open for you.

A win-win arrangement would be to arrange with your organization to take an informal leave. This gives your organization the opportunity to replace you if it chooses to do so, and gives you the opportunity to discuss options with your organization when you return. If you leave on good terms, were a high-level performer, and are up front about everything, an informal leave will more than suffice. Most employers will be happy to have their talented employees return, will want to keep the door and the dialogue open, and can even create something for you when you are ready to return if that is in the cards.

Planning for a Break[3]

Whether you are planning for a break or taking advantage of transition time for longer breaks, here are some considerations, questions, and issues to think about, and recommendations.

Get Your Finances in Shape

One of the core questions you need to answer for yourself when you are considering a break is: How much money do I need for the period that I want to take off? A deal breaker for taking time off is typically your short-term financial picture. Can you afford a break? Do you have enough money to pay for your basics and the quality of life you require? If not, what sacrifices—trade-offs—are you willing and able to make in order to build a reserve to fund your time off? How quickly can you do this or how long will it take to amass what you need?

To be honest, planning financially to take a break can be a hard sell. It isn't typical for us to "treat" ourselves in this way, and yet unscheduled time is becoming the new status symbol, as it is in such scarce supply. What is needed is a change in your mindset; you need to consider taking a break to be an investment in your career, not an indulgence. As with a mortgage, you can amortize the investment over a period of time. If taking a break helps you to be more productive, to sustain a career longer, or to be happier while pursuing a career, then it's probably worth planning for.

If you are part of a dual-career couple, can your partner serve as the primary "breadwinner" for a while (more on this later)? If you are not part of a couple or you are already the primary support of your family, how can you manage to take a break? One way is to make a midterm plan for a break in, say, 2 years' time. In the meantime, you can develop a baseline budget (more on this later), cut back on expenditures, and save for the specific purpose of taking a break. You will be setting aside money for your break on a regular basis, just as you would set aside money for buying furniture or for an expensive family vacation. Some tips on how to cut back on expenditures appear later in this principle.

Assess Your Financial Picture

As a base, you need to know your financial picture. How does your balance sheet look—what are your assets and liabilities? How much money and fairly liquid assets do you have? What are your cash inflows and outflows? Budgeting, tracking expenses, and financial planning are discussed more in depth in Principle 4.

In general (not just when you are preparing to take a break), the common wisdom is that at a minimum you need a 3- to 6-month cash reserve to cover any unplanned event such as being laid off. What are your sources of income (revenues coming in)? What are your expenses (money going out)? Which of your expenses are fixed or fairly fixed, such as house, rent, car payment, insurance premiums, and school loan payoffs? Which expenses are variable, such as food and eating out, clothing, entertainment, and travel?

Wants versus Needs

What most of us find is that there is a substantial difference between what we require and what we desire. For instance, we may desire a new car every few years or a fabulous vacation each year, but we don't require it. We may covet a bigger house or the newest high-tech gadget, but we don't truly need it. If you can adopt a mindset of making even small changes or trade-offs, you can begin to build your reserve to fund your break. We're careful not to call these sacrifices, because they are not. Rather than having the attitude that you are doing without or giving up, adopt the mindset that you are choosing to build toward your larger goal of your time off.

The Latte Factor

In his book *Smart Couples Finish Rich*, David Bach relies on common sense rather than eye-glazing financial formulas and theories. A sample of his advice is his talk about "the latte factor," the idea that a couple that spends $10 each day for a morning coffee, a muffin, and a newspaper could instead sock away the money and accumulate $1 million in 20 years. Take the idea of the latte factor and apply it more broadly and you will see that there are all sorts of possibilities.

Saving Money Best Bets

This list is only a starting point. What are other ways that you can think of?

- If you go to the theater twice a month, try going only once. If you are a movie buff and you must see the movies, then at least try to go during the reduced price show times or to wait until the films are available on videotape or DVD. If you eat out three to six times a week, try to halve the number of times. Thaw, microwave, or boil on the other days if cooking is not your strong suit. If you must take a fabulous vacation, go during the off-season, plan ahead for savings, or go at the last minute, when great deals abound. Take care of your car and go longer before buying a new one. Think about ways to lower your house payment or rent—refinance your loan or rent out a room in your place. If you are lucky, find someone who will let you house-sit in lieu of rent, which will save you a big chunk of money.
- Instead of buying expensive gifts, make them. One of the best gifts we received this past Christmas was a big glass jar filled with the ingredients for making chocolate chip cookies (chips, flour, nuts, and a favorite recipe). A gift that is always appreciated is the gift of time. Coupons to "cash in" for walking a friend's dog while she or he is away or a personal tutoring session in salsa dancing are examples.

You get the gist. Be creative, and keep your goal in mind. Remain focused in building your reserve for funding your break. The money saved by using these tactics will be worth the effort.

Making Extra Money

In addition to or instead of saving money to fund your break, perhaps you will want to make extra money. If you have a hobby in which you excel—woodworking, swimming, piano, writing, computers, languages, cooking—brainstorm easy ways to turn that into extra income. Maybe you can teach piano to adults, set up the computer networks for small businesses, do proofreading or editing for corporate publications, teach English to international executives and their families, or provide ready-to-eat meals for time-strapped working couples.

You might sell some stock or take on an extra work project after hours or on weekends for a while. Perhaps you will accept a higher-paying but less-than-ideal job for a year, with the goal of squirreling away 35 percent of your salary each month. Once again, be creative. Think about ways in which you can cut back, apply your talents in new moneymaking arenas, and live differently in order to fund your break.

Considering Your Significant Others

Principle 5 discussed the importance of taking your significant other into account when you are making career decisions and plans, and how to do this. If you are considering taking a break, you will want to think about how your significant other will be affected. Then have some open discussions about your viewpoints and objectives. Identify areas where there's potential conflict, determine what changes there will be for each of you, and problem-solve together, talking through your concerns.

Practically speaking, you will need to think about how long a break you ideally want to take, and when. How long is contingent upon how long a break you can afford. What is the maximum length of time your finances can sustain you? Is it a month, 6 weeks, 3 months, 6 months, a year, a few years, indefinitely? Also, think about when you will take a break. Is there a best time to do it? If possible, in making this decision, consider both your significant other and your boss, your team, your organization, and so on. Trying for the best possible outcome is not easy, but with thoughtful planning, it is often doable.

Dual-Career Couples—Making It Work

The successful dual-career couples with whom we've worked consider their relationship to be a true partnership. Over the years, they have traded off roles if one career needed to take priority. They have made choices based on mutual respect and on what matters to them, both individually and as a couple. They have been led by a foundation of values and dreams for the future. Indeed, having a supportive, loving, and complementary spouse is a gift. If you have this type of relationship, discussing and following through on your need for a break are easier to handle. If you do not have a supportive significant other, making the case for taking a break becomes more difficult. Other sources of support, as discussed in Principle 5, can be helpful.

Over the years, we've heard and participated in the discussions on the unique challenges and opportunities that dual-career couples encounter. We touch here on a few of those that are most relevant to managing your career. What follows are key questions and issues for you and your significant other to discuss. We suggest approaching them together and having "checkups" with each other quarterly or annually to assess how you are doing or to make changes in your plans or your direction.

- What do you value, individually and as a couple? Being happy? Being comfortable? Status? Security? Material wealth? Friends and family?
- What are your top priorities overall?
- Do you want children? If yes, when preferably?
- How important is it that one parent be home with a new baby, and for how long? For example, do you both want one person to be able not to work for the first few years? How will you decide which of you that will be? What alterations in your life or lifestyle will you need to make? How will you blend children and work?

- What are your aspirations 5 years out, 10 years out, 15 years out, and beyond—individually and as a couple?
- How will you deal with those areas where your aspirations diverge? For example, will you compromise? Will you methodically take turns, honoring one of your aspirations one time, then the other's aspirations the next time, or will you be less deliberate about it?
- When ideally would you like to take breaks during your lifetime? Can both of you take a break at the same time? When do you want to retire from working as you know it?
- What do you need to accomplish between now and each of those points, from 5 years out to retirement?
- What is your action plan—an ideal one and two or three fallback scenarios?

Getting the Word Out

In addition to significant others and finances, there are some logistical issues to think through when you are considering a break, especially if you are currently in a significant role in an organization and you want to leave in the best possible way for everyone. The considerations revolve around who, what, when, where, and how to tell.

- Who needs to know what, and when?
- Where and how will you tell them?

The people who obviously need to know include your boss, your closest colleagues, those with whom you work, your staff, vendors, clients, strategic partners, and colleagues inside and outside the organization. In general, you'll want to let anyone who is important to you, your work, and your future work know about your break. In getting the word out, not all people are created equal, and so you will probably want to tell different people at different times. You will want to phase your communication. As a general rule, you would tell your boss first out of respect, then your team and your close colleagues, and then make any broader communication.

Ideally, developing a communication plan and a transition plan are your responsibility; you shouldn't burden others with it. The communication plan would include what you tell to whom, when, and how. The transition plan would include the status of your current projects—where you are on them—and what you can finish by the time you leave, and whom you will transfer work in progress to, including providing background and transferring knowledge to help get the person who is taking on the responsibility up to speed quickly.

We've found that a simple email to colleagues, first those inside the organization, then those outside, suffices. The points to cover are

- You are leaving X organization/Y role.
- Why (as appropriate).
- What you will be doing, briefly, e.g., taking time off to ___.
- How to contact you during this time.
- Any information about a successor and the transition.

One particularly effective note that we received from a class act who had worked for a top-tier investment bank and then a top-two executive search firm and who recently landed at a hot high-tech company as a recruiting executive went something like this:

Dear Friends and Colleagues,

Well, I know that there are silver linings. I had a fantastic opportunity to work with you when I was at ABC Investment Bank, and I have enjoyed a great deal our keeping in touch with my move to the West Coast as director at BBC Executive Search. With the market and hiring picture slowdown, I've recently been laid off. After 7 years of working nonstop, I'll be taking some time off to enjoy time with my family and friends, travel, and look for my next job.

Do keep me in mind as you hear about opportunities. I am interested in x, y, z roles in high technology or consumer products. Ideally I'd like to stay around San Francisco and the Bay Area.

The best way to contact me for now is:

E-mail address and mobile telephone number

Best regards,

Elizabeth Grace

Source: S. Taguchi, "Reality Bytes" work-life skills seminars, "Managing Your Career for a Lifetime," Stanford Graduate School of Business, 1997.

Smooth Transitions

In your transition planning, shoot for whatever is the least disruptive for others. Remember that above all, you are your reputation and your integrity. You owe it to those you care about in the organization, and to yourself, to do your best until the very day you leave.

Show consideration and generosity. Make sure that everything is in the best possible shape before you take your break.

Depending on how much time you have, try cross-training others on your key responsibilities; organize your files so that it is easy for someone else to come in and pick up where you left off; when you need to, document what you are working on and what is left to be done; and discuss with your manager what role you will play in finding and training a successor.

Make sure to develop a status report giving all your current projects and where you are on them. Be clear and realistic about what you can finish before you leave. Think about what needs to be transferred and to whom. Make sure you have briefed the people who will be taking over, in person if possible, even if you have only a short meeting. Give them all your files and notes, and provide contact information for everyone with whom you have been working. Give them the scoop on any land mines, context, or behind-the-scenes information that they would not easily find out otherwise. Strive for smooth hand-offs.

No Burning Bridges

Whether or not you end up returning to the organization, keeping up positive relationships with your former employers and colleagues makes good business sense. Maintaining strong bridges for a future return or for a return in another capacity is an essential element of the transition plan for a personal break.

Think about your willingness to serve. If a successor or a colleague who will fill in for you during your break has not been found, you will need to ask yourself how willing and able you are to help out, and for how long. We would advise you to do as much as you can, but to set your boundaries. You want to be gracious and, as we have just said, maintain those relationships. But if your employer is one who will take advantage of your gracious behavior, you will have to make sure that you are not sucked into staying on indefinitely until the organization finds someone to replace you.

Determine what is reasonable and doable. For example, perhaps you can be on call for emergencies and to finish up any major projects for up to 6 weeks after the beginning of your planned break. Maybe you can agree to spend a few days with your successor, once he or she is recruited, to make the transition, and perhaps you can offer to be available by telephone or email as needed.

Chilling Out

Make sure to take some downtime and R&R to make your transition into your break. With Type A personalities and overachievers, a common difficulty that we've seen is that they fill up their schedules during a break to the same level of busyness as when they were working. This may be OK for a week or so, but doing it for a much longer period defeats the purpose of taking time off in the first place. Too-full schedules leave little space to reflect or relax or do any of the other *R* words: reenergize, rediscover, rebuild, rebound, repot, rejuvenate, renew, and so on. Even if you "relax" by keeping superbusy, we strongly encourage you to make time for R&R during your break. How long you do this is of course a personal choice. We suggest that you spend long enough on R&R to truly wind down before you wind back up.

When one of the authors took a year-long break in between jobs to care for an ill parent, she had great difficulty *not* overfilling her calendar as she was accustomed to doing. So one day she took the drastic measure of throwing away her day planner! She made a conscious attempt *not* to have scheduled activities, appointments, and to-do lists. Her goal was to not pursue any goals during this time! Taking this drastic step helped her to refocus her time and energy away from work and onto the important personal priorities on which she truly wanted to spend time.

Mini-Breaks

If it is not possible for you to take an extended break, mini-breaks can be a tonic for inspiration, creativity, feeding the soul, reconnecting with yourself, and clarifying what you are trying to accomplish and what matters to you. Mini-breaks can be taken each day, each week, or each month. Their purpose is to replenish whatever is running low in your life: energy, motivation, fun, or purpose.

There are plenty of possibilities for mini-breaks. Essentially, a mini-break is time taken off from your usual routine and work in order to have fun. According to the dictionary, *fun* means "being distracted." Do something that will reenergize you, inspire greater creativity, or clear your mind of the clutter so that you can resume your focus more intensely. Your mini-break doesn't require a lot of time, money, or effort. The following is a list of possibilities. Add any others that might appeal to you.

- Get out of yourself and do something for someone else.
- Read a book.
- Learn to knit.
- Take the first 10 minutes after you get home from work for you.
- Invite friends over for a Scrabble party.
- Volunteer to read children's stories at your local library.
- Host a slumber party, with pizza, a movie, and staying up late.
- Indulge in a film or museum.
- Do something physical: Take an aerobics class or ballroom dancing lesson; Rollerblade; go for a scenic walk; challenge your neighbors to a friendly game of basketball or foosball.
- Focus on inner work: meditation; yoga; listening to an inspirational book on tape.
- Pamper yourself in whatever way makes you feel like you are taking care of yourself.
- Plan and take a weekend getaway.
- Make something with your hands—make a topiary, design a birthday card from scratch, try a new recipe, or draw with washable chalk.
- Be a beginner—try your hand at something you are not comfortable with to stretch yourself.
- Engage in kids' play—fly a kite, doodle with a science experiment, or set a play date with your best pal.
- Change your physical space—rearrange the stuff on your desk or your furniture, declutter, or introduce a new, creative element.

- Spend time with friends and tell stories.
- Explore something you've been curious about.
- Risk failure.
- Take on an unaccustomed challenge.
- Show someone that you care about him or her.
- Discover something new.
- Make someone else feel better—take your dog to a nursing home to visit; call a friend who is in a bad stretch; perform a random act of kindness.
- Volunteer for a worthwhile cause—tutor someone; work on a community event; help sign up voters.
- Learn a new word each day for the next month and use it in five sentences.
- Keep a diary—a journal.
- Say out loud to yourself what you are most thankful for in your life at the beginning of each morning for a year.

But Will It Hurt My Career?[3]

Yes, taking a break could hurt your career. When you are embarking on something new or bold, there is always the chance that the result may provoke a setback rather than a move forward. Whether breaks will help or hurt your career depends on your attitude and your implementation. How do you feel deep down about what you are doing? Are you committed to and confident of your choice? What can you do to offset any insecurities or make your path smoother? How do you plan to take a break and then prepare for reentry later on? Thinking through these issues in advance can help you decide whether taking a break is for you.

Worst-Case Scenarios

In one of the author's work, while in industry, an especially rewarding role was to help executives and managers who were either considering a career change (within or outside the company) or in need of time off, to decide how to overcome the potential obstacles of taking a break and to keep it from being a career-limiting move in the longer term. What follows are a compilation of the common fears about the worst that could happen and suggested solutions.

Worst Case 1: Lack of Financial Resources

"I just can't afford to take time off. I need the money from my job and don't have enough savings."

Suggested Solution

Start planning in advance so that you can build a reserve that will support your time off. Cut back your discretionary expenses by a target percentage (for example, 10 percent). Save more money than you do now—either spend less or bring in more money to create your financial support. Review the earlier sections in this principle "Saving Money Best Bets" and "Making Extra Money." Develop a budget if you don't have one. Get to know your financial picture. Figure out what you need to do in order to fund your break.

Worst Case 2: Excuses, Excuses

"The organization needs me. My team needs me. My new boss needs me. My family needs this particular lifestyle. I am successful now; do I chance it? I've worked so hard to get to this point—I would be crazy to give it all up. I might never be able to jump back into the race again. . . ."

Suggested Solution

These are all valid concerns. That is why you need to be clear about why you are taking a break. What is important to you? Is taking a break something that you philosophically believe in? Is it something that you truly need and want to do? Does it speak to your current values? Can you visualize the benefits? Muster the courage to do it. It's time to put your career choice into the context of the rest of your life.

Worst Case 3: Pangs of Guilt

You may feel guilty about being "indulgent." So many of your talented friends have been laid off or are working in unfulfilling jobs. Your parents taught you the value of hard work. Why do you deserve the time off?

Suggested Solution

Why *don't* you deserve time off? Are you unworthy? Think of your break as an investment, not an indulgence—a means of sustaining yourself (and your career) for a long time.

Worst Case 4: People Will Think the Worst of You

You worry about what others will think of you. Will they feel sorry for you because you don't have a job and so you have decided to take time off (wink, wink)? Will they feel that your days will be empty and boring?

Suggested Solution

The reality is that some people would never take time off and cannot imagine the benefit to anyone else of adopting this strange behavior. Many pockets of society revere a strong work ethic, wealth, and more traditional definitions of success, such as prestige, status, and money. Taking breaks runs counter to conventional wisdom. There will be skepticism about why anyone would take time off voluntarily, without being forced to do so. Some people will not "get it," and that is OK. You're doing this for yourself and your career, not to gain others' approval.

The best advice is to articulate for yourself (clarify) why you are taking a break. Bring those people that matter to you into the thought process and/or decision early on. Hope for their support, but be willing to go ahead with your choice without it. Figure and accept that some people in your life or at work may think that you are selfish or that taking a break is not a smart move. How could anyone give up a great job or a steady income, given the tight job market? That is their opinion, but remember why you are doing what you are doing. No regrets. What matters is that you know why you want to take a break and that many of those whom you truly care about understand and support it. You don't need acceptance from everyone to prove the legitimacy and value of your personal choice.

Worst Case 5: Pressure to Take a Break Later

You may receive "helpful" advice from those who are well intentioned. They will urge you not to take a break now, but to wait for a better time. You may hear refrains like "Stay a few more years in your job," "Save more money," "Get more experience with this job under your belt," or "You will create a huge hole in the organization/team if you leave now."

Suggested Solution

If you have carefully thought through your decision to take a break, you will know your range of dates for your break. Be flexible to the extent you can be, but at some point you have to untie the string. It is nice to feel indispensable and needed, but life will go on without you. Hopefully, you have done your best to bring along people who can step up to the plate and fill your place. In fact, change, fresh perspective, and new ideas and energy will be good for those you are leaving behind. It's the work role you are stopping for now. Your relationships and affection for the people will continue.

Worst Case 6: Outdated Skills and Knowledge

Your field is competitive, with many talented people vying for a limited number of jobs. If you take time off, your skills and experience could become outdated. Taking yourself out of the flow will be risky. You and your knowledge could become obsolete.

Suggested Solution

Staying out too long without retooling your skills and knowledge and letting your experience lapse and become outdated are very realistic concerns.

During the time you are away from work, you will need to devote some effort to staying abreast of your field or industry or to retooling your skills and knowledge for a move to a new arena. Depending on the degree of difficulty in keeping yourself updated, you can do this in concentrated chunks of time throughout your time off or at the end of your time off as you are planning for reentry.

Keeping yourself in the know and in the flow does not have to be a chore. It can be built into your enjoyment. Plan a weekly lunch to meet with colleagues who are in the know and talk shop. Ask them to share things of note that are going on in their companies. Maintain your subscription to your professional journals and magazines. Participate in the annual conference. Savor a book or two on the leading-edge thinking or goings-on in your industry. Take an evening course on the latest practices or new technologies relevant to your field.

Worst Case 7: I'm Lost—Where to Begin?

It's all overwhelming. You are very uncertain, and you don't know where to start.

Suggested Solution

If the concept of breaks overwhelms you, reread this principle (and also Principle 3, on risk taking) and then ask around to identify a few people in your field or your next choice of one who have actually taken a break. Call them in confidence and let them know what you are thinking. Ask them to tell you how they did it. What were the mistakes they made and the lessons they learned? What advice do they have for you? Would they do it again? What was the worst thing that happened as a result? What were the positive outcomes? Talking with others can help you decide if taking a break is for you.

Worst Case 8: Flat-Out Fear

You may have major self-doubts or momentary crises of confidence. A jumble of many fears will come together and create a seemingly insurmountable fear.

Will you be able to jump back into the world of work? What will people really think of you? Can you afford to do this—literally, in terms of your finances, and figuratively, in terms of letting go of a great job?

Suggested Solution

May we offer you the sage advice of other writers, philosophers, or leaders whose prose was eloquent: "Nothing ventured, nothing gained." "The only thing we have to fear is fear itself." "Anything worthwhile is worth working for." "If you don't do it, you'll never know." "Nothing great was achieved overnight." If you have thought through the issues and questions in this principle and your system shouts "go," then go for it. Take a break. You deserve your sabbatical. Make use of it. If you have made a wrong decision, you can change your mind. Nothing is irreversible. If the organization has given your job away to someone else, use the impetus to try something new in your organization or try another organization. And one more quote, from a Turkish proverb: "No matter how far you have gone on a wrong road, turn back."

Attitude

Much in life is about attitude. You can see the glass as half empty or half full. You can approach your choices and decisions with positive optimism or negative pessimism. Yet it's much more complicated than black or white. For the purposes of your career management in particular, if you have decided to take time off, then be happy about it. This is not an uninformed giddy or naïve happiness, but rather acceptance of the idea that the break was your choice. Again, understand—be clear about—why you are doing what you are doing. Embrace the break as a natural progression—a valuable step in your career journey.

Read *The Power of Positive Thinking*, by Norman Vincent Peale. Talk with a particularly supportive friend. Keep focused on what you are hoping to achieve with your break. Visualize some of the new, exciting opportunities that you may consider after your break. Or just reflect on how lucky you are to be able to take a sabbatical. Be grateful that you have the knowledge of yourself and what's important, serendipity, time, money, supportive significant other, or whatever it was that brought you to this point. If all else fails, think about all the individuals who would love to take a break and how lucky you are. Then stop second-guessing yourself and start using your break for its intended purpose. Don't squander it. You'll be back in the flow of things again before you know it and looking forward to your next break!

Readying Yourself for Reentry

When you reenter the working world, you may be returning to your old organization in your previous role or a new role. More often than not, however, you will have decided to make a more substantial job change. Perhaps you will be going to a different company or a totally new industry or field. Perhaps you will opt to do similar work, but in a different mode—for example, you will consult on projects, allowing a more flexible schedule. Or perhaps you will start your own business or join a new partnership or alliance.

Whatever the role in which you decide to reenter, it is imperative that you develop a strategy and a plan for reentry. Give yourself time to focus on preparation—1 month or more, depending on how long you took off and how difficult it will be to make the change you are considering.

If you have been doing your homework periodically throughout your break, you will have used some of your time for such things as self-assessment and career discovery, building any new skills needed for a career change, or keeping abreast of your field. After you have completed this inner work, you are ready to formulate your action plan.

Give yourself ample time to plan for your next move, conducting a job search and reorienting yourself to being in the swing of things. Take a close look at Principles 7, on planning, and 9, on implementing your strategy. These principles discuss in depth ideas and to-dos for developing and implementing a job search or career change action plan. Utilize our five-phase career management model to guide your efforts. As context for the journey on which you are about to embark, think through some of the more practical issues:

- When do I want to start working again?
- Why am I reentering—what is it that I want to accomplish?
- Where do I want to reenter—my former/current organization or a new one? Do I want to return to my former role or take on a new role? Do I want to be in the same industry/function, or a new one?
- What is my action plan, including best- and worst-case scenarios?
- What resources—people, information, or others—can help me?
- What are the milestones? How can I measure my progress toward my objectives?

Lean on Me

Reach out to others and ask for their help as you ready yourself to reenter the world of work. Rely on your significant other, your family, and supportive friends or colleagues. Ask an old boss or a friend in the field in which you are interested for a reality check on your action plan. Tap into your relationships as informational resources as well as for advice or emotional support for your career change plans.

If you are returning to your previous organization, but in a new role, initiate discussions about opportunities and timing with HR and with the manager who supported your taking time off. If your skills and knowledge have lapsed, try as you might have to keep them current, then find out what you need to do to get yourself up to speed. HR or your manager will be able to suggest an internal class, outside training, or other resources for your learning. Your manager or others with experience inside your organization can also provide coaching, or even a quick briefing for you.

To further close the gap in skills and experience, especially if you are making a move to a totally different field or industry, you will need to put forth more effort. Initiate your own search for resources. Review the information in Principle 9 on researching industries, companies, and jobs; new-age networking; and informational interviews. Take an evening or weekend class; read some books; join your professional association; seek out people in the organization who can informally mentor you. You will make it through.

Case Study: A Bodacious Break—
A Thirty-Something's Journey from High-Tech
High Performer to Pastry Chef

Carol Escueta Ramos's journey is an inspirational and audacious one: She decided to step off the finance fast track at Intel, then took a 6-month break before enrolling in the Culinary Institute Academy's (CIA) baking and pastry arts program.

After earning her MBA from Stanford in 1996, Ramos joined Intel in Silicon Valley, where she was quickly promoted three times, reaching the level of senior finance manager in less than 5 years. She was also on the road to vesting of her stock options, which even with the overall stock market woes would have amounted to a lot.

Ramos's upbringing—her parents were well-educated, disciplined engineers who owned their own company—had a lot to do with her taking the traditional/responsible path for most of her 33 years. Ramos's parents had always stressed the importance of studying hard, getting into good schools, working diligently, finding a respected company and job, and saving for the future. Ramos had been doing remarkably well on all counts.

Recently, however, Ramos's "vague sense of dissatisfaction" had led her to a thoughtful conclusion that had been lingering at the back of her mind for a few years. She says, "I wanted something more or something else out of life. I wasn't unhappy at my job, and I was good at what I did, but I wasn't truly happy with it, either. Intel was great. I liked the people I worked with. I was on an upwardly mobile career path, and my financial future looked good. . . . The biggest realization was knowing that the next promotion would be to controller, and I had absolutely no desire for it. When you don't want the next step in your career path, it's time to change careers."

Ramos also notes that her values, which she was provoked to reflect on by a book that she had read, entered into her decision to take a break and follow her passion for baking. "I asked myself, am I living according to my values? . . . The answer was 'sort of,' and that wasn't good enough for me." She has not taken any of this lightly, and she has carefully handled the pitfalls, risks, and moments of doubt. Ramos has made it through with flying colors.

She has dealt with others' initial shock at her decision to put job fulfillment before job security, power, or prestige. She has gained the support of those whose generation grew up with the notion that if you have a steady job, you have it made, so why give it up.

Ramos has reset her view about people who take breaks. She confides, "I was always partly envious, partly baffled by people who took a lot of time off from work. I was envious because they had time to do things that I felt like I couldn't when I was working full-time, such as traveling and socializing . . . and contrarily, I was partly baffled because I couldn't imagine how people could stand having all that time with nothing to do. I was used to such a frenzied pace of life that it seemed that anyone who was not working must sit at home and twiddle their thumbs. I now know that isn't what happens at all." Ramos used her 6-month break to work out, visit family and friends, travel, indulge in her favorite hobbies of reading and fiction writing, and prepare for her CIA program with research and baking regularly.

She has also reevaluated her self-worth "without the usual markers to judge" how she is doing in life. "Since I'm currently unemployed, I had to realize that a job isn't who I am or shouldn't cause me to like myself more or less, depending on what it is. . . . My friends who know me well are happy for me that I am taking such a bold step and following my dreams."

Her story starts with a childhood activity that turned into a lifelong passion. Given that her mom and dad worked full-time, Ramos and her sister were latchkey kids and were on their own to amuse themselves after school. When she was 12, she started baking, mostly from the cake or brownie mixes that her mom bought for her to use. Ramos loved the process of baking. It was gratifying to her to experiment with recipes, mix the ingredients, and a short time later produce "wonderful aromas" and gooey-tasting treats that she liked a lot. She would often bring her friends and work colleagues home-baked treats, and she began being asked to sell her treats to friends for special occasions. As a result, she started up a small business on the side, "Homemade by Carol."

Will she ramp this business up after she finishes her program? Ramos answers: "For once in my life, I don't have a set plan for what I'll be doing after the program is over. I plan to use the time in the program to explore what the opportunities are, make contacts in the industry, and learn as much as I can from the best in the business. . . . I want to keep myself open to as many options as possible so I don't miss anything. For the first time, I am relying on gut instinct and heart instead of rational, logical analysis and letting my brain decide. The truth is, at this point, I don't know what I'll do after the program—but the great part is that I'm not afraid of finding out."

Excerpts from Our Interview

Q: How have you handled your finances to sustain your time off?

A: Even before I decided to pursue this career path, I'd always been a saver, thanks in large part to the influence of my parents' "earn a dollar, save at least 50 cents/spend a dollar, get 50 cents change" mentality. Fortunately, I also never got into status symbols or toys for the wealthy or other signs of conspicuous consumption. Other than my condo, I had no big liens on my salary after I'd paid off my MBA student loans and my car (I still drive my dented 1994 Integra and will continue to drive it for as long as it gets me from point A to point B). So I built up some savings to help fund the time off. But the biggest factor contributing to my being financially able to pursue my dream was the set of stock options that vested over the 5 years I spent at Intel. Through good timing in terms of when I started at Intel in 1996, perseverance in plugging away even when times were sometimes rough on the job, not abandoning a stable company for the dot-com craze, and not cashing out options too early, I was able to consider it a good investment in myself.

Q: What questions did you have to answer for yourself or what did you consider before deciding to take a break?

A: Being of a practical nature, the first question I considered was, "Can I afford this?" Other questions soon followed: How much will it cost, how much do I need, what will I be giving up if I do this, what will I gain if I do this. I basically did a qualitative ROI analysis—given all the investment of time, money, and risk I'll be putting into this, is the potential return going to be worth it to me?

I also asked myself what I wanted to accomplish in the 6 months before I started at CIA. I've *never* had that much time off before, and I didn't want to waste it.

Q: What are the pitfalls—caveats—to look out for when taking a break?
A: Be honest with yourself about why you want to take a break or make a change. The right motivation will get you through all the self-doubts, outside criticism, and any other challenges you'll run across. It helps you keep your thought clear, and you can turn to your right reasons when times get tough to help you through them.

Plan carefully and be practical. It sounds nicely Gen-Xish to take some time off and go find yourself or rejuvenate, but you need to be practical and make sure you can afford it. It doesn't help your self-esteem to take time off and then have to rely on others to support you financially through it. Not only will you not have the usual "markers" of how you judge yourself—a job or salary—but your self-esteem could go lower if you feel that you had to be subsidized by someone after you'd spent so much time being independent. The discipline of planning ahead, saving up, and not buying big-ticket items that you might have really wanted also helps you affirm (or abandon) your goal as something being worth the sacrifice you're making.

Q: What are any lessons learned or advice from your experience and choices—anything that could help others think through if they should take a break, when, how, and what to do about it?
A: Ask yourself what you really want. Are you burned out, unhappy in your job or career or company? And will taking a break solve those problems or just postpone them? If I had decided I just needed time off from work and taken a leave of absence for 6 months, then returned, I think I would have been in the same state of faint content/discontent within a few months of my return. You sometimes get to the point where no amount of time away from something will help and you need to leave permanently. Or sometimes you honestly just do need a few months off. Only you will be able to tell the difference, so you have to ask yourself some tough questions and be honest with yourself about the answers. As I said previously, it's all about having the right motives. If your motives feel right, then it's that much easier to plan for the break, decide on your next steps, save up for it, and execute it.

Q: How do you think taking the break helped your career over a lifetime?

Part 4

Take Action to Manage Your Career

With this principle, we begin Part 4 of our book: "Take Action to Manage Your Career. You've learned from your past, assessed your present, and envisioned your future. Now it's time to integrate it all—to develop and implement action plans to get the career you want and to keep working on these plans. Attaining career clarity and acting on it is a lifetime process, a continuous cycle of learning and application.

In Principle 9, "Just Do It," we provide a wealth of practical, hands-on strategies and resources specifically geared to job seekers and career changers. In Principle 10, "Own Your Career," we guide you to build on the discussions from all the earlier principles. This principle will help you to see the big picture, putting together all 10 principles to create the life and career that you want and to keep it developing boldly, dynamically, and in a way that is meaningful to you.

We also provide some inspiring advice and lessons learned from our interviews with diverse visionary business leaders who have artfully managed their own careers and guided the careers of others. They share their views on what it takes to keep a career successful, thriving, and enduring.

Principle 9

Just Do It

"What we have to learn to do, we learn by doing."
—ARISTOTLE

Career Model for a Lifetime[1]

The ninth principle in attaining career clarity is developing and implementing your job search/career change strategy and plan. We cover the how-tos for you to follow once you've determined that you want to make a job or career change. Our five-phase career management model (see Figure 9-1) can be used throughout a lifetime of job moves and career changes, successes and setbacks. This model underscores the fluidity of your work life, the importance of planning, the benefits of continuous learning, and the need to be tenacious and creative when pursuing your career plans. The five phases can guide you in a career that is ever-evolving and as dynamic as you are.

In brief, we suggest that you put effort into and follow through on five critical phases as you are thinking about, planning, and executing a job search or career transition. These are

Self-knowledge: Reflect on your values, preferences, interests, and skills and competencies.
Career discovery: Explore imaginatively. Research broadly, and generate options creatively.
Focus: Understand your best fit and determine what you will target.

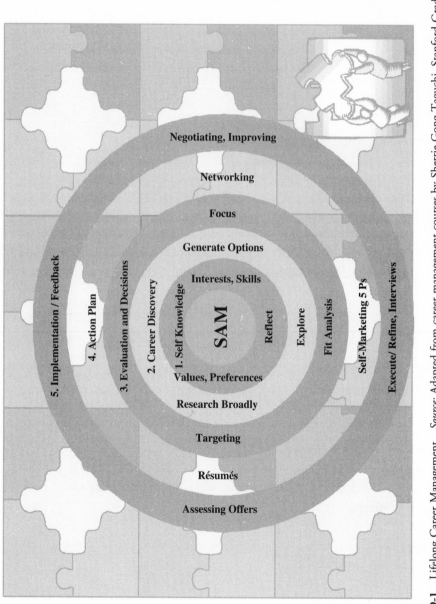

Figure 9-1 Lifelong Career Management *Source:* Adapted from career management courses by Sherrie Gong Taguchi, Stanford Graduate School of Business and Karen O. Dowd, Darden Graduate School of Business. Graphic designed by Keith Wilson, London, England.

Market planning: Create a self-marketing plan using the "5 Ps" model. Prepare for a job search by creating a wining résumé and using networking for your and others' advantage.
Implementation/feedback: Execute and refine your interviews; negotiate and assess offers; continuously monitor and improve the process. This phase involves focused monitoring of your plan, reassessment, and learning from both your successes and your failures.

Continuous Movement: An Ongoing Journey

Whether you are looking for your first job out of school or making your twenty-first job change across a diversity of industries, this career management model can guide you. This principle is especially for those of you who are results-oriented and who gravitate toward practical how-tos and to-dos that can be acted upon. We discuss core activities for each of the five phases.

A key point to emphasize is that after you have gone through these five phases, you start all over again when you are ready to make your next career transition or job change. You may also need to repeat a phase, returning to your basics or revising, before you can move forward again. The cycles and your journey are continuous, ongoing, and ever-evolving because you are dynamic—in constant motion, like your career.

Knowing versus Doing[2]

Using the Nike slogan "Just Do It," we advise you to embrace the principles in our book, then put these concepts into action, or turn your "knowing" into "doing." We have discussed the value of knowing yourself and what you want from your career in the context of your life vision, your interdependencies with people, your risk profile, and so on. Use this knowledge to develop a plan and implement it when you are ready for your next career change. This section will discuss getting to know your specific career options in more depth, including industries and job opportunities, and what you need to plan and do in order to achieve your goal. Only by knowing first can you then do.

The Bigger Picture

In your planning, be tough-minded and optimistic about what you want. Give yourself time to dream, but temper your dreaming with informed decisions about what it is realistic for you to accomplish. Allow time to set goals and objectives, then work on attaining them with fortitude and enthusiasm. Formulate an action plan and deliverables for yourself, making sure to establish milestones along the way. Reward yourself when you have reached each milestone. Celebrate your big and small wins. Each milestone is an accomplishment in itself.

Remember that there will be hurdles, setbacks, and frustrations. Principle 2 discussed ways in which these can be turned into powerful learning. Remain aware of them as you anticipate what's next, take the time to seek feedback, and learn how you can improve along the way. Be patient with yourself. It takes time to consider your options, research possibilities, and decide what you really want to commit time and effort to. Leverage all the resources available: books, the Internet, career services staff, and career coaches. Above all, as we mentioned in Principle 5, remember that people will play a significant role in your journey. As Barbra Streisand belts out, "People who need people are the luckiest people in the world." So share your aspirations and objectives with other people and get your significant other's input or help. Talk with someone you can trust when you are disappointed or want to share a triumph.

Making a job or career change also may require that you build new skills or fill in an experience or knowledge gap in order to reach your goals and take action on your plans. For example, perhaps you have never done any self-assessment and will need to work on that before moving forward. Or, more specifically, you may need to build communication or marketing skills before making a leap to a new industry. Do a gap analysis. All of this will take time. Take the time you need, but *carpe diem:* Seize the day. Develop your plan. Work your plan. Learn what you can do better at every step of the way. Go for it. Just do it.

We have seen what one motivated individual who prepares thoughtfully can accomplish. It's like watching an athlete get ready for a marathon. Your journey is not a sprint. Your work life is a continuous unfolding and an endless process of self-discovery. Achieving a bold, dynamic, meaningful career is a journey that takes a lifetime, with many twists, turns, and familiar and new terrain. We know that you will find the resolve and resources to try your best.

Rules of Thumb for Timing

Realistically, the amount of time you spend on each phase is very specific to you and your situation. A general rule of thumb is that for every $10,000 the job you are shooting for pays, you will need 1 month for a job search. That means that a job with compensation of $65,000 would require approximately 6.5 months of focused effort, and a job paying $150,000 would require 15 months. The amount of time you need will depend on factors such as the extent to which you have already done your self-assessment—how well you know your interests, preferences, and values. These may change over time as your life circumstances change. They can serve as anchors for you that you can refine for each job or career move.

How much effort you put into your next career move also depends on realities such as how established your network—your relationship base—is already, whether you have figured out how to use an interest or hobby for paid work, or how long your budget or your finances will allow.

Phase 1: Self-Knowledge

The first phase of the career management cycle is to reflect on and gain knowledge and understanding of your values, preferences, interests, and skills and competencies. We will not spend a great deal of time on this phase in this principle. Principle 1 offered many self-assessment exercises and tools used in the field for career discovery and management. In the self-knowledge phase of a job search or career change, you are soul-searching, to discover and reflect on what's important to you now. Using your work in Principle 1 as a guide, you should now be able to answer with greater clarity the questions that will guide your efforts and shape your job search plan and strategy.

Take some time now to reflect on the following:

- What are your core values?
- What are your core strengths?
- What skills, experience, and abilities do you want to utilize in your next situation? (These may be very different from those at which you excel or those with which you have worked previously.)
- Where do you want to be living?
- What kind of life do you want to be living?
- In what type of organization and work environment do you see yourself?
- What role or roles do you see yourself performing in your next situation?

Seek to understand what you truly want and don't want in your next situation, in an organization and its culture and environment, and in your specific role—the job content and the people with whom you will work and/or whom you will manage. Keep coming back to this as you go forward in your job search planning and implementation.

Distractions and Derailers

Seeking and accepting knowledge about yourself is challenging for many reasons. The temptation to please others or to meet societal expectations; the lure of money, status, or power; or the daunting challenge of making a bold career move can blur your vision for your future. (One of our respondents advised, "Leave the 'applause-seeking' side of yourself at home!"). On the other hand, self-doubt or confidence lapses can hamper your progress. Further still, the herd mentality, fear of failure or losing friends, blind spots about yourself, and lack of knowledge about what a specific job or career encompasses are other types of background noise that can derail you in this phase.

In the self-knowledge phase of your career management efforts, the key is to listen to yourself—to your own inner voice. Turn off the background noise. This doesn't mean that you do not take others' viewpoints into account. The focus, however, is on you. Tell yourself to have no regrets. No shoulda-coulda-woulda for you! Do your best for this point in your career until you are ready to have another go at your "what's next."

Phase 2: Career Discovery

The second phase in the career management cycle is to explore and dream. Research broadly. Generate options creatively. Embark on your journey to explore industries, functions, fields, jobs, and organizations. Keep your research broad, and generate as many options as possible in terms of industries, companies, jobs or roles, and organization specifics (size, geographic location, and so on).

Mind and Eyes Wide Open

Open your mind and consider the following examples:

- An investment banker who wants more time with his family and who is excellent in golf and at developing client relationships becomes a golf pro, teaching at a local club and offering private lessons. He translates his preference and interests into a new career direction.
- A management consultant who decides that the partner track is not for her switches into HR with a consumer products company, her area of focus while consulting. She applies the experience she gained from leading the recruiting efforts at top schools and her love for mentoring others. Her stand-up presentation skills are also useful for her new role in HR.
- A school math teacher who is active in her investment club, really enjoys giving advice to people, and worked in her family's business when she was growing up transfers these skills and interests to work in a bank, making loans and providing advisory services to small business owners.
- A vice president of finance volunteers for his alma mater's class reunion fundraising efforts and finds that he enjoys "working" in the school—especially the intellectual stimulation and collegiality. He later initiates a job as COO for the school.
- An entrepreneur who sold her successful software business after two others failed joins a venture capital firm as an "executive in residence," working with and advising the firm's portfolio companies. She is particularly valuable for her knowledge of what it takes for a

company to prosper, the land mines at various stages of growth, how to build a team, and how to work with potential investors and a board.

- An HR director who has always been known for her integrity and her open, direct communication and who enjoys creating new employee services and programs changes fields to PR, joining a firm that is respected for its work with socially responsible companies and products.

- A laid-off airline customer service manager moves into operations management in the retail industry. She applies her skills at resolving conflict, working with customers, and logistics and her strength in complex reservations databases to a new role in managing facilities, overseeing the group that handles IT and the computer network, and overseeing inventory management systems.

- A marketing executive in the hospitality industry switches to a portfolio career of teaching marketing at the local college; consulting to nonprofits that need new value propositions, new positioning, and strategic competitive assessments; and advising several start-ups.

- A long-time faculty member becomes active in local community theater groups and begins taking courses to prepare for a second career in real estate.

Be Bold and Audacious

You get the picture. The examples just given show some creative methods of "translating" one's preferences, interests, skills, and experiences into a career change. What it takes to get your mind brainstorming with out-of-the-box, audacious, broad options is to be bold and unabashed during this phase. Think with no or few constraints—develop the most far-reaching set of possible jobs or careers that may be a fit with your preferences, interests, and values and with the skills, abilities, knowledge, and experience that ideally you'd like to be using in your next move.

Your Wish List

You'll want to develop a list of industries and the kinds of functions and jobs they offer. List all the industries and functions that you can imagine working in and that you have an interest in based on what you have learned about yourself in the self-knowledge phase. At this point, nothing is off limits. It's still time to imagine and to dream.

Research Industries, Functions, Companies[3]

Sources are abundant and can be overwhelming if you are not selective. You will need to use your time wisely. Key resources for your research include school cohorts; your career management center professionals or alumni office, particularly if it provides career services for alumni; friends and colleagues past and present; and those outside your immediate circle. Also helpful are web sites and databases such as the U.S. Business Browser, Lexis/Nexis, Hoovers Online, and Wetfeet.com; business periodicals and news sites such as businessweek.com and cnet.com; trade-specific journals such as *Variety, PR Week,* or *Telecommunications;* and books that are representative of your targeted industry, like *The GE Fieldbook,* by Jack Welch, *Katharine the Great,* about the late Katharine Graham of the *Washington Post,* and *Newton's Telecom Dictionary.*

Other good leads.[4]   You can also generate good leads by using the resources that financial analysts track, those that salespeople draw on to find their next potential customer, and lists of the "best." This includes tracking companies that are consistently beating analysts' earnings expectations, following mergers and acquisitions, and looking at companies on lists such as Most Admired, Fastest Growing, Most Socially Responsible, Best for Working Women, or Coolest. Companies that are in the headlines because of their growth plans or those filing for patents and trademarks may also have exciting job opportunities.

Use the web to your fullest advantage.   Gary Alpert, CEO of WetFeet, Inc., shares his insightful perspective about the role of the Web in job searches and provides some valuable advice. He says,

> The Web has fundamentally changed the way that job candidates, from entry level to experienced professionals, conduct a job search. Here are some recommendations, based on our depth of experience, for making

the best use of Internet resources for your job searches and career management.

First, carve out a significant amount of time, especially at the early stages of your job search, to develop your personal and professional networks. No amount of Web surfing will substitute for the personal introductions and insights into a company's hiring process that your "real world" network will deliver. . . . The Web provides a wealth of resources in this area if you know where to look. Just remember, though, that at the end of the day you have to get out from under the keyboard and start meeting some people!

Second, combine your networking activities with a healthy dose of company, industry, and career research to learn more about yourself and the companies you are applying to in order to maximize the return on your job search investment. In the research arena, the Web is arguably the best resource available to you 24 hours a day, 7 days a week. The trick is to know how to use it. Here are a few quick tips.

Use the job boards, big and small, general and niche, but don't stop there. Don't limit yourself and your "universe" of opportunities. Many excellent job opportunities are never posted to a general-purpose job board.

So, where are these jobs? One place to look is individual company web sites. Job seekers consistently tell us that company web sites are the number one place they look for jobs on the web. . . . Recent studies have suggested that Fortune 500 companies' own web sites publicize up to three times as many open positions as do the major job sites. Also, companies that take talent seriously are investing a lot of time and money in offering job seekers a good online experience in their career sites. . . . Our research has consistently shown over the last several years that as many as 25 percent of candidates rule out applying to a company because of the poor quality of its web site for job seekers.

Another place to look for "hidden" jobs is to identify a short list of companies with which you are interested in pursuing career opportunities and to approach them proactively. This is where your networking and communication skills will come in handy, but once again the web can also be extremely useful in helping you research and target individual companies. In addition to using sites with huge databases of companies to research, like WetFeet.com and Hoovers.com, I recommend that you check out the "Best/Top/Most Admired Company" lists at major publications like *BusinessWeek, Fortune,* and others more tailored to the specific industries or issues that you are targeting.

Two valuable articles at WetFeet.com are: "Ten Creative Places to Find the Hidden Jobs" and "Career Related Websites for MBAs and Other A-List Talent." You'll find some gems that you may not have heard of before that could be exactly the right place for you.

And follow the advice in the rest of this book—both of the authors are true experts!

Some top research sites.   At last count, there were more than 2500 Internet sites related to employment and career management. The following are some that we recommend for learning more about industries, functions, and companies. Additionally, in Appendix A, we have listed 25 favorite useful sites. These are valuable resources for your research, in concert with your other, more personalized efforts.

Business Week Company Search, http://bwnt.businessweek.com/company/search.asp—utilize its extensive database of company information.

CorporateInformation, http://www.corporateinformation.com/— research corporate information in over 80 countries; access an index of 350,000 company profiles, a corporate records database, and 15,000+ company reports.

Fast Company, http://www.fastcompany.com/search/index—use the Fast Company Database and CareerCenter.

Hoovers Online, http://www.hoovers.com—conduct an advance search by area code, city, and industry.

JobStar.org, http://www.jobstar.org—access libraries, regional information, and the *Wall Street Journal* database.

Monster.com, http://www.monster.com—learn from its massive number of resources, links, and job postings. Particularly beneficial for its free career newsletters, 3000+ pages of industry information, and salary data. Can research companies by name within the United States and an impressive global network.

The Riley Guide, http://www.rileyguide.com or
http://www.rileyguide.com/busrank.html—tap into their fount of
employment opportunities, job resources, help on targeting and
researching companies, salary guides, extensive list of industry and
function information, links to business directories, professional and
trade associations, and so on. The second site listed allows you to
research rankings of companies, such as the Fortune 500.

WetFeet Press, http://www.wetfeet.com or
http://www.wetfeet.com/research/newsletters.asp—check out its
expansive resources, including the Insider Industry and Company
Guides and the CareerWatch and Salary Newsletters. You can do
company, industry, and career research; get advice on résumés and
interviewing; and find a job through its full-time and internship
listings.

Dimensions to Evaluate

As you conduct your research, seek information that will help you evaluate
whether the industry, function, or company is a good fit with your values,
preferences, interests, and objectives. Concurrently, strive to "get smart" on
the industry, learning its unique challenges, needs, and issues. Figure out the
industry's terminology (its vocabulary), and discover what jobs or roles are
in high-growth mode or in critical demand. Eventually, develop a list of two
or three industries that are of primary interest to you, and do some more
detailed research on those.

This is a sample starter list of questions and issues to research:

- What does this industry actually do (make or offer)?
- How does it add value to the customer?
- Who are the major players and the up-and-comers? How do they
  differ?
- What are the critical success factors for a company that outperforms
  the others?
- How does the trend look in terms of metrics such as performance,
  size, and growth or contraction?
- What are the different models of doing business?

- What does the future look like for this industry?
- Does the type of talent that the industry seems to hire have common qualities or experience?
- What does the hiring picture look like over the past year? Over the past 2 to 5 years? Over the next few years?
- Who is there in the organization that I know? This may be an alumnus or alumna of a school you have attended, a family friend, a colleague of a favorite professor or former boss, your yoga instructor, or your doctor's husband. How can I most easily reach this person?

Researching Companies[5]

In doing your due diligence, probe and dig to answer questions such as these:

- How does this company compare to its competitors?
- What are its points of difference?
- What is the company's culture? What are its values and personality, its aspirations?
- Who are its leaders—the CEO, CFO, COO, and heads of major groups?
- What are they like? (Read their bios and their quotes on the company web site.)
- How does this company value (or not value) its people? Does it have a track record for development; internal promotion when possible; diversity; ethics; international assignments; investing in continuous learning for employees; taking risks on broad, cross-functional rather than vertical moves?
- What is the company's record in hiring great people? What kinds of career portfolios have its professional hires had?
- What is the general sense of the company's level of innovation, turnover, and commitment to developing and keeping its employees?
- What are its specific recruiting plans for entry-level or experienced candidates? What about upcoming events such as industry career fairs? Who are the key recruiting contacts? What are the dates to note, positions it is hiring for, locations, and recruiting team members (if available)?

- Review the company's job descriptions, check out its web site, and ask for quick assessments of the company from any cohorts or colleagues who have worked with or know about the company.

Gut instincts.   Even the most thorough research can sometimes miss some deal-breaking information on a company. As part of your research, you need to trust your gut instincts to decipher what may not be so transparent about a company's values, culture, or dealings. Take these indicators about a company seriously as you decide whether to pursue it. How do you get at this information? At the end of the day, what is your sense about the company? What is the "feel" you get from your experience with it? What do its competitors have to say about it? Do you have gnawing concerns?

Much of this will need to be taken with grains of salt, but if competitors echo the same refrains consistently, you should at least factor those into your perspective. For example, at extremes, do you hear frequently that Company A is socially responsible and treats its people well, and that Company B is underhanded and plays to win at all costs—like a Trojan horse or the "scorched earth" approach?

Reading the telltale signs.   Look around you when you enter the company's offices. Are people enthusiastic? They don't have to be smiling and bouncing off the walls with energy, but do they look happy? Do they appear to be rushed, stressed, dispirited, indifferent? How is the morale among the people with whom you are interviewing or meeting? How are the PAs, the administrators and secretaries, treated? Are employees fearful of giving you wrong information or making a mistake? Do managers criticize their staff or colleagues in public? Are people talking in hushed tones by the water fountain?

What do the executives, especially the CEO, say or espouse, and do they seem to "walk their talk"? Do their words and deeds match up and ring true? Have you heard or read about the CEO, for example, stating that diversity of ideas is valued, but then surrounding him- or herself with "yes" people and openly blasting back when challenged? Has the company just laid off 25 percent of its workforce but continues to indulge its senior team with unneeded travel and the accoutrements of success like expensive perks and "toys"?

In order to make the most informed decisions about what organizations to focus on in your job search, let both your disciplined research and your gut instincts guide you to or away from taking the next steps with any organization.

Phase 3: Career Focus

Focus in and winnow down your choices based on evaluation of your fit with the opportunities. Decide on what you will target: industries, roles or functions, organizations, locations, cultures, or something else.

After you have researched your possible solution set of industries, functions, and companies broadly, it's time to make some decisions. Determine where and how you "fit" and set your focus. You will want to winnow down your choices based on your self-knowledge, what's important to you now, and what is realistic given your background, potential, timing, and objectives. Decide which industries, career opportunities, and companies you will target in your marketing plan and job search activities.

How you go about determining your focus is more an art than a science. A fair amount of listening to your instincts, coupled with your assessment of your industry or company research and how it fits with your self-evaluation, is required. Some people take the approach of eliminating anything that just won't work. For example, you may want to make a change to entertainment from education, but based on your research, you would have to either make a cross-country move or start at the very bottom, and that is just not realistic for you at this time in your career. Some people edit out anything that they are not excited about. The key is to make decisions and to focus.

Ideally, you will end up with one to three industries and at least five to twenty-five companies within each industry. Your target list can be fluid, added to and subtracted from as you start implementing your job search plan.

So that your efforts and time are utilized where you most want them, prioritize your list. Identify industries and companies as A, B, or C, for high, medium, or low effort or dream, great, or good prospects.

Where the Jobs Are

In formulating your list of targeted companies from the set of possibilities, the reality of the market must come into play. Start with your wish list, then sniff out whether the companies on your wish list have openings in the kinds of jobs in which you are interested. Every time you have to remove an organization from your list because it is not hiring, replace it with a similar company that is hiring.

Ferreting out where the jobs are requires a mix of tactics. Be resourceful, tenacious, and creative. Make the most of your targeted companies' web sites and job postings, top job and career management web sites, people whom you know and those whom they know, job advertisements, newspaper ads, industry networking events, your school's career center or alumni career services, and selected career fairs.

Appendix A provides a short list of the "best of the web," our 25 favorite web sites.

Phase 4: Market Planning

The fourth phase in the career management cycle involves developing a self-marketing action plan, including updating your résumé and networking for your and others' advantage. This principle is dedicated to those of you who are in active job or career transitions. The market planning phase of our career management model is also relevant to a transition to retirement or some other lifestyle change.

Self-Marketing 5 Ps[6]

For phases 4 and 5 of the career management model, we adapt the classic marketing 5 Ps for your job search or career change efforts (see Figure 9-2). Use the marketing 5 Ps as an overlay to the five phases of the career management model. The 5 Ps are

- Product
- Place (distribution)

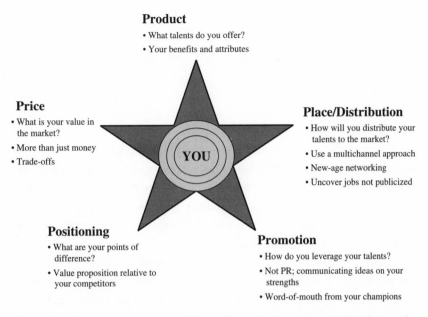

Product
- What talents do you offer?
- Your benefits and attributes

Price
- What is your value in the market?
- More than just money
- Trade-offs

Place/Distribution
- How will you distribute your talents to the market?
- Use a multichannel approach
- New-age networking
- Uncover jobs not publicized

YOU

Positioning
- What are your points of difference?
- Value proposition relative to your competitors

Promotion
- How do you leverage your talents?
- Not PR; communicating ideas on your strengths
- Word-of-mouth from your champions

Figure 9-2 The Marketing 5 Ps and the Branding of You *Source:* S. Taguchi speeches: "Managing Your Career for a Lifetime," Professional Business Women of California Conference 2001 and "Marketing Yourself with the 5 Ps," University of California, Berkeley, 1984.

- Promotion
- Positioning
- Price

In this career context, the *product* is *you*—you're a "brand" or a business of sorts. Think of yourself and your job search as being the product—you are what you have to offer. *Price* translates into what people—in this case, employers—are willing to pay for the package of skills, abilities, knowledge, and experiences that you bring to the table. *Promotion* is not the distasteful self-promotion, but rather the more sophisticated, higher-level skill of self-leveraging or self-marketing. *Place* means how you distribute your services or product to your customers and deliver it from one place to another—what channels you use. We recommend a multichannel strategy; this will be discussed later. *Positioning* refers to identifying your points of difference vis-à-vis other candidates—other viable contenders for the jobs or careers you want. Positioning also means developing your "value proposition" (what you have to offer) as part of your market plan and implementation.

P 1: Product

If you are your own business and your own product, what are your attributes? What are your benefits? What do you have to offer in terms of your experience, and how might this be applicable to the desired job? What skills, abilities, knowledge, and personal qualities will you bring to the organization or role? What do your customers (the organizations that are the potential buyers of your talent) need and want?

The most powerful and widely used representation of what you have to offer is your résumé. Yes, it is true that it's not your résumé that gets you the job, it's you, but your résumé is definitely a critical door opener. It is a "cost of entry" for doing a job search—almost everyone needs one. Your résumé is what gets you screened in or out and what determines whether you ultimately are invited for an interview.

Winning Résumés[7]

An effective résumé is a critical part of your self-marketing plan. It is a strategic communication that highlights your objective, competencies, qualifications, accomplishments, and future capabilities as they relate to the job or career change you are seeking. It is a focused sketch of your educational, professional, and personal background that is tailored to the position you are pursuing. Your résumé should be straightforward, logical, easy to read, and intriguing. The objective is to develop a solid, winning, general résumé as a base. You can then customize this résumé for targeted applications.

Especially if you will be changing industries, your résumé is extremely important in helping you stand out from other candidates and garner further interest. Most recruiters make quick judgments about résumés. Most of them scan a résumé in just 2 seconds to 2 minutes. For electronic résumés, there are many books available on the how-tos; however, most companies' résumé databases and candidate tracking tools are designed to screen out, rather than screen in, résumés. When you submit a résumé electronically, include as many words from the job posting description as you can in that version of your résumé. Also minimize fancy graphics that may turn into gobbledygook when viewed or printed out.

Types of résumés. There are essentially three types of résumés. For templates, a useful web site is http://careers.yahoo.com/careers/resume.html

- The *reverse chronological* résumé the type that is most widely used in business and other fields. Education and work experience (organization names and titles) are listed with the most current first and the oldest last. There can also be a section of the résumé entitled "additional information" or "other." This section covers volunteer activities, community service, personal interests, and hobbies. For highly technical fields, another section on "technical/computer skills" for highlighting language competencies (e.g., HTML), certifications and training, professional affiliations, and the like can be added. Many job sites have résumé templates and builders.
- The *functional within chronological* résumé can be extremely valuable to those who are making substantial career changes. This kind of résumé focuses on major skill areas within a chronological context. Three to five skill-based subheadings relevant to the job you are seeking are highlighted. Under each, you list the responsibilities and accomplishments that pertain to each skill, drawing from the sum total of your experience. Organizations for which you worked, date ranges (month and year), and job titles can be listed as one separate section before the skill subheadings and bullet points. Examples of skill subheadings are creative problem solving, client relationships and customer service, business development, project management, leading teams, negotiation and conflict resolution, communication and presentations, recruiting and development, financial analysis and reporting, innovating and launching, and fundraising.
- The *functional* résumé is similar to the functional within chronological except that you list your most important and relevant work experience and your educational background in order of their importance to the role you are seeking rather than chronologically.

This type of résumé can be confusing, but it can work wonders, particularly if you have hopscotched industries and functions and you want to put your most transferable experiences and achievements first.

Work experience section.   This section of your résumé has the most important substance. For your work experience section, focus on your accomplishments and achievements rather than simply listing your tasks and responsibilities. Begin each description with an action verb, and try to specify the result you achieved or the impact you made on your organization. Illustrate compellingly and concisely what you accomplished. In general, consider what you accomplished in your work to be viable for your résumé if one or more of these statements applies:

• Your contribution produced something that was important to your organization, the employees, or your clients or stakeholders.
• You achieved results with fewer resources, under budget, before the deadline, and so on.
• You made something easier, simpler, better, or faster.
• You achieved something for the first time or performed remarkably given the circumstances.
• You or others were proud of what you did; it made a difference.

Accomplishment statements—PAR.   A compelling accomplishment statement is composed of three parts:

1. The *problem*—the issue that you solved or the need or challenge that you met; a major undertaking.
2. The *action*—what you accomplished and how.
3. The *result*—what was the benefit or outcome for the organization? Try to quantify or calibrate the result.

Examples of phrases that can be used to quantify accomplishment statements include "improved quality or response time," "increased profits," "reduced costs," "grew the business," "strengthened morale," "enhanced productivity," "lowered turnover," "designed a new program," "created a new process to improve, reduce, or change," and "decreased failures, shrinkage, overtime, or downtime."

Qualifying and calibrating.   We are talking about the fine points here, but these can make a big difference. Whenever possible, quantify or calibrate what you accomplished. Quantifying is using numbers or specifics to describe the result—the impact of what you achieved. Calibrating is providing some context so that your result can be better understood in relation to the whole of what you accomplished.

Some examples of quantifying are

- Led design and testing of $20 million operations control software that allowed Fortune 100 client to save $100 million annually.
- Created and ran educational course on IBM workstation service for internal and external customers, which resulted in a 62 percent reduction in service response time.
- Managed four-person team to reengineer the labor planning process for a major airline client, resulting in a 10 percent reduction in cost.
- Identified market share decline in cola beverage products. Designed and implemented new promotional point-of-sale displays that stopped share loss and 1 year later had increased market share by six points.
- Taught new employees advanced customer service and administrative processes that generated a 30 percent reduction in complaints.

Some examples of calibrating are

- Invited to stay on as third-year investment banking analyst. Consistently ranked among top 5 percent of peer group.
- Devised successful strategy to survive a crop-damaging freeze by using industry knowledge to save 95 percent of permanent acreage versus industry average losses of 50 percent.
- Transformed lowest-ranked battle damage station of 34 crews into top-performing unit. Reduced crisis reaction time from over 10 minutes to less than 2 minutes. Achieved "perfect" inspection score.

- Youngest in-residence choreographer in repertory's 25-year history. Innovated postperformance artist-audience talks and assisted in major fundraising campaign for new season.
- Graduated first in class, NYFD; selected for media training to serve as press spokesperson.

Common Résumé Problems

For ideas on how to handle the most common résumé problems, refer to Appendix B. We answer:

When to use a functional/skills-based résumé
What's best when you are changing careers
Dealing with gaps in unemployment
What to do if you have no degree or one from an unknown school
How to handle when you've worked for company that's not well known
What to do if you had no formal job title or if it did not reflect your real responsibilities

Targeted, Timely, Relevant Cover Letters

A résumé is not a stand-alone document. To be most effective, a résumé needs an intriguing cover letter to introduce it and set it up contextually. Cover letters need to be targeted, timely, and relevant. The cover letter should briefly explain how you learned of the opening, why you're interested in and qualified for the position, and what the hoped-for next steps are. The best cover letters are focused, not a mass mailing. These are some of the finer points about cover letters that we have taught over the years.

- Address letters to a person, and make each letter unique. Ideally this person would be the decision maker/hiring manager, HR point person, or whomever you are asked to send your résumé to. It could also be someone you know within the organization (asking her or him to refer your letter and résumé to the appropriate person).

- Keep your letter brief, about three-quarters of a page or less. The maximum is 1.5 pages.
- Use simple and direct language and a balanced tone. Try not to be either too formal or too casual. Your letter should sound as if you are speaking to the person—as if you are engaging him or her in a conversation.
- Focus on the needs and style of the organization. Try to identify through your research what it wants and needs, and its culture. Write your letter with this in mind.
- Do not repeat details from your résumé. That would be redundant and a waste of valuable attention time. Craft a few compelling, overarching statements for your letter that will intrigue the reader and make her or him want to read your résumé.
- Avoid arrogant statements, shameless namedropping, or uninformed assertions at all costs.
- Do not use too many adjectives. Try to be concise, using the fewest number of words to say what you mean. Make every word count.
- Avoid jargon, pat phrases, and the trite, e.g., "I am a self-starter," "You will not find anyone as enthusiastic or qualified as I am," "You won't be sorry for taking a chance on me," or "I can help you meet your challenges."
- Let your interest and enthusiasm shine through.
- Use paper for your cover letter that is coordinated with (the same stock as) the paper you used for your résumé. Off-white or cream is usually the best, and a subtle weave or texture is nice.
- Read, reread, and review your cover letter and your résumé. Ask someone else to proofread your cover letter and your résumé for typos, grammatical errors, and anything that does not make sense or sounds boastful.

An outline. A cover letter consists of four main parts:

Introduction. Explain who you are and why you are writing. Mention your referral if you have one. Ask for an informational interview, or ask to be considered for an interview if you are writing about a specific job opportunity.

Interest highlights. Summarize what interests you about the company, its needs and challenges, and/or the overall industry.

Compelling examples. Describe what you can offer. Highlight a few relevant examples or specific experiences that would be valuable to the organization.

Next steps. State clearly who to follow up with, when, and how.

Refer to the section on cover letters in Appendix B.

Follow-Up and Next Steps

All the planning in the world will not benefit you if you do not follow through. Here are some examples illustrating when and how to put into action your next steps.

Requesting an interview for a specific job.

I learned about your 'a b c' job from ___ (person referring you, the job ad, etc.). My ___ (#) years of experience in the ___ industry and strengths x, y, and z, make me an especially strong candidate. Additionally I am a quick learner, have a positive attitude, and work well with customers (list a few personal qualities relevant to the role and industry). I would be excited about hearing more about your needs, discussing the opportunity and how I can contribute. I will call you next week to schedule an interview . . .

Requesting an informational interview.

Doug Affleck, who worked with you at Google suggested I get your advice and insights. I am making a career shift out of tech and am very interested in The Gap and the retail industry in general. You successfully made the transition and I would really appreciate about 15 minutes of your time to answer some questions. I will call your admin to see if there's a good time we can talk during the next few weeks. I hear you travel a lot so however is easiest for you, I am flexible.

or

Madison Mulligan, a mutual friend, recommended I contact you. She said it was great to see you at your recent B school reunion and told me about the exciting work you are doing in making documentaries. After years of consulting, I am interested in making a change to something like you're doing. Madison tells me you would be a terrific resource with lots of advice and ideas. Could we meet for coffee or a drink? If your schedule doesn't allow, I could ask some questions even by email. I'll call you to see what works. Many thanks.

P 2: Place (Distribution)

In the marketing 5 Ps, *place* means the channels you will use to "distribute" yourself to the market. How will you deliver what you have to offer to the market? Will you respond to a job advertisement; apply to job postings on targeted companies' web sites or other employment sites; or follow up on job leads from friends, colleagues, former clients, or others? Will you attempt to work through an executive recruiter, approach HR, or go directly to the hiring manager? If you are currently a student, will you use on-campus interviews or network in through an alumnus or alumna?

Many people find tapping into their relationship base incredibly helpful for identifying opportunities and connecting with someone within the organization who can make an interview happen. For years, networking—working through others and relying on contacts—has proved effective. A multichannel approach, using many routes to distribute yourself to the market, is best. Beyond responding to job advertisements, working through executive recruiters, and the more traditional channels, two of the more challenging but potentially fruitful ways to distribute yourself are networking and informational interviews. We focus on networking in this section; we will discuss informational interviewing later in the principle.

New-Age Networking

In Principle 5 we discussed networking, particularly expanding and diversifying your relationship base. This section guides you on a new-age networking for an especially tough job market and details how to use it to your advantage for your specific job search or career change. For many people, networking has come to be considered distasteful or an outdated concept. It conjures up the perception of people being used as a means to an end. Cultivating a relationship with someone and then subsequently using that person to help you get something you desire sounds manipulative.

New-age networking is most focused on cultivating a diverse, rich relationship base in which one both gives and receives over time. The concept is more about making people a priority in your life and helping others reciprocally, which gives your own career deeper satisfaction, meaning, and purpose. Essentially you want to build multiple and diverse interdependencies and connections that make up a unique dynamic relationship "database." It's about expanding your circle of friends and career connections and establishing, nurturing, and changing it over a lifetime.

In most job markets—both boom times and tough ones—starting up, developing, and tapping into relationships is essential. This means both asking for help and giving it in return frequently and freely. Not only is expanding your circle of friends enriching, but doing so also expands your job and career horizons and opens up new directions and opportunities at many times when you least expect it—often when you really need it.

The hidden job market.   It's still true that most of the best jobs are not widely publicized. They are not advertised to the masses. Most people never find out about these plum jobs. You've probably heard stories about someone getting a to-die-for job by knowing someone in the organization who told him about it. Perhaps you know someone who got her job because a former colleague, who was leaving her job on the QT, wanted to go the extra mile for her company and recommend a worthy successor.

Cultivate your relationships in both traditional and novel ways. Realize that relationships take time to build. Frequently, what you can ask for depends on the depth and longevity of the relationship. Many people, however, are naturally helpful. Even if they barely know you or the person who referred you, they are happy to do a good deed: to recommend someone talented for a job, to give an informational interview, or to suggest ways to learn about an industry or a company. Whether you are in a job search or career change or not, keep your relationships alive. In addition to the overall benefit of making people a vital part of your life experiences, a ready-to-go relationship base can serve as an incredible resource for your career when you need to tap into it.

How to cultivate your career connections.   Stay in touch with recruiters you had a connection with during prior interviews and those organizations that you considered working with. Drop them an email from time to time or keep them updated on your contact details. Remain in contact with your classmates from your undergraduate or graduate programs. Selectively participate with other alumni (graduate and undergraduate) who host events in your area. Attend some of your school's alumni events and reconnect with faculty and administration. Find out who is on your school's advisory council and if it is appropriate to contact them. Stay connected to your favorite professors, deans, and career management center, alumni relations, admissions, and corporate relations staff. Remember to take time to keep in touch with your staff, colleagues, managers, and clients from former jobs. Don't be bashful when you need to ask for referrals from friends of your family and their friends; your doctor; your yoga instructor; or your pastor, priest, rabbi, or spiritual adviser, who may know people in the industries or companies you are targeting.

This does not have to take a burdensome amount of time. A simple way to keep your relationships going is to create a database of contacts and their current contact information—for example, an email distribution list. Likewise, make sure that these people have your current contact information. An en masse email will do (suppressing their email addresses, however, so that their addresses cannot be used for spam email). You could also send a yearly holiday card or newsletter, a short note, or an email greeting card. This is about all that most people have time to read anyway. If you are in a job search or career change mode, you can call specific people or personalize an email to them at that time.

Expanding your circle of friends.   Expand your circle of friends by doing one or more of the activities mentioned here at least once every 3 to 6 months. Even if you spend only a few hours a month, you will be building something worthwhile over time. Your relationship base will be enriched substantially, given the cumulative effect!

Volunteer for your city's next big event—a community clean-up day, a Black and White Ball, a bid for hosting the next Olympics, the annual dog or garden show, an art and wine festival, or a summer BBQ. Spend your lunchtime on a holiday at a soup kitchen or helping others. Involve yourself in your school's alumni activities, your church, a worthy cause or non-profit organization, or your children's schools or sports teams. Initiate something with your neighbors. Take a few extra minutes to talk with and get to know the people at your gym, those waiting at your dentist's office, or those you don't already know at work. Participate on the planning committee for your organization's holiday or summer event, or serve on a committee with colleagues from other departments. Join a softball or other sports team.

Engage with those you meet at work-related events such as conferences, classes, trade shows, and online communities. Sit by people you do not already know for lunch or dinner during these events. Follow up with a speaker or presenter about ideas that provoke further discussion. Offer to write an article or provide a session for your local or national professional association. Join a book club or other clubs with people who share your interest in reading but may come from diverse industries and fields.

Sincerity and reciprocity.   If you have cultivated your friendships when you are not asking for anything, you will find it easier to ask people for help when you do need it. The fundamentals are to be sincere, direct, and reciprocal. When you ask people for assistance with a job or career change, tell them, without going into detail, what you would appreciate from them. Let them know what you are considering and how specifically they can help you. Don't be bashful about saying that you need a favor. It may be as simple as asking someone to keep you in mind for opportunities in her or his organization or industry or to give you an introduction to the head of her or his department. You might give people your résumé and ask them to refer it to those in their organizations who might be interested in your experience. On the higher end of involvement, you might request a referral to their favorite executive recruiters, an informational interview, or actual input into your job search strategy and plan. It never hurts to ask, but be careful not to keep going back to the same people over and over for help.

If the people you ask for assistance say no to your request, that's the worst that can happen. You can thank them for being straightforward, ask them to let you know when their schedules free up, and move on. Be tenacious. Perhaps in the future, the time will be right for asking them for help. If people reject your request for help, it is typically because of something that is going on with them, not because of you. They could be too busy, overwhelmed with their work or home responsibilities, insecure about their jobs or careers, going through personal stuff, or maybe just overloaded at present. Maybe you approached them at a time when they had just finished helping many others and they felt that they had nothing more that they could give right then. Try again later, but if someone says no a second time, remove that person from your active lead list for a while.

Give those people who will help you a copy of your résumé, to update them quickly on your background. Include a brief note about the industries, companies, and jobs that you are targeting. You're not doing this to be pushy, but rather to familiarize them with your background. Take the lead and be proactive about any next steps. For example, call or email them in follow-up. If someone gives you names of referrals, ask for the easiest way to get the referrals' contact information. Perhaps you can connect with the person's administrative assistant to ask for the referrals' email addresses and go from there. Use your sensitivity radar to ensure that you are active but not inconsiderate. Show your gratitude by expressing thanks profusely. Above all, remember the golden rule: Do unto others . . . When you are asked to help someone, whether for a job search or something else that is within your power, do it. Give back. Help others as much as you can.

Phase 5: Implementation/Feedback

Although in a sense you have been actively "doing" throughout the previous four phases, in phase 5, the focus is on taking action and building momentum. You immerse yourself in the doing: preparing for and putting yourself through the paces of interviewing, conducting your due diligence by asking informed questions during the recruiting process, negotiating compensation, evaluating offers, and deciding which you will accept.

In phase 5 of the career management cycle, you implement your action plan and go for what you want to achieve. Send out your cover letters and résumés. Contact people for informational interviews, and follow up. Review your channels for finding out about jobs and pursuing your candidacy for them, and determine which are best. Put into action your multichannel approach to self-marketing. Make cold calls and branch. Do your compensation homework. Essentially, work your plan.

Cold Calling and Branching

Sometimes, no matter how much you have researched industries and companies, tapped into your relationships, or expanded your circle of friends, you will not have any leads into a specific industry or organization. You will need to contact people you do not know—cold—and try your best to persuade them to do something you are asking. You will need to take some risks, put aside any fear, and do some branching or cold calling.

With branching, you know someone who knows someone in a targeted company. You will use that entry point—the someone you do know—and branch from there. If you are successful, you will end up with several valuable, relevant contacts within the company. To illustrate branching, suppose that you know Jon. Your brother Sam is a friend of his. You contact Jon, let him know of the connection through your brother, and tell him briefly what you're interested in. You then ask Jon if there is anyone in the organization that he can recommend that you call. For example, perhaps he can suggest someone in Human Resources with responsibility for recruiting, the head of his group who does a lot of hiring for the company and may have some openings right now, or a colleague in the group that you think you are interested in. You keep branching out by making contact with those people. Sometimes you will strike it lucky. Sometimes they will not be able to help you. Whether or not they will help you, you ask them for recommendations to others in the company with whom you could talk, and so on and so forth. It's like a tree—starting from the roots and branching out every which way.

When you do not know anyone and there's no chance of branching, you will need to try your hand at cold calling. You have no hot leads, no names, nothing, but you can prepare to do your cold calling. Study the company web site and look for an organization chart or an annual report. Often the names of the executive team, the managers of groups you are targeting, and other key people such as the head of recruiting will be featured on the web site. If this information is not in the organization chart or the annual report, look for other material. Web sites regularly feature company spokespeople or managers who are quoted in press releases, recruiting materials, and other media. Ferret out the best person for your objective: a head of HR or recruiting, Finance, Marketing, or Manufacturing. If need be, find out the name of the CEO, CFO, or COO.

Write to this person, or, if you are feeling bold and are more convincing over the telephone, consider calling. If this sounds scary—which for many people it is—write a script or talking points. Practice talking into a tape recorder or with a friend over the telephone. Rehearse a few times and think about how you would handle various worst- and best-case scenarios so that you are prepared.

For example, what will you say if you can never get past the administrative assistant to the person you are trying to reach? What will you do if you get the person (surprise) right away on the first ring? What if the person has 15 seconds before dashing off to a meeting? What if the person is rude and discouraging? What will you do if the person says that he will call you back but does not follow up? What if she is super busy but gives you 10 names of people to call on the spot—but it's up to you to find out their contact information on your own?

Much of your handling of these scenarios will be instinctive, and you will also learn on the fly, getting better as you go along. However, the more thought you give to anticipating these what-ifs and determining what you would say and do in follow-up, the better. If you prepare, you will make a better first impression with the person and build your confidence by putting forth the effort.

If you are taking the route of sending a letter, review the cover letter advice from earlier in this principle. Send the letter and a copy of your résumé via email, fax, or post. FedEx or express mail seems a little overdone. Our advice is to email the person or, if you can find out his or her phone number, call after hours and leave a brief message introducing yourself. Let the person know why you are calling and tell her or him that you will be sending a résumé so that she or he will have a snapshot of your background. Send the résumé in hard copy by mail. You are being personal, yet unobtrusive, with the call or email, and then you are saving the person the trouble of printing out a résumé by sending him or her a copy. An old-fashioned hard copy résumé looks better as well.

Informational Interviews

Informational interviews should focus on three areas:

- Connecting with the individual
- Researching the field or industry, job or function, and organization
- Developing your next steps

Once you have sent your letter and résumé, wait a week or so, then follow up. Ideally, call or email. Try to pick a Tuesday, Wednesday, or Thursday for touching base, not a Monday or Friday. Try not to call first thing in the morning, at the end of the day, or around lunch. People tend to be more harried at these times, and you want to catch them when they may have some time for you. Ask the person if he or she has received your information (if not, you'll have to summarize it in a minute) and repeat your request for an informational interview, about 15 minutes of the person's time.

If the person agrees, schedule a time to talk and ask if he or she prefers that you come to his or her office or call. If you are talking by telephone, offer to call the person and confirm the best number for you to call. For instance, on that date, you may need to call the person's mobile while she or he is in transit, or you may have to ring the person's administrative assistant, who will connect you to a direct line.

Prepare your list of questions ahead of time. The next section includes ideas for questions that can help you probe for the information you need. The questions for researching industries and companies that were given earlier in this principle are also useful.

When you conduct the interview, start off by saying that you want to be sensitive to the person's time, and so you will start right in with the questions, if that is OK. Begin with a few easy ones, such as the person's background and how he or she got into the industry or company; what the person likes or doesn't like about the job or the organization; and the biggest changes over the time the person has been in the company.

Throughout your time together, show interest, enthusiasm, and respect. Be an active listener. Take notes so that you remember what was said and you have something to refer back to later. Honor the time commitment. It is up to the person to decide if she or he wants to extend the time she or he is spending with you. Toward the end of the conversation, be bold and ask for three things:

1. Feedback, especially constructive, on your fit with the industry and/or company and your chances of making a move into it. Ask for suggestions as to how you can you improve your candidacy in general—what can you do to be more competitive?
2. Recommendations of a few colleagues who might have job opportunities in your area of interest or who might be willing to speak with you, even informationally.
3. Permission to keep in touch with her or him periodically. Ask the person to also keep in touch, especially if she or he hears about opportunities or thinks of other information that would be helpful to you.

Thank the person enthusiastically for giving you his or her time. Genuinely show your appreciation and follow up with a handwritten thank-you note within 3 to 4 days. If the person really went above and beyond to help you, and your budget allows it, follow up with a thoughtful gesture. Send flowers, a book on something you talked about, or something inspired by your observations in the person's office. Perhaps the person likes high-tech gadgets or unusual picture frames, or has a penchant for kooky pens. The key point is to personalize the thank-you.

In summary, Table 9-1 provides dos and don'ts to keep in mind for your informational interviews.

Quick-start questions.[8]   If the informational interview has time constraints, asking these questions can provide you with a solid start.

- Please tell me a bit about your background. How did you get your start in this industry?
- What's the company culture really like?
- Describe a typical day or week.
- What advice would you offer to someone trying to break into this industry?

Table 9-1   Dos and Don'ts for Informational Interviews

Do	Don't
Be wise with your time	Take a contact for granted
Be thoughtful and professional	Have a defeatist attitude
Treat each contact like a client	Let a no or a rejection make you stop
Be respectful of the person's time	Be afraid to ask for other referrals
Be generous in your thanks	Forget to reciprocate

Source: S. Taguchi speech to recruiting executives: "Hiring and Keeping Top Talent and What's Next in Your Own Career," International Telecommunications Conference, Sao Paulo, Brazil, 2000.

- What are the critical success factors for X job (the job that you are interested in)?
- How are your goals and objectives established and measured?
- How is success rewarded? How is failure handled?
- What do you like the most and least about the industry? About the company? About the job?
- Given my background, what can I do to be more competitive for this job or industry?
- How would you approach a job search for this organization or industry?
- Could you recommend other colleagues with whom I can speak? Is it OK to use your name when I contact them?

If you have more time for an interview or if you have multiple informational interviews, consider asking values-based questions so that you can cover more ground. Asking different questions of different people you interview will net you a broader set of data upon which to draw.

Evaluating fit—values-based questions.[9]   When developing your list of questions, you want to revisit what you discovered about yourself and your values during phase 1, seeking self-knowledge. Here are suggested questions to ask that will help you to evaluate the fit between your values and those of an organization and the people with whom you will work. The questions are based on the concept of values-driven work, originated by the Career Action Center, now based in Cupertino, California, in 1995. The questions guide you to uncover an organization's values, both those it espouses and its actual values.

Intrinsic Values
- How would you describe the organization's values?
- What are its aspirations?
- How are decisions made here?
- What makes someone successful here?
- How much turnover is there? What are the main reasons for it?

Work Content Values
- What are the top three competencies that someone would have to have in order to do well here?
- Where do most of the people here come from—what is their prior work experience or education?
- What kinds of common qualities do employees possess?
- What do you need in order to do your job effectively?
- Tell me about someone's failure on the job.

Work Environment Values
- How are sales at your company store?
- How is morale?
- What kinds of things do people do at lunchtime?
- How often do people work on weekends or through holidays?
- How do people share information and communicate?

A lead, not a job. It is true that you are not asking for a job in an informational interview. Remember, however, that many an informational interview *has* resulted in a job or a viable lead to one, at that time or in the future. Some of the most rewarding stories from our career coaching are those involving the generosity of people helping each other, leading to happy endings and new beginnings.

At a minimum, informational interviews are valuable, experience-rich sources of information about an industry and/or a company that a web site, book, or other publication is hard pressed to provide. Informational interviews allow you to see the human side of the organization. They offer you an opportunity to discern firsthand realistic opportunities, cultural fit, and foundational knowledge concerning what it would really be like to work there. At best, informational interviews catapult your hat into the ring and get you a better vantage point on how to get into the flow of the company's recruiting process.

P 3: Promotion

To some people, self-promotion is a necessary evil in a job search or career change. Self-promotion has received a bad rap over the years because people have associated it with bragging, puffing up one's background, arrogance, or attempting to make a competitor lose.

Rather than self-promotion, we are encouraging proactive communication about who you are and what you have to offer to a job or an organization. You communicate your ideas about what you think are your gifts and talents. This means acknowledging what is good about yourself and letting it shine. You should be somewhere in the range between being modest and being zealous, but you should be charming about it. Our brand of self-leveraging is about knowing what you have to offer—your gifts and your strengths—and being confident about them. It means taking your package of skills, abilities, knowledge, and experience and letting others know about it and see it in a positive, genuine light.

Self-marketing is about the way you present yourself with your résumé and in person, how you prepare for each step in your job search process and display your knowledge and professionalism with everyone you meet. It is being self-assured that you have a lot to offer and the humility and willingness to learn whatever it is that you need to learn in order to contribute meaningfully to an organization. Self-marketing effectively means that you are proactive and strategic, and that you understand your customers, your competitors, and yourself. It's about finding the intersections of what your customers (the companies or organizations) need and want, what other candidates (competitors in the marketing sense) have to offer as they vie with you for the opportunities, and what you have to offer that is of value, particularly what is unique.

Word of Mouth

Promotion in the marketing sense also can result from what others think about you. Promotion about you from others can prove to be potent viral marketing—word of mouth. Others who know you can generate a healthy buzz about you to support your job search or career change efforts. They can share their opinions about you and your abilities in general or your viability for a specific role. When other people refer you for a job, serve as a reference for you in the recruiting process, or tell an inquirer "off the record" what they think about you, they are basically promoting you. This kind of promotion can turn out to be a substantive factor affecting whether you do or don't achieve the job or career change you want. You have heard the phrase, "what goes around, comes around." How you treat people, especially when you do not need anything from them, is quite telling.

P 4: Positioning

By positioning, we mean how you are positioned vis-à-vis the competition. What do you have to offer that is unique to you? What are your strengths—your points of difference? In this case, your competition really means the other contenders for the job that you want. Based on what you know, what are the trade-offs that you think the company would have to make if it hired you rather than one of the others? By reading between the lines or from information gleaned, determine where you are in the pack of contenders—are you the front-runner, or are you in the middle of the pack? How can you improve your position with the decision makers? A mature, confident way to glean information is to ask an interviewer with whom you have connected particularly well something like, "I am really excited about this role. Could you tell me in general about other candidates being considered and how I compare?"

Here's another, more direct approach: "Your job is my top choice among those I'm considering. I'd appreciate the opportunity to address any shortcomings you think I have vis-à-vis the other people you are talking with." Here's a case in point: We recall advising a young woman who was up for a director's job, for which she had only half the required years of experience and did not have the advanced degree preferred. This young woman took this direct approach. The senior vice president interviewing her told her of her two shortcomings—"concerns," as she called them. They were (1) how she would handle managing people more than double her age, and (2) whether she could be tough and unpopular along with being liked and nice. The young woman addressed both concerns head on, without being defensive, including some backup examples of experience managing older people and being tough yet respected. She got the job. A side benefit was the open communication that this interaction established between the young woman and the executive who would be her boss.

P 5: Price

Although all of us would like to think that we are a premium product, and therefore eligible for the top compensation if the job is offered to us, this may not be realistic. The days are long gone when each successive job change meant a 10 to 20 percent increase in compensation. In these times, some job changes and career moves may even require a decrease in compensation. This may be the case, for example, when you are changing industries, functions, or locations, or when you do not possess all the qualifications for the job or are not the ideal candidate and require an up-front investment of time or training.

The key thing about price is to do your homework diligently. Know what the industry is paying and what the market is for people with your background. There are many resources for this. They are discussed later in the compensation negotiation section of the principle.

In summary, when you are considering your "price," you will want to ascertain the company's compensation philosophy and get a sense of what the salaries are for various job groups. Looking at the job listings on the organization's web site, looking at the Internet and industry resources we recommended for your research, or talking with personal contacts in the industry or company will provide you with some information. The job description will give you a range. At the appropriate time (further along in the process, after preliminary interviews and when you think you have a shot at receiving an offer), clarify whether the range is the whole range or only to the midpoint. Some job postings list the minimum and the midpoint of the salary "band," or range. This makes a big difference. We advise you not to ask about money up front, because this could be perceived as indicating that money is your most important priority. Also, it is amazing how flexible some salaries or total compensation can be if the organization really wants you. There may indeed be a range, but it may be more flexible if you allow the natural progression of your learning about each other.

Preparing for Interviews[10]

Getting interviews and getting offers are two milestones in your job search progress.

Prior to getting to the interviewing stage, ideally, you will have researched the industries and companies with which you are interviewing and marshaled every resource to your advantage: cohorts if you are a student, alumni and professors of schools you have attended or are attending, career-center resources, informational interview contacts, and referrals from former work colleagues, among others.

Before you begin your interviewing, revisit your self-assessment work. Reflect on what you're looking for, what's important to you, and why you are going into the interview. Think about your values, interests, and preferences—the kinds of roles and responsibilities that are most stimulating to you. Consider your top five criteria for choosing a company or accepting an offer. What drew you to interview with this company for this job? Why are you excited about talking with the organization?

Reflecting on these dimensions will keep you focused in your interviews and keep you from wasting time (yours and the interviewers) on interviews for jobs that you aren't truly interested in

Unfortunately, a significant number of people are poorly prepared for interviews. The most common feedback we hear from recruiters about interviewees is

- Lack of preparation
- Poor communication (not listening, too tentative, rambling, evasive, dominating, clamming up)
- Little knowledge about the organization

- Lack of clear career focus or goals
- Arrogance
- Geographic or other inflexibility

Study your marketing plan and think about your 5 Ps. What would you say about each? Articulate to yourself what you have to offer: your skills, experience, education, talents, and strengths. What makes you unique? What are your points of difference? Understand how these make you a good fit for the opportunity the company is offering, so that you can make the fact that you *are* a good fit clear to the interviewer.

Formulate a clear picture of how you think you can add value in the job and the organization for which you are interviewing. What can you do or offer that will make an impact on the organization's business needs and challenges?

Anticipate the questions you'll be asked. Everything that is on your résumé or that has come up during any interactions or communication you have had with the organization or interviewer is fair game. Mentally note the key points that you would emphasize for each question you can imagine the interviewer asking. In addition, be prepared to handle any illegal, unfair, or politically incorrect questions in a firm but graceful manner. And remember: If it's on your résumé, you could be asked about it. Make sure that everything on your résumé is accurate and that it will "check out" if a firm hires an investigative organization to do a background check on you.

Behavioral Interviewing

Behavioral interviewing[11] is the most popular interviewing approach used today. The premise behind behavioral interviewing is that past behavior is the best predictor of future behavior. Rather than basing questions on trait theory (tell me about your creativity or hard-working characteristic) or hypotheticals (what would you do if ____ or how would you handle ____), behavioral interviewing focuses on an individual's past actions—actual experiences he or she has had that will be a good indicator of his or her behavior in the future.

Familiarizing yourself with this approach will be a good background as you prepare for your interviews.

The idea is to think about examples of past performance. For example, questions will start with phrases such as

- "Give me an example of a time when you _____."
- "Describe an experience in which you ___."
- "Tell me about a situation in which you ____."

Some common phrases that recruiters use to fill in the blanks are "used creativity," "mastered or learned something quickly," "adjusted to a change," "asked for forgiveness—not permission," "took a risk," "made a big mistake," "did something bold," "solved a complex problem," "were conflicted ethically," "ran with the ball, even though it wasn't your responsibility," "overcame an obstacle or the odds," "influenced a difficult group of people," "dealt with a crisis," "faced failure," and "conceived an idea and put it into action."

Practice Makes Better

Ask a friend, a work colleague whom you can return the favor for, or a family member to take you through your paces. Videotape it if you can. If you are fortunate enough to have access to a career center, your school's alumni career resources, or a friend who happens to be an experienced interviewer, use these resources over and over until you feel comfortable with your interviewing skills. With every practice run, solicit honest feedback. Invite constructive criticism and work to improve in those areas.

Good Vibrations and Manners

Be on time, enthusiastic, and professional in your interviews. When in doubt, dress more formally (most of the time, a suit and tie for men, a pantsuit or jacket and skirt for women). Don't overdo the accessories (scarves, jewelry, perfume, makeup). Bring extra copies of your résumé, just in case. Make sure that pagers and mobile phones are turned off. Present a firm handshake and maintain eye contact when you introduce yourself. Wait to sit until after the interviewer does, or until he or she offers you a chair. Don't rush to fill in silence. Think before you speak; take time to formulate your thoughts. Invite the interviewer to contact you further for follow-up questions.

Show enthusiasm, but modulate it to the interviewer's. For example, you would not bounce off the walls with zeal if your interviewer was more monotone or reserved. A notch or two above the interviewer is the maximum variation. Speak with clarity and confidence. Close the interview with a handshake, a smile, and a genuine thank you; make a positive last impression. If something embarrassing happens—you spill your coffee on the interviewer, you've worn different color shoes, your pen has leaked onto your jacket pocket, or you have a brain cramp and forget what company you are interviewing with—laugh at yourself, apologize, and move on gracefully.

For more on preparing for interviews, visit www.WetFeet.com or www.JobTrak.com.

When It's Your Turn to Ask Questions

Develop at least three questions for each interview. Here are some examples:

- What keeps you in the company or makes you most excited about working here?
- What has your organization done over the past few years to change the competitive landscape?
- Please give me some examples of the kinds of career paths other people in this position have followed within the company.
- What's a recent challenge or problem that your group has had, and how did you approach it?

We provide a more comprehensive list of questions, focusing on what stage you are in, later in this principle.

In almost every interview, the interviewer will ask you if you have questions. It's important to note that the interviewers are not just being polite. They genuinely want to answer your questions. They also may be using what you ask to gauge whether you have done your homework on the company, how interested you are, and whether you have differentiated yourself from other candidates who are vying for the role. Asking questions is a key component of the interview process. Perhaps more crucially, by asking informed questions throughout the recruiting process, you are conducting substantial due diligence on the organizations and the jobs you are considering.

Strategies in developing thoughtful questions. Here are some strategies to use in developing thoughtful questions:

> *Think about what stage you are at in the process.* Are you attending a company's information session or an open house or its booth at a career fair? Are you in the preliminary interview with HR or less senior people? Have you been invited back to meet with a larger group and the hiring decision maker? Have you been made an offer but are still talking with people in the organization?
> *Know yourself and keep in mind a clear impression of what's important to you.* Now that you've done your homework and soul searching, what's really important to you? What are the deal breakers that you need more in-depth information on? A few thoughts include the company's culture; the best estimate of the impact of an upcoming layoff, merger, acquisition, or expansion; and examples of how top performers have developed in their careers—broadly or more vertically. You'll want to try to get at those things that you cannot find in the company's published, more surface publications or that you haven't easily been able to glean from your research or your interactions.
> *Develop a core list of questions, then tailor them.* Generate a core list of questions that could be used with all the organizations with which you are interviewing. For a specific interview, apply what you have learned about the organization to tailor some questions specific to it.
> *Stay in tune with the interviewer.* Keep yourself in the flow of the conversation and interpersonal dynamics. Use your judgment as to what will show your enthusiasm and interest and help you shine in terms of your knowledge, insights, and thoughtfulness about the industry, the company, people, culture, and/or specific ways you will be able to add value in the job.

Recommended questions for each stage in the recruiting process are outlined here. Clearly, you wouldn't ask all of these questions. In fact, you want to read the signals indicating that the interviewer's time is up and that's enough. We provide a more comprehensive list here to give a variety of questions that will meet all kinds of interview situations.

Anytime Questions
- What do you see as the top-priority challenges for the company or the group?
- How do you measure performance—define success for yourself?
- What do you think gets lost about your company in the recruiting hubbub that I should know?

Some Time before the Interviews
- Chitchat:
  - What's your background?
  - What do you like most or least about working for X?
  - How is your recruiting going this year?
  - I read about X (something you read about or researched, such as a potential acquisition or a foray into a new market) . . . that's exciting.

During Preliminary Interviews
- At the end of the interview: Are there any issues or concerns that you have about my candidacy? I'd like to have a chance to address them. (Yes, be bold.)
- I remain enthusiastic about the possibility of working with you; what are the next steps (if the interviewer has not outlined them)?
- What are your deciding factors for choosing whom you'll pursue further? What is the timing?
- How have you liked working with your organization? What have you disliked?
- When you look back on your experience with your company, what would you be proudest about? What regrets would you have?
- I get the sense that your culture is very x and y (for example, risk taking and fast-paced or collegial and flexible). Is this an accurate assessment? What more can you tell me about what it's really like to work here?

Preparing for Compensation Negotiation[12]

There are numerous resources on negotiating compensation. Here we discuss some of the more strategic issues and give you some guidance on the pitfalls you may encounter and the approach to use.

Remember that compensation is more than just the dollars. It is the sum total of the elements you are negotiating:

Base salary	Timing of first salary review
Sign-on bonus	Bonus target
Stock option grant	Vesting schedule
Title	Benefits
Start date	Vacation
Relocation support	Professional development
Spouse/partner assistance	Home purchase assistance

Negotiation Strategy and Tactics[13]

If you've gotten an offer that you are excited about, that is an enormous achievement in itself. Now you start the delicate process of negotiating, although to some extent, every interaction with the organization that you have had to date has established either debits or credits for you. Yes, the organization has compensation ranges or bands for your role, job classifications, perhaps grade levels, and other such restrictions. It has a historical perspective on what it has offered people with backgrounds commensurate to yours in the past. The subtle reality, however, is that your debits and credits, in addition to other subjective factors, will play a part in your compensation package.

Factors that influence your compensation are how you have treated people throughout the recruiting process, how people value your various qualifications relative to those of others inside the organization or top contenders for your job, who likes you and who does not (yes, this is the sad reality), what the market is paying, the amount of talent available, and to what extent you are a scarce resource. There are numerous books and many resources on the art of compensation negotiation. Here are some quick insights and tips distilled from our career coaching and work in Human Resources over the years.

Remember that almost everything is open to negotiation, but you do not want to come off as a prima donna, overly pushy or demanding. Throughout all your interactions with those in the recruiting organization, you are building either debits or credits. Ideally, you are building a positive relationship, whether you get and accept an offer this year or reconnect with the company in the future.

It is critical that you do your homework beforehand so that you know how big the ballpark is and what flexibility you have to ask for more. Some of the best sources of information are your classmates who have worked in the industry; some leading HR executives in the field; leading compensation experts such as iQuantic, Hay, and Watson Wyatt; or many of the job or career web sites.

You could also ask your contacts in the industry or company, touch base with your school's career center director or alumni, or ask someone who recruits for the field.

Research what the market rate is for the industry, the company, and people with your background. Factor those things in with what's important to you, what you absolutely need, and what you'd be over the moon about.

Negotiation Play Book

In summary, try these tactics when negotiating.

> *Do your homework.* What is doable for the industry, the company, and the job you have been offered? What would your background warrant on the market? Try WetFeet.com, FutureStep, or other leading web sites to get an indication.
>
> *Know what's important to you.* Is it base, bonus, title, career growth potential? Figure out your floor (the lowest you'd be willing or able to accept). Be realistic about your background and what that is worth in the market.
>
> *Negotiate as if you are on the same side of the table.* Try for a win-win, or at least give-and-take. Remember that you are already *in* a relationship with this person as a colleague.
>
> *Try to get a reading on degrees of freedom.* In which components do the person making the offer and the organization have some

flexibility to improve the offer? Most of the time base pay is fairly
set, but often there is a band (a range) for it. More flexible
components of the total compensation package are possibly a sign-on
or year-end bonus, eligibility for a pay increase sooner than annual,
additional vacation time, work schedule, and professional
development support.

Be gracious but firm. It may be a tough job market, but the ideal
situation is one where both parties—the offerer and the offeree—feel
good about this deal. Refer back to your self-assessment from
Principle 1 and remember what is most important to you. Money
isn't everything, and compensation is not just about dollars. As one
of our clients, a woman who's the primary breadwinner in her
family, said, "I've never taken a job for money alone, but I have
turned down an otherwise interesting job because the numbers
didn't work." Take a job where both the monetary and the
intangible benefits work for you.

Intangibles and Perks

In considering compensation, remember that intangibles and perks are part
of the overall package. These often get discussed together; however, a simple distinction is that perks are the more concrete benefits that a company
provides for its employees, individually or collectively, whereas intangibles
are those things that you cannot touch, see, and so on. Intangibles and perks
do not have a specific dollar value, but they can be very important in the
decision to accept a job offer. For example, perks are such things as lunch
provided at staff meetings, holiday or special event celebrations, and a quarterly training stipend for outside conferences or continuing education. Intangibles are liking the people with whom you would be working, being excited about the company's products or senior management, and the fact that
the job offers you intellectual stimulation and a chance to continue learning. Resonating with the company's values and being given an opportunity
to broaden your career are also intangibles. The key point about intangibles
and perks is to factor them into your consideration of offers. Understand
how important they are to you in your decision to accept or decline the
offer.

Evaluating among Offers—Three Alternative Methods

Following are three proven strategies for evaluating offers and choosing *the* one to accept:

- Use the McKinsey 7-S framework to evaluate each company or organization.
- Create a simple T account, noting your debits and credits for each job offer.
- Calculate a quick weighted average.

The McKinsey 7-S Framework[14]

The first strategy involves adapting the tool first introduced by consultants at the strategy firm McKinsey & Co., the 7-S framework. This tool is generally used by companies for strategy development. However, it can be adapted meaningfully by individuals as well. The 7 Ss are strategy, structure, systems, staffing, style, skills, and superordinate goals. To utilize the McKinsey 7-S framework, you would assess each organization on these seven dimensions. For company A, evaluate its strategy, structure, systems, and so on. What are the pluses and minuses? Do the same for company B. How do one organization's 7 Ss compare to those of another organization? Which organization is the most compelling to you, based on your priorities?

T Accounts

The second strategy involves borrowing the concept of a T account from accounting. Make a T account, a simple uppercase T, for each organization and offer. Above the top of the T, write the name of the company. In the space on the left side of the T, list the debits. On the right side, list the credits. The debits are the negatives about the organization and the offer. These are the minuses or the not-so-good things about the organization or the offer itself. The credits are the positives about the organization or the offer. These are the pluses.

Company A	
Debits	**Credits**
Lacks diversity	Nice People
Could get bored	Entry to industry
Up and coming competitors	Great compensation package
Not enthralled with location	Prestige brand-name company
Career paths seem rigid	Good mentors/managers
	Quality of life

Company B	
Debits	**Credits**
Unproven management	Career broadening
Lots of politics	International exposure
Star culture and competitive	Smart people
High cost of housing	Intellectual stimulation
Questions about morale	High growth mode
	Lots of responsibilities

T Accounts Can Be Helpful in Clarifying the Pluses and Minuses of Each Organization/Offer

Figure 9-3 T Accounts for Evaluating Options *Source:* Adapted from "Understanding Your Values and Negotiating Your Best Compensation Package," Sherrie Gong Taguchi, Stanford Graduate School of Business, Alumni Womens Conference, 1997.

After you have developed a T account for each organization or offer you have received, it will be fairly easy for you to ascertain which organization and offer has the most credits.

Figure 9-3 gives an example of the use of T accounts.

Weighted Averages

Weighted averages have been used effectively in business and other disciplines for years. We apply the concept here to choosing among organizations and job offers in the home stretch of your job search. It incorporates your priorities and the weights (levels of importance) that you assign to each of your options. It can guide your decision making by connecting what is relatively most important to you to the way in which each organization or offer meets your priorities.

For this exercise, develop a prioritized list of the five to ten things that are most important to you in a job and an organization. Figure out what's most important to you in choosing among your options. Examples may be the people, intellectual stimulation, location, scope of responsibility, and compensation. List your priorities in order on the left-hand side of a sheet of paper. Next to each priority, in parentheses, indicate a weight for each (e.g., values a fit may be assigned a 30 percent importance and location may be weighted as 15 percent). The percentages should total to 100 percent.

Across the top of the page, put the words "Offer A," "W. A. (weighted average)," "Offer B," "W. A.," "Offer C," "W. A.," and so on (see Figure 9-4).

Using your gut instincts, and without overthinking, rate each offer on how well it meets each priority, using a scale of 1 to 5. A rating of 1 is low, and 5 is exceptional. Do this for each of your priorities in each column.

After you have completed this rating for each of your offers, multiply the weight you assigned to each priority by each offer's rating (1 to 5). Add up the scores for each offer's W. A. column.

The offer with the highest score—the highest total weighted average—is the best for you based on what you have indicated is important to you and how each offer meets your priorities.

Feedback and Improving

An ancient proverb says, "It's what you learn after you know it all that counts." Continuously monitoring how you are doing and reassessing your action plan are critical so that you can improve, refine, and keep learning

Example 1

My Priorities	Weights	Offer A	W.A.	Offer B	W.A.	Offer C	W.A
Fit with culture/people	30%	3	0.90	2	0.60	5	1.50
Learning/ development	25%	3	0.75	3	0.75	4	1.00
Boss/Executive Team	15%	1	0.15	3	0.45	5	0.75
Location	15%	2	0.30	5	0.75	4	0.60
Total Compensation	15%	5	0.75	3	0.45	1	0.15
Total	100%		2.85		3.00		4.00

In this example, Offer C is the best choice

Example 2

My Priorities	Weights	Offer A	W.A.	Offer B	W.A.	Offer C	W.A
Fit with culture/people	25%	4	1.00	4	1.00	3	0.75
Learning/ development	20%	5	1.00	4	0.80	3	0.60
Stability	20%	3	0.60	3	0.60	4	0.80
Flexible schedule	15%	4	0.60	2	0.30	3	0.45
Socially responsible	10%	5	0.50	2	0.20	1	0.10
Job help for relocating	10%	2	0.20	4	0.40	3	0.30
Total	100%		3.90		3.30		3.00

In this example, Offer A is the best

Figure 9-4 Using Weighted Averages in Evaluating Options *Source:* Adapted from "Understanding Your Values and Negotiating Your Best Compensation Package," Sherrie Gong Taguchi, Stanford Graduate School of Business, Alumni Womens Conference, 1997.

during this job search or career change and the next time you cycle through. In Principle 2 we discuss learning from successes and failures in more depth. Here, we give some specific advice related to your job search strategy, plan, and implementation.

Learn from your successes and your failures throughout all phases of your career discovery, planning, and implementation. Seek out feedback; reflect on how you are doing and how you can improve; figure out solutions. Keep improving. At every phase in your process, take time to reflect on your performance. Strive for continuous improvement. Reflect on what is working and what is not. How can you do better? Feedback can be likened to doing a bug report on yourself and your performance in your job search or career change efforts.

Ferret out any bugs, glitches, and gaps in your performance. There will always be some. Even the most spectacular efforts can be improved. Just as a new software application or product launch is guaranteed to have bugs, so will your plan and your execution of it. Making sure that you have a process in place to identify your bugs and to follow up quickly to fix them is important. Some bugs are within your control and can be fixed, while others are not. Some gaps or areas of improvement can be corrected midcourse, while some may take a while. The key is that you are proactively learning what you can change and doing it.

Triumphs and Setbacks

How do you figure out how you are doing? At every step—each milestone along the way—seek out feedback and incorporate it into what you are doing. Analyze yourself critically. What did you do really well? How could you have done better—taking specific steps for follow-up, having more learning or depth, or asking someone else for help? Were there definite mistakes? What did you learn from them? What can keep you from repeating them in the future? What were your successes—your triumphs? Celebrate those. Who made your life easier—provided encouragement, shared knowledge, bounced ideas, or took you through your paces to hone a skill? Take the time to appreciate what you have accomplished as well as to analyze how you can improve. Focus particular attention on identifying tangible steps to improve. Ask yourself:

- What is working and what is not?
- Where can I improve?
- What help or advice do I need?
- Where can I go for resources or expertise?
- Are there gaps in my performance that need filling in?
- How do I stay motivated to keep up my momentum?

Feedback and Fixes

Do you have knowledge gaps? For example, are you not up to speed on industry lingo? Do you not grasp the company's business model or competitive landscape? Do you have skill gaps? For example, are your résumé and cover letter writing skills not sharp? Do your interviewing skills need work? Remember that knowledge is attainable and skills can be developed—even mastered. Be critical of yourself to the point of learning, not browbeating. Seek objective feedback from others when you can. Ask for it from others early and often. Then learn from what you have gained from them and do better next time. Apply what you have gleaned.

When you conduct an informational interview, ask your interviewee for feedback on the questions you asked. Were they on target? What other questions would have been important to include in your research?

Is your résumé not attracting attention? You can seek professional advice on your résumé. Ask a career expert or someone in the field to take a look at it and give you suggestions. Are people not returning your calls? Tape-record yourself or ask someone in sales or marketing to listen to your spiel and offer some pointers. Do your informational interviews lead nowhere? Why? What can you refine in your approach and technique?

Find out the bugs in your process—what is wrong or below par. How can you fix these things? If the number of bugs is overwhelming, focus on things that you *can* control and on the highest-priority ones that are preventing you from achieving your career objectives.

Easy fixes are things like better anticipating the questions that you will be asked in interviews. Perhaps you need more practice or coaching in interviewing. For example, you can ask a friend who is an excellent interviewer to do a mock interview with you and videotape it.

Maybe you need to develop a more organized tracking system for your job search activities, noting the status of each and keeping names, dates, and follow-up items updated.

Could you use more research on the industry? You can set aside time to do more in-depth research to learn more about an industry or an organization. Are you consistently being told that you are overqualified or underqualified for the types of jobs you are pursuing? Step back and rethink what roles within your targeted industries are a good fit for your background. If you are trying to make a leap to another industry or a different function, perhaps you could use more experience in a certain area or develop a skill as an interim step.

After every interview, ask for constructive feedback. Most interviewers appreciate the idea that you are humble enough to ask and eager to improve. Some will not give you feedback because of the instructions they have been given on interviewing (the potential legalities) or because they are too busy. It may also be that you really have no deficiencies—rather, it's a competitive situation, and other candidates are stronger overall. Many people will be helpful and give you feedback. When they offer it, be gracious; don't be defensive or argumentative, and remember that it is just one data point—one perception of how you presented yourself that one time.

Some improvements will take longer. You may need to gain more experience in a particular field, perhaps with a volunteer project. You may need to find a mentor. Perhaps you will want to take a short course at a community college or online or to embark on a full-blown graduate program to build your knowledge and repertoire. Moving closer to what you want may also mean that you accept a role that brings you a step or two closer to your goal as a strategic move toward the role you ultimately want.

Iterative and Cumulative

Learning from both your successes and your failures is a pivotal part of your career management process. Incorporating feedback—your own and others'—to learn and to improve is imperative, iterative, and cumulative. Monitoring your progress and making adjustments is a natural part of the career management process. Completing this phase allows you to learn continuously and be even better prepared for your next job search or career change.

positions you well for a program of continuous learning and for restarting the career

Recession Proofing Your Job Search Skills

To weather the tough job market, here are some timely articles with focused, specific advice, to help you as you develop your job search action plan and "just do it."

They are available at: http://www.wetfeet.com. Search by author, Sherrie Gong Taguchi or by the article title.

Getting a Great Job in a Weak Market

Keeping Up Your Job Search Momentum (When it's in Overtime)

Ten Creative Places to Find the Hidden Jobs

Surviving and Thriving in a Tough Job Market: Top Ten To-Dos to be Your Best

Surviving and Thriving in a Tough Job Market: Acing the Interviews

Ten Executives Discuss What They're Looking for When They Interview Candidates

What to Say When It's Your Turn to Ask Questions in An Interview

Decoding the Interview and Evaluation Process

Résumé Makeovers: How to Stand Out from the Crowd

Get Results with Your Cover Letter

Seven Tips for Smarter Compensation Negotiation

Career Related Websites for MBAs and Other A-List Talent

Case Study: Job Search Strategies and Plans—A Tale of Two Kellogg and University of Chicago MBAs, Class of 2002

Like many bright, accomplished MBAs from top schools, Dan Levine and Leslie Joy's main goal for 2002 was to get a job. Both, however, aspired to much more than that—they wanted to go into roles and organizations that were a fit with their values, have work and colleagues that they enjoyed, and have the opportunity to contribute significantly and to keep on learning and developing.

Levine was born in New York City and was raised in Westchester County, the son of an attorney father and a teacher mother who took time out from work to raise him and his siblings. Joy was born in Detroit, Michigan, and raised on a farm in rural Missouri by her mother, an attorney, and her grandmother, a housemother at a sorority house. Her parents had divorced when she was young.

Although they came from different backgrounds, the two are similar in that they understood the importance of having a plan and working their plan in a decidedly down market. They embraced taking responsibility for their careers. Both are self-aware and know their values, preferences, and interests. They both could easily tell us what was important to them—the top five factors influencing their current job and organization choices. They took the time to formulate a strategy and a plan for their job searches, and they were determined in implementing their plans. Along the way, Levine and Joy both learned from their mistakes and setbacks, as well as their wins, adapting as needed. Here are their compelling stories.

For his job search/career change, Dan Levine focused on consumer-oriented companies and a role that would leverage his marketing experience and interests and lead to general management. Leslie Joy targeted a location in Florida and the hospitality industry—hotels, airlines, and convention centers—followed by commercial real estate.

Dan Levine

Levine's eclectic and well-rounded education at Brown, the University of Melbourne, and Kellogg and his work experience at Patagonia, Sprint PCS, Outward Bound, the *Congressional Quarterly,* and Schroder's Bank in London prepared him to aim high while being anchored in reality. His strategy was to start broad, talking with as many companies as possible, then to focus in on those that were a fit with his values, skills and strengths, and interests.

Through ongoing self-assessment, reality checks, and input from his school's career counselors and other informal advisers and mentors, Levine was able to clarify his short- and longer-term objectives for this stage in his career:

- To join a company where he fit in culturally, to develop management skills, and to learn about a new industry
- To contribute in a marketing-oriented role at first to build a specialty, keeping a generalist mindset, then to broaden out to general management

Says Levine, "My main goals throughout business school were to find an opportunity where I could learn a great deal, find a company that was a good fit culturally . . . with good mentors and a belief in general managers. Also, after a pre-MBA career with extensive travel and frequent moves, I wanted an opportunity where I would not have to travel as much and where I thought I could stay and grow within the firm over a number of years."

Levine's plan included beating the grass, researching companies, making connections, working his network, conducting informational interviews, talking to alumni, knowing his résumé inside and out for the interviews, and getting feedback from his informal advisers (former bosses and other colleagues with more business experience than he that he keeps regularly consults with about jobs, career direction, and educational decisions).

Although he doesn't put too much credence in self-assessment tests, he feels that self-assessment is something ongoing and that what he has done to date has helped him to highlight his desire to strive for both professional and economic success and work/life balance.

Simply put, to generate options for his job search, Levine wrote letters to companies that had an interest in Kellogg MBAs and those where he knew colleagues enjoyed working. "I did a lot of networking within the companies I was targeting, whether it was with Kellogg alumni, friends of friends, or simply names of other employees that I got from interviewers."

At press time for this book, Levine had landed a great role with Vanguard's Institutional Division as a marketing manager. Levine had networked into Vanguard through a "friend of a friend," which led to the friend's sending Levine's résumé to a colleague. After an informational interview with that colleague, Levine was invited in for an interview. Levine says, "I both let people (my friend) know what sorts of things I was looking for and then was open to opportunities and experiences that came along."

In his words:

Q: Looking back on your successful job search, what did you learn?

A: I learned that there are always opportunities, even in a down economy, but that I needed to stay open-minded about locations, companies, and positions. I also learned to be well prepared for interviews. Getting by on personality and rapport was never enough if I did not have strong examples and vivid stories to support my experiences and qualifications.

Q: What advice on marketing themselves do you have for those carrying out job searches?

A: The interviews and companies where I had the most success were the ones where I had taken the time to really get to know the company and the industry and, having done so, felt excited about the opportunity. By being well informed about the companies I was targeting, I was able to present myself and highlight my skills and abilities in a way that best represented to the company what it was looking for. I never departed from my résumé, but I did shape my message depending on the company and the opportunity.

Q: What's been the biggest challenge in managing your job search/career change?

A: It sounds funny to me, but it's been to realize that managing your career is indeed something that needs to be done well. That in the end, I am the only person who can do it. Somehow, post-college, everything just flowed, and I did not give my career a lot of thoughtful consideration as I moved around and took on new challenges. . . . Somehow my whole career has taken on a new degree of seriousness in my mind as I have been considering my options and my life post-Kellogg. . . . Up to now, my career has largely been developed by the organization. I have realized that I need to start taking more control from here on out.

Leslie Joy

Leslie Joy had already achieved a successful career in the hospitality industry—in Hong Kong for a decade and in New York—before starting her MBA program at Chicago. Joy was director of sales and marketing and performed in manager roles for Inter-Continental Hotels and Resorts, the Island Shangri-La, and Hilton Hotels. At the age of 35, Joy realized that while her bachelor's degree had served her well so far in her career, in order to move into senior management and to feel comfortable and confident of her ability to deliver as her managerial scope increased, she needed a "more comprehensive understanding of business." Joy notes: "I wanted to understand finance, accounting, strategy, and other areas of management in more depth. Getting an MBA was the logical way to achieve this. . . . While some people did cringe when I told them I was returning to school at my age, I really did want to go back to learn." Her return at an atypical age illustrated her zeal to accomplish many things during "the short time we have on earth. I've never been one to let society's norms dictate choices for me."

Joy also embraced her overarching objectives: "In life to be fulfilled both personally and professionally. That means being a wife, a mother, and a respected peer to my business colleagues." Her moves have been motivated by her itch to take on more responsibilities and challenges.

Joy began her post-MBA job search with clear goals and objectives. Logically, she notes, she wanted to find a job, but she goes on to say, "As I approach this opportunity to reenter the workforce at age 38, it means more than just getting a job. I place a good deal of emphasis on finding a job I like. I've had jobs that I didn't like, and it's a miserable existence. I know what works for me and what environments enable me to make valuable contributions, so right now I'm striving to endure this anxiety-ridden period of uncertainty for the payoff later of a really interesting, fulfilling, and fun job."

Joy targeted Florida because of her desire to join a significant other, the climate (after a decade in the Orient, she knew that she liked hot, humid, sunny weather), and the hope that being located in Miami would result in job responsibilities in Latin America so that she could retain her global perspective in her work. She chose the hospitality industry because she knows that she likes it very much, and she also explored commercial real estate after having a taste of that during her summer internship. Recently, given the unique challenges of a geography-constrained job search and the job market, Joy has adapted by widening her net. She has also included in her search her functional top choice roles (in marketing or sales, development, asset management, or strategy), but in a new industry if neither hospitality nor real estate works out.

Joy used multiple entry channels to make the moves she has made so far in her career. In the early years, she relied on newspaper ads. She made her next move through her own research, targeting a firm by reading and learning about it. Later her moves were more a matter of cultivating relationships. Joy identified key players within the Hilton organization, for example, and pursued opportunities directly with the vice president of sales, Asia/Pacific. For her move to the Island Shangri-La, she again identified a key manager and initiated a conversation that led to a job. From that role, peers began to have more of an influence on her job changes. She heard from colleagues about great opportunities and pursued them to success.

Her current strategy and plan have been thoughtful, disciplined, and fluid. To deal with the extra challenges of being geography-bound, she says, "First, I think that intrinsically I had to get comfortable with the fact that I might not find the 'ideal' job in my preferred industry if I wasn't willing to move anywhere. It made me think very hard about the type of functions I enjoy and then correlate them with other types of jobs that may be available in Florida. For example, if I couldn't do development for a global hotel group because most of that work is located in headquarters offices, which are not in Florida, what other type of job would lend itself to development-type work, such as investment analysis, scouting out potential partners, strategy, and so on?

"Second, research is enormously important. You can't progress without knowing who the players in your area are. For me, that included many cold calls/emails to Chicago GSB alumni to extract industry updates and additional contact names and numbers. It also involved hours and hours of Internet research through employment web sites and online search tools such as OneSource.

"Third, I've enlisted the assistance of a select number of executive recruiters (headhunters) whom I have great respect for."

Being realistic about the extra challenges of focusing on Florida, such as doing her job search from Chicago, not being in or knowing the local market, not having a ready relationship database or track record there, and not being readily available to meet folks for lunch, coffee, or networking opportunities, she sketched out a workable plan.

She was fluid with respect to the types of jobs she was looking at and applying for, but also disciplined in her tactics.

Joy outlines: "I have a large three-ring binder with alpha tabs that I use as my 'bible.' All correspondence (cover letters and résumés, printed job descriptions, company web site information, notes to myself) are filed in the binder. I use dated notes as reminders for follow-up calls. My plan includes daily review of the binder and follow-up calls. I note the dates and the actions I have taken."

To generate job leads, Joy used select Internet resources like Monster, CareerBuilder, Hot Jobs, WetFeet, Flip Dog, and 6 Figure Jobs and industry-relevant resources such as Hospitality Careers, Hospitality Online, and Careernet. She read the local and regional newspapers to keep up with local business news. "Fundamentally, my plan is a constant sending out of résumés for targeted jobs. Online searches are an integral part of my daily routine Monday through Friday. I take weekends off." Joy's plan also incorporated networking with Chicago alumni through emails and cold calls and connecting with executive recruiters, as noted earlier.

At press time, Joy had successfully made the move to Florida and was making great progress on opportunities that she was excited about. She had received many valuable leads for known job openings from the people with whom she had been able to network personally and was in discussions with key senior executives at hotels she had focused on.

In her words:

Q: You've seemed to do well in making significant career changes and directions. How did you do it?

A: My motivation to make moves was always a desire to try something new and to challenge myself with entirely new environments and responsibilities. I think the best "navigation" device I possess is my intuition. . . . If it seems like the right thing to do, then I do it. . . . While I am a believer in the old adage "nothing ventured, nothing gained," I also trust my gut. I talked with lots of people to get diverse perspectives, loaded up on research, and took the time to analyze the research, but I always listened to my gut instincts.

Q: What have been the biggest challenges in managing your career, and how did you handle them?

A: One challenge has been how to make a transition. In other words, when a job became routine or I felt that I needed a change, how to identify where to go next and how to get there. . . . Another challenge has been to sell myself into that next job. Some of my transitions were dramatic and I didn't have the traditional background for the work, so I am used to being able to sell my skills and value-added to firms. I think that comes from knowing yourself well and also knowing what you don't do well and being very up-front with people.

Q: Looking back over your career and your current search, what are some of your lessons learned that may help others?

A: "Patience and persistence both pay off. . . . Reputation in how you do your job and how you treat peers, customers, and others is all very important. . . . I've learned to respect people with opposing viewpoints. You can always learn something from them. I've also learned not to accept something that I'm not comfortable with . . . to say no to people, especially my bosses."

Q: What are your thoughts about work/life balance and the role money plays in your career choices?

A: The balance is becoming more important. Overall, I've loved my jobs and, thus, my career. . . . There was no real balance in my twenties and early thirties, as I worked in high-pressure, demanding, travel-oriented roles. . . . As a single career woman, financial security has played an important role in my drive to succeed—not the driving force, because I've taken jobs for less pay, but I had student loans from undergraduate school to repay and the desire to earn "enough" disposable income to collect art, and so on.

Principle 10

Own Your Career

They must often change, who would be in happiness and wisdom.
—Confucius

The tenth principle for attaining career clarity is to direct and "own" your own career. This principle has two main sections. In the first, we give guidelines for pulling all the principles in this book together and approaching your career as part of your overall life vision. In the second, we offer hands-on advice for what to do once you have achieved the career that you want. Eleven visionary executives who have artfully managed their own careers and have a gift for developing others offer practical insights and wisdom on what it takes to gain career clarity and to sustain a bold, dynamic, and meaningful career over a lifetime.

Work in the Context of Your Complete Life Vision

One of the core themes of this book has been the idea that work is just one dimension of life. We take a holistic and integrated approach, encouraging you to use the principles in this book to create your life and career mosaic. Work can be a miserable part of your life or one that brings you immeasurable satisfaction, personal growth, *and* money.

So Now What?

Once you have achieved the career you want, what do you do with it? Well, if you consider the bigger-picture context that your career is just one dimension of your life and that your work now is just one snapshot or image in a larger mosaic that evolves over time, then you balance enjoying the moment and being grateful for what you have accomplished with embracing the idea that your career deserves continuous effort. You own your career over your lifetime. To keep it fit, in shape, and healthy, you need to marry working at it, nurturing it, building it, and changing it with enjoying it, loving it, and being satisfied and content with it.

Guidelines for Owning Your Career

During the many years that we have coached executives, managers, and those who are just starting out in their careers, some core themes have emerged concerning the attitudes, strategies, and skills that are critical to attaining career clarity. Some of the most important of these are discussed here. These lessons are enriched by words of wisdom from some extraordinary executives who are masterful at managing their own careers and guiding the careers of others.

Seek "Career Amplitude"

We enjoy watching the Winter Olympics, and we especially enjoy seeing the new Olympic sport of snowboarding. The snowboarders' success is measured by the degree of "amplitude" they achieve, a combination of the height they achieve and the grace with which they achieve it. This is a great metaphor for your career: What level do you want to achieve, and by what measure will you know that you've succeeded? Unlike in the sport, however, in your career it's you who have the power to measure your success, not some commentator or judge!

Adopt an Attitude of Career Self-Reliance

It begins with the attitude. Adopting an attitude of being career self-reliant is important to owning your career. Accept that you, and no one else, are in charge of your career—you are responsible for it. Remember that a manager is one who allocates resources toward organizational objectives. You're the manager of your career. You're the one who is in charge of formulating objectives and deploying your resources to meet your objectives.

Remember that Bad Things Sometimes Happen to Good People

We know there will be mistakes, failures, and hard knocks (see Principle 2). We have advised on numerous careers in which bad things did happen to good people. These people were on the receiving end of political machinations, various forms of bias, jealousy, unfair competition, or their own weaknesses.

The positive element in all these cases, however, was that these individuals prevailed. They picked themselves up, dusted themselves off, and, yes, at times started all over again. They were not only self-reliant but extremely resilient. In fact, the silver lining was that they all learned from their situations and next time around did many things differently that affected the outcomes. These success stories provide excellent examples of "making lemonade out of lemons."

Plan an Entry Strategy

How you enter a new job as part of a new organization or group, or a new career, project, or role can make the difference between success and failure later on. In particular, the first 90 days in a new role are critical. You've heard the old adage about starting off on the right foot. Anecdotally, you probably can recall colleagues in your own organization who have come in, gotten up to speed quickly, acclimated to the culture, and gone on to do exceedingly well. On the flip side, you've probably also encountered colleagues who had loads of anticipated promise and impressive credentials, but who never quite got off the ground. They never fulfilled their potential, and they often ended up either leaving the company or being asked to do so at some point.

People form initial impressions of your competence and cultural fit. Your new boss or business partners, colleagues, direct reports, clients, vendors, and others are judging how you fit in, how your actions will affect them, and how much or little to give to their new relationship with you. Unintentionally violating the company culture, not reading between the lines, communication gaffes, and other missteps—while you can recover from them—can derail you.

Much ado about something.   Watch out for some common missteps. Here are some examples of some of the more subtle ones that we have seen:

- Your department's existence is being challenged by several key senior managers. You don't pick up on the seriousness of your team's risk and the need to deliver better financial results immediately.
- You fail to see the political warfare between two of your direct reports until it affects a key project's success.
- You break a communication norm by sending a broadcast email instead of speaking with the relevant colleagues in person first.
- You realize after starting your new role that you need more competence in speaking before a huge audience. Not having this skill will mean failure in your role.

Consider the 5 Cs for successful entry.   The 5 Cs[1] is an action-oriented framework that is designed to help you ensure your success during those first few critical months in a new job or new organization. The 5 Cs framework was developed by the author in her work with new-hire orientations and in coaching executives to integrate effectively into the company's culture.

The 5 Cs are
Core values and culture
Context
Communication
Connections
Core competencies

Here's how to apply the 5 C's to your career:

1. *Learn the core values and the culture.* Take the time to go beyond the espoused values and culture of the organization and particular work groups. Get to know, listen to, and observe people, particularly those in leadership roles or those who are well respected. See what

their actions and behavior indicate is *truly* valued, not what people *say* is valued.

2. *Pay attention to context.* Context as defined by Webster's means "the circumstances around an act or event; the parts of a discourse that surround a word or a passage and help to explain its meaning." Understand what is and is not being said. Look for what is related or relevant to a particular situation or decision.

3. *Understand communication norms.* How do people communicate— both informally and formally, verbally and nonverbally? How does one seek out or hear valuable information? Who are the "go to" people, the people who usually know what's going on and can help newcomers decipher it? Is the organization and/or work group an email, voice mail, or talk-in-person culture? How does important information get shared—through formal meetings or informal exchanges?

4. *Build connections with people.* Be a student and learn about people. Take a genuine interest in what they do, how their role fits into the whole, and what their backgrounds, motivations, and ambitions are. Get to know HR. This group manages the people "processes," but, more important, it can be an advocate in your career development and coaching. Who are the culture gatekeepers; the leaders and mentors; the go-to, helpful people; the people to be careful around?

5. *Focus on core competencies.* What do you need in order to perform well in your role? What are your gaps, and how can you fill them? Identify any areas that need to be strengthened early on, while you still have time to initiate your own learning or improvement program.

Refer to Appendix E: "Getting It Right – Due Diligence and Entry Strategy."

Manage Your Career Inside and Outside Your Organization

Take the time to do career check-ups—to assess where you are and how you are doing. Generate ideas for what's next and how you will get there. Manage your career both inside the organization and outside it. Use all the internal resources available to you: development discussions with your manager, HR programs, job postings, informal advisers or mentors, and learning about other groups or jobs on your own time. Couple this with an active external focus. Join and become active in professional associations and service organizations. Become a thought leader in your industry. Make sure you do not become complacent, isolated, or unprepared.

Look to the horizon.   Make a point of being aware of what's "out there" beyond your organization. Find out what opportunities are available in your field in general and what opportunities you might be interested in for the future. What's the market like? What are high-growth sectors and industries? Which skills and competencies are in the highest demand, and which are becoming obsolete? Stay connected with others in your field or those in potential new fields.

Consider where Babies and Marriage Fit In

Although we are unable to discuss this in depth, it is a vexing issue for our generation. For both men and women who desire marriage or some other committed relationship and/or children at some point, this needs to at least be on the radar screen—even if not with a strong signal for now. Sylvia Ann Hewlett's recent book *Baby Hunger: The New Battle for Motherhood*[2] caused quite a stir, as her research findings were received with both affirmation and panic. Hewlett concluded that a generation of high-flying women has put careers before babies, but that only about 30 percent made that choice deliberately; the rest made it by default and have regretted it. She goes on to make several points that were directed toward women but are applicable more broadly to men, too.

Hewlett's main point was that you should use your brain to look at and to think about your whole life, not just your education and your career. If you want partnerships and family as part of your future, she noted, they should be an intentional consideration that requires effort. Hewlett introduced the concept of "backward mapping"—figuring out what you want in your future, then planning backward, understanding, for example, the realities of fertility and age.

This resonates with our encouraging you to view your career in the context of your life in total. Make informed, active choices and decisions to achieve your work/life vision.

Be Committed but Not Blindly Loyal

Some people think that loyalty is stupidity and that you should always look out for number one. We couldn't disagree more; however, there is a difference between blind loyalty and being committed to the people you're working with, your organization, and doing the best work you can do.

In spite of the changing employer-employee contract, both employees and employers can care about and be committed to each other while keeping business needs in mind.

For example, an organization may have to lay off 15,000 people, but it can do this with consideration for those employees who must lose their jobs. It can be thoughtful in its decisions, honest in its communication, and helpful with career transitions.

Employees may accept an opportunity elsewhere, but they can ensure a smooth handoff of responsibilities, assist the company in finding a successor, and agree to complete the highest-priority projects before leaving, possibly even pitching in and doing double duty while they are in their new job at their new company.

For example, when one author managed the HR aspects of layoffs for Bank of America, Dole Packaged Foods, and Mervyn's Department Stores, the senior managers were similar in philosophy. They believed in the importance of treating employees with respect, and they were committed to caring enough to implement the layoffs as painlessly and thoughtfully as possible. This included regular and open communication about what was going on, active efforts to find other jobs in the company for those who were being laid off, and career transition services for those people for whom jobs could not be found.

Be Open to both Vertical and Horizontal Moves

As we said earlier in this book, the old model was moving up the proverbial pyramid—promotions all the way to the top, with more money, more responsibility, and a higher title each time. However, career-broadening moves—sideways (lateral) moves or zigzagging up and down or up and out (spiral)—can bring career satisfaction and powerful learning through experiencing new responsibilities, challenges, and roles.

Develop Relationships with Executive Recruiters

Jana Rich, managing director at Russell Reynolds Associates, a top global executive search firm, suggests that you find the best-quality executive recruiters who focus on your industry and your geographic area. Rich suggests evaluating executive recruiters on the following dimensions:

- Look at what searches the recruiters get—are they positions at the right level with the most interesting companies in the industry?
- Do the recruiters get quoted in business articles relevant to the industry and geographic area?
- Are they respected in the industry by their clients (companies), candidates (those they help place), and peers?

She goes on to advise that once you have identified these recruiters, you should cultivate key long-term relationships with them. "For example, if they call with a search in which you aren't interested, call them back anyway and try to provide them with some good referrals—they will remember! The recruiters might even note in their large databases that you are someone to be regarded highly because of your helpful behavior." Other advice that Rich offers is "to use the opportunity of talking with recruiters to find out what is going on in the market, who is hiring at what levels, any interesting compensation trends that might be occurring."

A caveat, however, is that if you are actively seeking a job, you need to understand that while the recruiters with whom you have developed a relationship will want to hear from you, they doesn't work on your behalf. A recruiter can help only if that recruiter or his or her colleagues is working on a search that is appropriate for you. "If they aren't, it is not a good idea to call them persistently. If you've developed a relationship with them, they will remember you!"

Work with select executive recruiters. Rich has three recommendations for working with recruiters:

- Be honest about any reservations you have throughout the process—there should be no surprises at the end of the process or wasting of your or their time.
- Keep them in the loop; they can be an objective voice and even an ally to you throughout the process. Call them after any interviews, and make sure they have your timely feedback and interest.

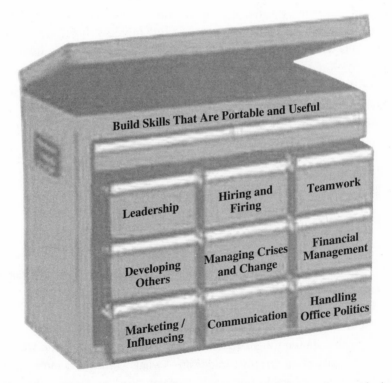

Figure 10-1 Skills/Competencies Toolkit. *Source:* Expanded from various works by S. Taguchi: presentation for the International Placement Directors Conference, 2001, contributions to The San Francisco Chronicle's "Workers Dozen" career advice columns, 2002, and guest lectures for The London Business School Career Strategy Programme, 2002–2003.

- Give and take. Refer them to hiring managers in your company, and send them strong candidate referrals.

We like to think of reputable recruiters as an extension of your diversified network. They can be knowledgeable experts to develop in your relationship base for career connections.

Build Survival Skills for Your Toolkit[3]

In our work with organizations, some core skills and competencies have emerged as significant ones to have in your career toolkit. These are core skills and competencies that we suggest you develop and try to keep improving over time to remain employable but more so, highly marketable. These skills will serve as a strong foundation whether you are employed by an organization or self-employed and whether the job market is up or down (Figure 10-1). Through some lively exchanges, these 11 extraordinary leaders give an insider's view of these core skills and competencies that have made them successful in their own careers as well as in others' careers that they have guided.

11 Executives Share Their Lessons Learned

Leading, Motivating, and Inspiring Others

William F. Meehan III, director and chairman of the West Coast Practice, McKinsey and Company, Inc., and lecturer in strategic management, Stanford Graduate School of Business

To state the obvious: You can't be a leader without followership. But it is from this simple insight that one can derive in any situation what the requirements of an effective leader are—what will attract, motivate and inspire the followership one needs to accomplish an organization's mission and goals. No doubt, some things that followers want are specific to an individual context. But, in general, followers always want a few things: a mission, a set of goals and values that inspire them in some meaningful way, usually by creating some greater sense of purpose; an opportunity to contribute in a way that they believe allows them to reach their own personal and development goals; a leader who, whatever his or her style, communicates in a way that reinforces the importance and value of that individual; and a sense of loyalty that extends beyond the narrow tasks to be accomplished.

Hiring and Firing People

Libby Sartain, senior vice president of human resources and chief of people, Yahoo!

Over the course of time, as the business world has evolved, managers have learned many "scientific" approaches to hiring. Conventional wisdom tells us that if we develop a good position specification, and then match the skills and competencies of candidates to that spec, we will make a good hire. Well, maybe. . . . I have learned. . . . that there is much more to this formula. Often job fit is so much more than skills and background. At Southwest Airlines, we had a mantra "Hire for Attitude, Train for Skills." By the time a candidate has been screened enough to be interviewed for a job, one should assume that he or she can do the job, but what are the behavioral characteristics that make someone successful in an organization and position? That is what I like to focus on in hiring.

I like to pick a good fit with the organizational culture first. As far as having the best talent pool available, it is important to hire well, grow your own talent, and get rid of those who do not fit into the culture or cannot deliver results. I recommend that those decisions be made early, preferably within the first 6 months to a year in a position. When bringing people in from the outside, it is important to have a good orientation program, and clear expectations and understandings of how someone can succeed or fail.

Every company has strong players and those who are not so strong. Successful leaders cut their losses early. We all make hiring mistakes, even the best of us. A bigger mistake is to try to fix the problem by trying to change a person. This never works, wastes everyone's time and energy, and doesn't lead to high performance or productivity.

Ken Kam, CEO, Marketocracy, and top-ranked fund manager of the Marketocracy Masters 100 Mutual Fund

Hire A players: When you see a top manager who surrounds himself with yes-men and other sycophants, it is a sure sign of impending failure.

Tigers can't change their stripes, so don't hire immature people. A good measure of maturity is the level of insult it takes to generate hostility, anger, or outrage. Immature people are quick to take offense at the slightest provocation.

A Christmas tree metaphor: Don't expect everyone you hire to be perfect. If you can work only with perfect people, you will not have that many to choose from when you are building your team. Like Christmas trees, everyone has bad sides. Also like Christmas trees, you try to turn the bad sides toward a wall so no one can see them. In practice, this means that you hire people for their strengths, not their weaknesses.

Managing through Change/Problems/Crisis

Libby Sartain, senior vice president of human resources and chief of people, Yahoo!

Through my work, I have discovered some very simple lessons about leadership and working with people that are applicable in times of crisis, change, and uncertainty, in good times and in bad. While people can be very unpredictable under stress, we can assume that during turbulent times, people will seek safety and security and look to meet their most basic needs. This was something I learned in both my HR and my emergency response training.

The person who takes charge in a situation is often the leader, and sometimes that person may not have any qualifications for that role other than being willing to take the lead. During times of uncertainty, people want answers. While you may have to make up your action steps as you go along, you will not want to make up answers as you go along. Honesty and integrity are nonnegotiables in a leadership role. These lead to trust, and without trust, there can be no leadership. Being honest means that you may have to give answers that people don't want to hear. You may have to explain that you don't have any answers because of looming uncertainty. You may not be loved, you may not be popular, but you will be respected.

In helping to create a "Best Employer" brand and culture, I learned that people need and want to be led, not managed. People want to be inspired, and they want to feel valued. They want to know that they contribute to the cause, something bigger than themselves. They need a positive outlook. They need hope. They need to see an envisioned future. They need goals, clear expectations, and some structure.

In times of crisis, people need information, and they need to know how any crisis or change will affect them personally. They need to see that their leaders care about them as people.

It has become clear that courage, compassion, and creativity—along with clear vision and focus—are required to keep our companies and our people moving forward. Unmatched value, speed, accuracy, simplicity, flexibility, and effective communication characterize industry leaders in this marketplace.

During turbulent times, circumstances often change quickly, dramatically, and constantly. Yet people will be looking for consistency. People cannot count on leaders who are indecisive, are inconsistent, and do not communicate clear direction and goals. Only leaders who stick to their core values and principles have any chance of maintaining a semblance of consistency during tumultuous events.

Developing Others

Eric Snyder, vice president, Corporate Human Resources and Organizational Development, Travel Retail Group, LVMH (Louis Vuitton Moet & Hennessey)

A manager is a developer first and foremost. Team members feel very valued and a tremendous amount of loyalty can be established when managers genuinely show they care. This care means finding out what team members want to do and supporting them in reaching their goals. It also means continually checking in, asking how things are going, listening, and offering support and encouragement.

A valued team of employees paves the way for a manager to more effectively guide the team to maneuver through the obstacles and problems thrown any team's way. Many managers sorely underestimate the importance of the development of team members and ultimately the impact it can have.

Building a Team and Teamwork

Steve Anderson, partner, KPCB (Kleiner, Perkins, Caufield & Byers Venture Capital)

Two often-overlooked elements of building an effective team are diversity and process. There is strength in diversity of opinion and experience. I call it "getting the right DNA." If everyone is the same, the best solutions never surface. We would never have the microprocessor or commercial airplanes that can fly halfway around the world if we didn't have diversity of ideas coming to the table. Having diversity and difference of opinion creates overhead and a certain amount of hashing it out, but that's the only way to get the best ideas and answers.

"If team members only agree with each other, why bring them together? People have better things to do. Strength in diversity is about the classic components, such as backgrounds, experience, and specific expertise. More broadly, diversity includes styles and perspectives.

"Lay the framework. Clarifying process questions can make a significant difference in the end results. How will you work together? What are the roles and responsibilities of the various team members? How will the group communicate wins, problems, changes? How will you handle conflict or someone who is not coming through with what he or she is supposed to be doing? For big decisions and moving the ball forward, will you require consensus, majority rule, or something else?"

Financial Management

Andy Miller, vice president of finance & corporate controller, Autodesk

The dot-coms made perhaps the best case for why executives and managers, whatever their roles, need to have competence and even mastery in

and suggestions. Exceptional verbal communication skills are a core competency in all professions and at all levels of the career ladder. All that you know and all of your capabilities matter not if you are unable to communicate and establish rapport. You must be able to convince the jury, communicate construction specifications, or win the account. In the modern world of high-tech media with a generation raised on infomercials this ability is increasingly essential. Great minds and brilliant ideas can forever remain hidden behind inadequate communication skills. Talking is the core of human interaction, yet it is unfortunately lacking in most educational curriculum. It is worthy of investment and a trait that should not be overlooked by the aspiring professional.

Handling Office Politics

Simon Sutton, executive vice president, International Television, Metro-Goldwyn-Mayer

Simon's perspective is that politics aren't necessarily a bad thing. "Corporate politics involves the managing of interpersonal relationships in the work environment. What makes this different from other environments is the different power that individuals have, their differing ability to persuade others and manage resources.

"The important thing to realize," he continues, "is that people are driven by different agendas—for example, some very different fundamental agendas are ego/status, money, shorter hours, a fun experience, and so on. We often make the mistake of assuming that everyone in an office wants the same thing we do—but often that is not the case."

His best advice for handling office politics? "The best way to work with corporate politics is to further others' agendas while furthering our own. In short, have an awareness of what people want and why they want it, and then work with it. You can even ask people what they want to achieve (so many executives never do this). This is far easier if ego is not one of your own agenda items. It is simpler to work with others' agendas if we work without ego—ironically, this can often result in a furthering of one's own career."

Dave Murphy, the award-winning At Work editor, San Francisco Chronicle

Dave offers these three lessons on surviving office politics at work:

1. Let others win when you can. The best bosses and the most effective office politicians use power only when it is absolutely necessary. They know that you can get a lot farther by persuading people to go along than by forcing them. That's why micromanagers are so inept when it comes to dealing with talented people. By demanding that everything be done their way, they sap the creativity out of their staff. . . .

2. Be subtle in your alliances. Think of Rudyard Kipling's classic, "If": "If all men count with you, but none too much." Loyalty is a wonderful thing for your spouse, children, significant other, or dog. It's also useful at work as long as you know the difference between loyalty and blind faith. . . . Even if you work with your best friend, disagree in public once in a while. If you seem to be an ideological clone of one or two or ten other people, your credibility with everyone who is not in the clique is likely to suffer. . . . A different sort of problem occurs if the CEO listens to only a few key people. The boss misses out on hearing diverse ideas, and the company suffers.

3. Read the handwriting on the wall. Never, never, never listen to what people say. Watch what they do. If managers or influential rank-and-filers leave, watch where they are going . . . [and] who is replacing them. . . . If there have been layoffs, which people are getting targeted? Do you need more allies or more effective ones?

Influencing Others/Marketing Your Ideas

Jason S. Goldberg, executive director, International Broadband Strategy & Operations, AOL Inc., and former special assistant to the White House chief of staff, Erskine Bowles

Jason offers this overarching strategic career advice especially for twenty- and thirty-somethings who are starting out in their careers. It can also be applied by those who are longer into their careers but need to keep proving them-selves, starting over again, or establishing a track record in a new industry or field. In Jason's own words:

> Throughout my short career, I have constantly found myself in situations where I was the youngest, least experienced person in the room. Such sit-uations can be tremendously frightening and downright dangerous when one is not well prepared. Imagine briefing the president of the United States on the day of the Oklahoma City bombing at age 25. Or, taking a briefing from the Treasury secretary at 26. Or, presenting to a board of directors as acting CFO of a 350-person start-up company at 27. Or, pre-senting to senior executives of the world's largest media company at 29. Amazingly, I've found that the same rules apply when confronted with these circumstances as in any other business situation. As such, I've de-veloped three simple rules for myself. I hope these are helpful to those reading the book

- *Don't prove that you are smart; display that you are valuable.* The very fact that you were invited to the meeting—or that you got the job you are in, for that matter—means that the people you work with believe that you are smart and capable. Don't waste precious time and effort trying to display your intelligence. Attempted displays of intellect too often come across as obnoxious arrogance. Instead, go the extra mile to show that you are a valuable contributor to the team. Help the people around you come to their own smart conclusions and you will have displayed true intelligence.
- *Be principally objective and strategically opinionated.* Frankly, as a young person, your opinions are less important than your facts. Be the one person in the room who can speak objectively about the merits and demerits of all sides of an argument. Know and understand the analytical reasoning behind all possible options. If you display an unbiased, logical approach to problem solving, your recommendations will be heard, will carry weight, and more times than not will be followed.
- *Being well-liked is as important as, if not more important than, being well-regarded.* In the end, the business of doing business is all about

relationships. People who like doing business with you will do so willingly and with pleasure. People who don't like doing business with you, most definitely won't. They will avoid you and work around you. Be the person they turn to because they want to, not because they have to.

Case Study: Jim Collins, Best-Selling Author of *From Good to Great* and *Built to Last*, Educator, and Management Visionary Owns His Career Artfully

The real path to greatness, it turns out, requires simplicity and diligence. It requires clarity, not instant illumination.

—JIM COLLINS

Jim Collins has written two best-sellers, *Built to Last* (co-authored with Jerry Porras) and *Good to Great: Why Some Companies Make the Leap . . . and Others Don't*. He's been featured in *BusinessWeek, Fortune, Fast Company,* and the *New York Times;* earned two degrees (a B.S. in mathematical sciences and an MBA) from Stanford University; worked with the venerable McKinsey & Co. and Hewlett-Packard; and taught creativity and entrepreneurship at the Stanford Graduate School of Business. His inspired and accessible teaching style won him the highest honor from his students—the Distinguished Teaching Award in 1992. Taking his teaching to the next level and on a broader scale, he is now "a self-employed professor who endowed his own chair and granted himself tenure," having founded a research lab in Boulder, Colorado. He and his wife, Joanne, a "50-50 partner with all the voting shares" and a former Ironman triathlon champion who is now a track coach, chose Boulder in part because of their passion for rock climbing, something that Jim's been doing since age 12. The lab is in the old brick schoolhouse where Jim went to first grade.

These are a few facts about Jim's remarkable career, but still it is difficult to describe on paper the man and the depth of the substance, wisdom, humility coupled with faith in himself, and multidimensionality that are his essence. The written word does not do justice to Jim and his journey; we would need an IMAX theater for that. However, we will do our best to share his story and some valuable lessons that we can take away and apply to our own careers over a lifetime.

Jim has managed to combine his values, purpose (what he stands for), passions, and talents to create a career mosaic. He's melded together work that he is excited about in the context of his total life vision. Jim's work life has been achieved through some luck and some conscious career management, powered by a relentless curiosity, yet it has not been easy, breezy success. There have been bumps along the way.

The beginning of Jim's life was grim. His dad died of cancer at a young age. His mom scraped by on $200 per month. There were no Christmas trees for the family; instead, Jim and his brother had a Christmas rock that they painted red and green. Food was a luxury, and sometimes there was not enough. Jim learned early that life is always difficult—sometimes more and sometimes less. Luckily, the lows that life could bring have become a counterbalance for the highs. He shared in our interview that "when you come from nothing . . . and have been through a lot . . . you know you can survive."

Having faced the harsh realities of his early-life situation, and having faced the existential questions about life and death through close calls when rock climbing and the death of both his father and his grandfather at an early age, Jim appreciates that life is short. He embraces the idea that a life that is worth living is one in which you figure out what you want to get out of it, enjoy what you do, and are true to your core values.

In his book *Good to Great,* Jim articulates that "going from good to great in any endeavor is like pushing a huge, heavy flywheel, one turn upon another. At first, it takes a huge amount of effort to just go one or two turns. But with persistent effort, you eventually hit a point of breakthrough results. We need patience to build momentum . . . and not fall into a doom loop of frantically searching for a quick fix."

From an interview with him, and from having known him as a student more than a decade ago, it is clear that Jim is actively and artfully pushing the flywheel to create a bold, dynamic, and meaningful career over a lifetime.

Here are some lessons learned that are relevant to our own career management.

Jim learned what he stood for—what is important to him in his work—through an early "quarter-life crisis." At the age of 25, he found that he was good at his job at Hewlett-Packard, was paid well for it, but was miserable in it. He asked himself the "2 million in the bank and 5 years to live" question: "If I woke up one morning and had $2 million in the bank and 5 years to live, how would I be spending my time? What would I stop doing, keep doing, and start doing?"

In gaining clarity about his purpose in life, Jim spent time on understanding his core values, and they haven't changed over the intervening 15 years. His values have become his basic precepts, serving as a foundation for his work life. They are

1. The idea of relationships, long-term and lasting—marriage, friendships, family members, students.
2. The fundamental notion of respect—for others, from others, and for himself.
3. Sheer enjoyment. "It's vital to enjoy what you do, since life is so hard anyway."
4. Improvement and excellence for its own sake—for example, although he has been rock climbing for 30 years, he's recently hired a coach to help him keep learning and improve.
5. Integrity. Jim calls it "the front page of the *New York Times* standard." "Picture a videocamera filming you 24 hours a day—your conversations, the decisions that you make, how you are handling things. . . . I ask myself if I would be comfortable if all of that was revealed in detail on the front page of the *New York Times*."
6. Time with mountains and the outdoors. The mountains are "my cathedral."

Asked about his overall purpose in life, Jim says, "My basic purpose is to contribute through learning and teaching. . . . It is to harness my unquenchable curiosity and love of learning in ways that make a significant and lasting impact on the world."

When discussing how he's managed his career over the years, he notes, "There have been some great strokes of good fortune and blessings that I can't take credit for. . . . For example, I stumbled into circumstances and discovered what my talents are: basic intelligence, being a good teacher. . . . I've also been really lucky in people. Bill Lazier, who is still a mentor, gave me an incredible break to teach at Stanford, literally going to the dean, going out on a limb, and saying, 'Let Jim fill in some holes in the curriculum, and if he fails, I'll take responsibility.' I am also really lucky with my wife, Joanne. We've been married more than 20 years. . . .

"There's also been some conscious management to my career. . . . The single framework that I've used is to search for places where my passions and talents intersect. Earlier on I was trying to find where they intersect. Once I discovered that, I could focus more on looking out for or recognizing the opportunities where there are intersections."

He encourages others to "find and pursue three circles and where they intersect: (1) What you are passionate about and what's your purpose—what do you stand for? (2) What you are good at—genetically coded for—what would you do if you felt like a fish *in* water? (3) What people will pay you for—what is the value of your contributions?"

Other principles that Jim factors into his career management are his wife's valued partnership, putting money into perspective, taking some big-bet risks, and excellence and continuous learning.

Jim says of his wife, "Joanne is the person I work for. We have a 50-50 partnership, but she holds all the voting shares." Joanne is part of a three-person "executive council" that also comprises Jim and a long-time research associate. Jim makes no major career decision without the unanimous agreement of the council.

And what about the importance of money in career choices? "Money has never been a motivator," Jim notes. Rather, he's been driven by his passions and his purpose, and he keeps coming back to those. After his first bestseller, for example, Jim could have made easy money and lots of it by going the full-time speaking and consulting route, but he didn't. Each year he turns down an enormous number of consulting and speaking opportunities and other requests for his time. But he does appreciate the role that money and finances play in taking risks.

"I've taken a series of untraditional big-bet risks in my career, but I am fairly conservative financially, so I can take life risks. . . . I'm a value investor."

Jim's big-bet risks have included rejecting the traditional route of getting a Ph.D. in order to teach. While he was co-writing *Built to Last*, Jim spent 5 years living with his wife on $33,000 a year in a dank, basementlike house that was worse than most of his students' housing. He didn't know how the years of research and the book would turn out at the time, but he was passionate about it, and it fit with his purpose of learning and teaching. Jim's next big project, *Good to Great*, took another 5 years, and he didn't know how that would come out, either. The phenomenal success and, more important, the impact of both of those books on business and management is legendary.

Excellence and continuous learning are part of Jim's DNA. He views learning as a key to personal growth in order to remain vibrant but continuous over a long period of time.

Here are some excerpts from our interview:

Q: When you think about your research and teaching on next-generation great companies and new businesses, what do you think the people who work in them (or for themselves) will need to know in order to be effective in their careers and career management?
A: The whole idea of "first who . . . then what." The who question is "picking the right who's . . . the people you want to be with, work with."
Q: What are you working on now, and how will you figure out your next big thing?
A: I'm working on a project on how technology-based companies in explosive change arenas go from IPO to greatness when others don't—but I don't consider this a "big question." It is just another brick in the wall of understanding what makes for great companies. I've often been asked that question and haven't answered it. Also, we're creating a true e-teaching site—you won't be able to buy anything on it! It will use the medium of the Web as an intellectual driver . . . as a site for students around the world to access ideas. After that, the next big project I do will involve research and teaching and will draw upon my talents and passions, but I would be surprised if it has anything to do with business.

Rather than carefully planning out what's next for him, he will take a break in between projects as is his custom, going with the flow of his version of rest: "Although I never really rest. I rest by being actively engaged." He'll let his next big endeavor—whatever audacious idea it may be—come to him in its own time. His students will guide him to the answer.

And here's what he says about sustaining and owning a career over a lifetime:

> There's this understanding of the difference between your fundamental driving purpose that doesn't change versus the manifestations of the way you bring it to life and allow the manifestations to change. You might change from being a classroom teacher to being a basketball coach, but you're still a teacher. The essence of the long term over the course of a lifetime of work is that blend of continuity of change—that preserving of the essential core nature of what it is that you are and what you do with it, but being willing to be very open to perhaps fairly drastic changes in the way in which you bring it to life.

Jim is humble about the breathtaking success of his body of work, is very self-critical, and calls himself productively neurotic—not knowing all the answers. To this day, he does not feel super-successful, and he doubts that he ever will. "I am aware of my own shortcomings better than anyone, and of how much more there is to do," he says. "I'm very self-critical, always aware of what I could have done better." He surrounds himself with people who have known him for a long time and who are always willing to keep him in his place. Jim Collins is an inspiration, showing what someone can accomplish through learning from the past, facing the present, envisioning the future, and taking action to create his or her own opportunities to keep changing his or her life and career with simplicity and diligence, clarity and discipline.

Jim epitomizes someone who has actively created the career that he wants—one that is bold, meaningful, and dynamic. To hear him talk, though, he'll forever be on a journey and never be satisfied that he has reached a destination. He'll keep turning the flywheel as he keeps creating his career mosaic, living an inspired work life, and transforming himself, his students, and much of the world around him.

Appendix A

Best of the Web—Our 25 Favorites

Here are 25 of our favorite job or career management sites, with a brief description of each. We call out any unique features or resources that each site offers.

BrassRing.com (*http://www.BrassRing.com, http://www.mba-jobs.net*).
High-tech career events nationwide: Virginia, Massachusetts,
Maryland, California, Illinois, and so on. International job
resources for Austria, Belgium, Canada, Germany, and the
Netherlands. Special section for MBA jobs.

Campus Career Center (*http://www.campuscareercenter.com/*). An
online community for college students. Permits applying for jobs,
researching companies, and receiving guidance on job searches,
information on networking and career options, and interview and
résumé tips. "Ask the expert" feature.

CareerBuilder.com (*http://www.CareerBuilder.com*). A comprehensive
site with more than 300,000 jobs, a company search function,
pointers to employers and ad agencies, résumé advice, relocation
services, and layoff survival kit.

Career Journal (*http://www.CareerJournal.com,
http://www.careerjournalasia.com/, http://www.careerjournaleurope.com/*).
A premier career site for executives and senior managers. Access to
regional news, job listings, career advice, negotiation tips, career
indicators, hot issues, options, and benefits.

Career Voyager (*http://www.careervoyager.com*). Offers advice/guides,
search/portals, and general sites. A collection of job sites, research

resources, job-hunting news, interview questions, and information on job fairs, graduate schools, and professional associations.

Chief Monster (*http://www.my.chief.monster.com*). Provides job opportunities based on location, category, key word, and compensation range. Ability to benchmark your skills and compensation against peers. Offers networking circle, personalized real-time tools and information, and career strategy advice.

CNET (*http://www.cnet.com/techjobs/0-7067.html*). An excellent source of high-technology job postings.

ComputerJobs.com (*http://www.ComputerJobs.com*). Lists jobs by major cities and skill sets, e.g., ERP, new media, project management, database systems, technical sales, Unix, and so on. Special sites for entry-level jobs, H-1B visa jobs, and consulting.

Craigslist (*http://www/craigslist.org*). A popular site that posts listings from both small and large companies.

ExecuNet (*http://www.execunet.com*). Focuses on the $100,000+ executive. Offers executive-level resources, tips, information, and advice. Provides market trends, networking, and access to thousands of jobs.

Fast Company magazine (*http://www.fastcompany.com/*). An extensive online career center loaded with job search and career information. Check out "company of friends," a collection of 150 groups with 40,000 members for networking, online discussions, and so on.

FlipDog (*http://www.flipdog.com*). Offers a career center and resources such as expert advice, a semimonthly newsletter, and job searching 24/7. Permits researching thousands of employers. Neat feature for jobs around the world. Examples: figure painter in Great Britain, writers in Russia, nanny in Australia.

FreeAgent (*http://www.freeagent.com*). Targeted to consultants and freelancers. Provides gamut of services, information, and resources: personal 800 telephone number, voicemail, email address. Create an e-portfolio to let employers find you. Get an instant office, secretarial support, conference room facilities, and so on. Offers a bartering marketplace.

FutureStep (*http://www.futurestep.com/*). Executive search service for management professionals from Korn/Ferry International and the *Wall Street Journal.* Offers access to exclusive opportunities with companies worldwide. Fosters long-term career management relationship, including an assessment tool and feedback on best fits for industries and companies. Members can send résumés to companies.

Glocap Search (*http://www.glocap.com/*). Alternative asset search firm that recruits for VC firms, LBO funds, hedge funds, asset management firms, Fortune 1000 companies, and venture-backed start-ups.

Headhunter.net (*http://www.headhunter.net/*). Permits posting résumés, receiving information on jobs by email, searching for jobs by interest, and participating in online career fairs.

Heidrick and Struggles Management Search (*http://www.leadersonline.com*). Exclusive management and senior-level career opportunities. In partnership with BusinessWeek Online, offers extensive access to top employers, executive search firms, and venture capital companies.

HotJobs.com. (*http://www.hotjobs.com*). Top career site with jobs by industry or key word.

Jobs in the Money (*www.jobsinthemoney.com*). A job site dedicated to finance professionals interested in investment and commercial banks, Big 5 accounting firms, Fortune 500 and technology companies, and so on.

JobStar.org (*http://www.jobstar.org*). An excellent site, including information on the hidden job market, salary data, and *Wall Street Journal* stories on job hunting and career management. Searchable database of more than 30,000 middle- and senior-level positions, updated daily. Career centers and libraries for California and beyond. Personal electronic librarian to answer your questions.

Monster.com. (*http://www.monster.com*). Great "personal salary report" to find out your market value. Touts one million job postings. Can be used to research companies. Global network of experts and resources. Resources for self-employment or contract/temporary work.

MonsterTrak (*http://www.monsterTRAK.com/*). Used by 1000 college and university career centers, alumni associations, and MBA programs. Can be searched for jobs or internships. Offers a variety of job search tools. Offers employer showcase, career guides, helpful "major to career" converter, virtual interviews, career and alumni contacts, and a career advice library.

New York Times (*www.nytimes.com/jobs*). Great guide to how to use technology in job hunting; pointers to relevant web resources (online résumé preparation, work alternatives, networking in cyberspace, and so on). Job ads and collection of columns on careers.

SpencerStuart Talent Network (*http://www.spencerstuart.com, http://www.hunt-scanlon.com*). Valuable info on leaders on the move, industry statistics, and "best of the web" hot links to other Internet resources.

Top Careers (*http://www.topcareers.net*). An impressive site offering career and education information to top students and professionals worldwide. Lets you customize based on what career stage you are in. Information/resources for top universities and MBA programs, executive education, and career forums.

Appendix B

Résumé and Cover Letter Pointers

- Think about your résumé in two dimensions: content and style. The style centers on questions of formatting—whether you will use bullets or paragraphs, how you will show your dates (for example: right justified or in the left margin) and locations, and so on. The content is the substance of what you will write.
- Emphasize results and achievements. Quantify wherever possible.
- Stress skills, experience, and knowledge that are transferable to your current job search or career objective.
- Write dynamically and concisely. Make your résumé active and nonrepetitive.
- No *I, me my, the, a,* or *an.* These are eye "clutter."
- Remember that anything you bold, italicize, or capitalize will stand out to the reader, so make sure you use these options selectively.
- Watch out for other elements that can make your résumé look too busy, such as underlines, parentheses, and quotes. Try not to use these if you can help it.
- Make your résumé one page unless you have more than 15 years of experience. Then a two-page résumé is all right. Ideally use a 10- or 12-point font and one that is easy to read, such as Times New Roman, Arial, Architect, Garamond, or Palatino.
- Make every word count; don't fear white space and clean lines.
- Spell out names of cities, organizations, and countries; it is OK to use the postal abbreviations for states.
- Check meticulously for grammar and spelling. Let someone else who has a fresh pair of eyes and attention to detail read over it.

- Use action verbs.
- Develop problem/action/result (PAR) statements for the items on your résumé (see Principle 9).
- If you are changing industries, think about using a functional résumé rather than the more traditional reverse chronological résumé so that you can emphasize the skills, abilities, and knowledge that you have and the job you are seeking requires rather than your prior job titles, organizations, or industries.
- You don't want to include salary history or requirements, references, buzzwords or jargon, or reasons for termination.
- Don't include anything in the résumé that you would not want to be asked about or couldn't speak knowledgeably about.

Handling Common Résumé Problems

When to Use a Functional/Skills-Based Résumé

Use a functional résumé when you have different kinds of work experiences that don't seem to tie together or perhaps gaps in your employment. Figure out the common three to five skills that you used in all of your jobs. Use the ones that are most applicable to the jobs you are trying for. For example, if you are applying for marketing jobs, and in the past you worked as a financial analyst, a golf caddy, and a retail clerk in a computer store, you might use skill headings: Customer Knowledge and Service; P and L/ Financial Analysis, Creativity, Computer Skills, and Initiative. Then under each skill heading, list particular achievement statements from any of your jobs to show that you have that skill.

What's Best When You Are Changing Careers

When you are changing careers, it's a good idea to use a two- to three-sentence statement about yourself after your identification section. Usually this is centered so that it stands out. The purpose is to "set" your positioning with the recruiter before he/she starts reading the rest of your résumé.

For example, let's say that you have been in investment banking your entire career, but want to move into an operational role at a high-tech company. I might say: My investment banking work gave me valuable experience with a variety of high-tech companies and COOs. I worked closely with clients at all levels in operational roles. I used my strengths in analysis, problem solving, and financial management to understand their business and key challenges. My most enjoyable contribution was giving high-tech managers advice and ideas on their operational plans and measures for increased effectiveness.

Dealing With Gaps in Employment

Always make sure you are completely honest, however, you don't have to let a gap be a negative. If possible, note the gap, but give a short explanation for it. For example: Took six months off to care for terminally ill mother, or took one year off to try out for professional women's volleyball.

What to Do if You Have No Degree or One from an Unknown School

If you have no degree but have equivalent work experience, really emphasize your work experience section, showing that you possess the knowledge and skills required. List in the "additional info" section any training courses you have taken or self-initiated studies that are relevant to the job.

Example (if you have no degree): Studied operations and accounting through own initiative; participated in marketing seminars. Self-taught in finance through volunteer projects and various online courses.

If you went to a school whose name is not known, say something positive about it to give some context. If there is nothing you can say, then emphasize your activities by listing a few of them, or your academic standing if in the top 10 percent, or your thesis or fieldwork if it will help your candidacy.

Examples:
Mark Pearson School of Design
Leading school of fashion design in Northeast region for planet-friendly packaging and athletic apparel.

Rosalea Parella College
Oldest liberal arts college in Spain.

What to Do if You Have Worked for a Great Company but One That May Not Be Well Known

Add a brief description of it under the company's name.

Example:
Marketocracy
A visionary mutual fund management company that finds the best investors in the world by tracking the performance of more than 60,000 virtual portfolios. Recognized by *BusinessWeek* as one of the best.

Your job title would follow under the company name and description.

What to Do if You Did Not Have a Formal Job Title

Within the boundaries of being honest and not glorifying what you were actually responsible for, it's OK to create a title that reflects what you really did for the company. If in doubt and you are out in the open with your boss about doing a résumé, run it by him or her. It will be better for when he or she may be a reference for you as well.

Examples would be: "project manager," "operations manager," "HR assistant," or "team leader." You could also take the focus off a title and instead emphasize what functions/responsibilities you performed.

Example: Performed in a variety of roles as company's needs changed. Responsible for key activities including web site design, purchasing, HR administration, and HR/office management.

Cover Letter Outline

Before you begin writing your cover letter, ask yourself the following questions and jot down your thoughts.

Who? Who am I (in one sentence), and to whom I am writing? Think about the person to whom you are writing. How did I get his or her name? What are his or her job responsibilities, title, educational background, and demographics (age, gender, and so on)?

Why? Why am I writing now, and why should this person be interested in me? What would intrigue her or him and motivate her or him to consider me?

What? What do I have to offer? From my research, what are two or three needs or challenges that this industry or this specific organization has or faces? What strengths, experience, or knowledge do I have that will help it meet those?

When? When will my letter be read? How long will I give before following up? When is presumably the best day or time for this person's schedule?

How? How will the person feel about my letter based on my tone? How will I differentiate myself so as not to sound like everyone else? How will I intrigue the reader with what I have to say?

For more ideas and specific advice on résumés and cover letters, refer to: *www.wetfeet.com*, articles by S. Taguchi, "Résumé Makeovers: How to Standout from the Crowd" and "Get Results with Your Cover Letter." These include tips, examples, a worksheet, how to deal with common résumé problems and a list of 2003 action verbs.

Appendix C

Values-Based Questions for Evaluating Organizations

Intrinsic Values

What are the company's vision, mission, and purpose?

How are priorities decided on? What are the company's priorities?

What are the company's views on family commitments?

What programs and policies are there that support people with families?

What do you like and dislike about the organization?

How does the organization value women and people of color?

Can people be terrible managers and still be valued?

How open are people with bad news, problems, or other information?

What is the ideal profile for a top candidate for this job?

What would someone doing a bad job be doing?

Where do people go from here—what are ideas for various career paths?

What do you like most and least about your work?

How are resources allocated here?

Describe a huge accomplishment that someone in the group recently achieved.

Is it better to be fast or thorough if you can't be both?

What's a typical day or week for you like?

Are there seasons or cycles to the work flow? What are the highlights of each?

Describe the work environment here.
How do people feel about the organization?
How do people dress?
How long are typical days?
How do people celebrate successes?
How do people handle failures or mistakes?

Work Relationship Values

Do people work more in teams and collaboratively or individually?
To what extent do people do things together after work?
How easy is it to ask for help or resources?
Is consensus valued?
Do people challenge each other?
How is conflict handled?
How are differences of opinion handled?
Describe the politics that go on here. Can you cite a confidential example?
What examples are there of different groups working together?
How do the CEO and the executives interact with others?
What about internal competition? How do people compete with each other?
Are people most loyal to the company, their work groups, or themselves?

Expanded by Sherrie Gong Taguchi from *Values-Based Work Assessment Inventory,* Career Action Center, Cupertino, California, 1995.

Appendix D

Compensation Negotiation Tip Sheet and Resources

Here are additional tips and techniques for approaching your negotiations.

- Know yourself. This is a theme we keep coming back to. Then do your homework thoroughly. What do you need, which is different from what you might want? Refer back to Principle 4 to focus on your views on money, budgets, and personal finance. For the decisions at hand, think through the following issues:
- What is your walk-away, your absolute, minimum?
- What are some things that would be nice to have but that you might be willing to give up?
- What are some trade-offs that you are willing and able to make?
- Know whom you'll be dealing with and her or his mindset and style. How much latitude will this person have? Is she or he the decision maker or a broker? What could really make this person angry or stop the process? What would make you walk away? How can you negotiate as though you are on the same side of the table, continuing to build a good relationship, but achieving what is important to you?

Helpful Resources

The best bets for information are the following sources:

- People inside the industry or those in the actual organization. They can give you the straight scoop on the company's compensation philosophy, the components of compensation, and where you might have flexibility to negotiate.

- Selected web sites that will help you in understanding the going rates for the industry, function, and location. Review the industry and company research sites listed in Principle 9. Also, visit the company's web site and review its job postings and the compensation ranges. Study the top five competitors' web sites and do the same.
- Salary.com's salary wizard (*http://www.salary.com*). This shows market rates for numerous functions and industries in different locations.
- Other web sites, including
  - *http://homeadvisor.msn.com/pickaplace/comparecities.asp*. This site lets you compare cities by such dimensions as cost of living, school ratings, and crime rate.
  - *http://www.wetfeet.com/research/newsletters.asp*. This site lets you learn about compensation trends in various industries and fields.

Excerpted from: Sherrie Gong Taguchi, *Hiring the Best and the Brightest* (New York, NY: American Management Association – AMACOM Books, 2001), pp. 91–105 on compensation components, employers' perspectives on structuring offers, and negotiation talking points.

Appendix E

Getting It Right: Due Diligence and Entry Strategy

After you have received offers, here are some additional questions to ask before you make your decision on which to accept.

Your objectives in this final "due diligence" phase are: to fill in any information gaps you need to for making your best decision among the job options you have and to begin to transition yourself—set yourself up—for effective entry into your new organization.

Ask the Person Making You the Offer

1. What's the time frame for getting back to you?
2. What is your ideal time line for the start date—earliest and latest?
3. When will you be sending the formal offer letter? *Note:* If the company does not send such a letter, you could follow up with an email outlining what was discussed with you as a way of confirming it more informally, or—although some would disagree—I'd say trust the company and keep going based on your conversations while waiting for the letter. Some HR groups just don't send offer letters until after the offers are accepted.
4. If I have follow-up questions or requests, are you the best person to contact?

Find Out from Your Hiring Manager

1. What's your management style? How do you make decisions? How do you like to communicate? To lead people?
2. What do you see as the group's top priorities?
3. What are some things that it's important for me to know if I come aboard—what will make or break whether I'm effective and acclimate well?
4. How do you measure success for yourself?
5. How do you reward your people?
6. What's your view on developing people? Are there any examples that you are particularly proud of?
7. What's the worst thing that someone new could do coming into the group?
8. What do you see as the top three goals or objectives for my job? What are the metrics that you use to evaluate them and my performance?
9. How will my job performance be measured? How is the bonus structured—what percentage is based on individual performance, and what on the company's? What have been the general ranges of payouts over the past few years?
10. What are your ideas for how my role could evolve? What other opportunities would be logical or creative next moves?

Listen and Learn After You've Accepted the Job

I'd still like more information on x, y, and z—are there alumni from my school or some other people that you could put me in touch with?

11. Are there alumni from my school that I could contact? (*Or*, are there individuals who have been in this job for the past year or so with whom I could speak?)
12. Are there any upcoming events that I could participate in? For example, are there upcoming company events (e.g., an all-hands meeting, a company happy hour or gathering, a town hall with the CEO) that I could attend? (This is to get to know the company, the people, and the culture in more depth.)

13. Of those who have joined you and done really, really well, what was their entry strategy—what did they particularly pay attention to that helped them make the transition into the organization well and be effective quickly?
14. Are there things that I could be doing before I start to be better prepared?
15. How can I best ensure starting off on the right foot?

- Can you give me the names of some recent hires who integrated into the culture quickly and were productive fairly fast? I'd like to contact them, if you don't mind. Prepare your entry strategy. *Use what you've learned.* From asking your due diligence questions and the discussions with those in the organization, note the common themes about what they did to transition effectively into the organization. Pay special attention to what mistakes they made or regrets they have.
- *Stay connected.* If you won't start work for a month or more, communicate periodically with your new manager, team, or others with whom you've developed good relationships during the recruiting process. Brief emails or telephone calls will do. This will help you stay on their minds so THEY can prepare for you. It also shows your enthusiasm for starting.
- *Focus on those 5 C's.* Refer to Principle 10's discussion on the 5 C's for successful entry into a new organization. Think about in advance how you will gain a sense of the 5 C's—both formally and informally—and how you can apply them to transition effectively into your new job and organization.
- Give and receive feedback. In the crucial first 90 days in your new role, get feedback from your manager on how you are doing and how you can improve. Also, offer feedback on what you need to perform your best.
- Remember there will be missteps along the way. Try to remember, it's not how hard you fall, it's how high you can bounce.

Source: Longer versions appear in S. Taguchi, "Getting Set for Success—New Hire Orientations and the First 90 Days," *HR Magazine*, Society of Human Resource Management, the EMA Report, May/June 2002 and "What to Say When It's Your Turn to Ask Questions in An Interview," *www.wetfeet.com*, 2001.

Notes

Principle 1: Know Yourself

1. John Cook, *The Book of Positive Quotations* (Minneapolis: Fairview Press, 1993).
2. Adapted from various works, including Karen O. Dowd, "How to Really Assess Yourself," *BusinessWeek's Guide to Careers,* 1986.
3. An excellent tool for identifying skills, "Skill Card Sort," can be found through Career Research and Testing, Richard Knowdell, president, San Jose, California. Also see Barrie Hopson, *Career Builder, U.S. Edition,* ed. Karen Dowd and Tom S. Dowd (Leeds, England: Lifeskills Associates, 1986); Bernard Haldane, *Career Satisfaction and Success (Seattle: Wellness Behavior, 1993)*; and Howard E. Figler, *PATH (Sulzberger & Graham Publishing Co., 1993).*
4. Exercise adapted from David Bloom and Gary Villani, The Empower Group, New York, competency modeling presentation, 2002.
5. D. C. McClelland, "Achievement Motivation Can Be Developed," *Harvard Business Review* 43 (1965): 6–24.
6. See, for example, works by Maury Peiperl, who has studied 360-degree feedback for a decade (as mentioned in *Harvard Business Review,* January 2001).
7. Donald E. Super, *The Psychology of Careers* (New York: Harper & Row, 1957). Super expanded on his theory in 1980; see Donald E. Super, "A Life-Span, Life-Space Approach to Career Development," *Journal of Vocational Behavior* 13 (1980): 282–298.
8. Philip H. Mirvis and Douglas T. Hall, "Psychological Success and the Boundaryless Career," in Michael B. Arthur and Denise M. Rousseau, eds., *The Boundaryless Career* (Oxford: Oxford University Press, 1996).

9. Yourdictionary.com, *Merriam-Webster's Collegiate* (Merriam-Webster, 2002).

10. Adapted from R. Harvey Campbell, "Forbes Financial Glossary," Forbes.com.

11. Michael J. Driver, Kenneth R. Brousseau, and Philip L. Hunsaker, *The Dynamic Decision Maker* (San Francisco: Jossey-Bass, 1993).

12. A. H. Maslow, *Motivation and Personality* (New York: Harper & Row, 1954).

13. Edgar H. Schein, "How Career Anchors Hold Executives to Their Career Paths," *Personnel* 52 (1975): 11–24. See also Edgar H. Schein, "Career Anchors Revised: Implications for Career Development in the 21st Century," *Academy of Management Executive* 10 (1996): 80–88. See also *Career Management Seminar,* J. Beirne, K. Dowd, R. Muller, R. Scalise and N. Schretter (Vienna, VA: 1993) and Karen O. Dowd and Susan Doughty, "Know Thyself, Know Thy Market," *MBA Employment Guide* (Association of MBA Executives, 1986).

14. Douglas T. Hall, *Careers in Organizations* (Glenview, Ill.: Scott, Foresman, 1976), 201. For more information on protean careers, see the Career Orientation Index being developed by Douglas T. Hall and Jon J. Briscoe. The index is available from Douglas T. Hall, Boston University. For further self-assessments related to this topic, see Douglas T. Hall, *Careers In and Out of Organizations* (Newbury Park, Calif.: SAGE Publications, 2002). In particular, see the set of principles for organizations to follow in doing career development. See also p. 296 for steps for individuals and pp. 298–299 for further self-assessment questions. More assessments can be obtained in D. D. Bowen, R. J. Lewicki, D. T. Hall, and F. S. Hall, *Experiences in Management and Organization Behavior* (New York: Wiley, 1997), pp. 289–299, 294–300, and 307–313.

15. D. M. Cable and Jeffrey R. Edwards, "Value Congruence and Value Fulfillment as Competing Predictors of Work-Related Outcomes," working paper, Kenan-Flagler Business School, University of North Carolina, Raleigh-Durham.

16. Barrie Hopson and Mike Scully, *Lifeskills Teaching* (London, England: McGraw-Hill, 1981).

17. Adapted from an exercise that first appeared in Suzanne C. de Janasz, Karen O. Dowd, and Beth Z. Schneider, *Interpersonal Skills in Organizations* (Burr Ridge, Ill.: McGraw-Hill/Higher Education, 2002).

18. A longer version of this appears in Karen O. Dowd, "Preparing for Interviews," in Robert Greenberg, ed., *Career Planning Course*, an online resource available on the MonsterTrak.com web site, 2001. Another excellent resource is Sherrie Gong Taguchi, "Guide to Surviving and Thriving in a Tough Job Market" (*http://www.WetFeet.com*, 2001–2003). Series of articles on job search skills, career changing, and lifetime career management. In particular, see: "Ten Executives Discuss What They're Looking for When They Interview Candidates," "Decoding the Interview and Evaluation Process," and "How to Find a Great Job in a Weak Market."

19. Originally appeared in Karen O'Neil and Julie Johnson, *Career Development Center Manual* (Notre Dame, Ind.: Saint Mary's College, 1974).

Principle 2: Bounce Back from Setbacks

1. Quoted in an interview with reporter Catherine Saint Louis, *New York Times*, Dec. 9, 2001.

2. Daniel Goleman, "What Makes a Leader?" *Harvard Business Review*, November–December 1989.

3. Robert E. Kelley, *How to Be a Star at Work* (New York: Times Business/Random House, 1999). Cited in Karen O. Dowd, "Competencies for Effectiveness," *The International MBA Newsletter* (Floral Park, N.Y.: Kwartler Communications, Fall 1998). See also *The San Francisco Chronicle*, "*Workers' Dozen*" feature articles, January – December 2002. Advice and how to handle common career problems, Dave Murphy (editor), Sherrie Gong Taguchi and a panel of 10 other career experts.

4. An excellent resource to help you assess your level of engagement or disengagement with your job can be found in James G. Clawson

and Mark E. Haskins, "Beating the Career Blues," 2000, available from the authors, Darden Graduate School of Business, University of Virginia. See also E.H. Schein, *Career Dynamics* (Reading, MA: Addison-Wesley, 1978).

5. With appreciation to Jim Beirne, former director of staffing for General Mills, Inc., and Kathryn Van Ness, University of California at Irvine, who presented this at the National Association of Colleges and Employers National Conference, May 2002.

6. Michael B. Arthur, Priscilla H. Claman, Robert J. DeFillippi, and Jerome Adams, "Intelligent Enterprise, Intelligent Careers," *The Academy of Management Executive*, Ada, November 1995.

7. Philip H. Mirvis and Douglas T. Hall, "Psychological Success and the Boundaryless Career," in Michael B. Arthur and Denise M. Rousseau, eds., *The Boundaryless Career* (Oxford: Oxford University Press, 1996).

Principle 3: Take Measured Risk

1. Yoram Wind, quoted in Keith H. Hammonds, "No Risk, No Reward," *Fast Company*, April 2002, 86–90.

2. With special appreciation to Agnes Le, Stanford MBA, class of 2000 for her background research and sample illustrations for this principle.

3. Frank H. Knight, *Risk, Uncertainty, and Profit* (Boston: Houghton Mifflin, 1921).

4. William H. Beaver and George G. C. Parker, *Risk Management Problems and Solutions* (New York: McGraw-Hill, 1995).

5. Yourdictionary.com, *Merriam-Webster's Collegiate* (Merriam-Webster, 2002).

6. Definitions have been adapted from Forbes Financial Glossary, Forbes.com and Investorwords.com.

7. Adapted also from "Recruiting Trends, Themes, and Best/Worst Practices," led by Sherrie Gong Taguchi, International Placement Directors Conference in collaboration with Harvard Business School, Paris, July 2001.

8. Originally developed for this book by Sherrie Gong Taguchi, London, England, 2001–2002. Based on industry experience and research coaching executives and managers.
9. John N. Celona, *The Manual – Decision Advisor*, 3 vols. (Menlo Park, Calif.: Strategic Decisions Group, 1998). John N. Celona, *Decision Analysis for the Professional* (Redwood City, Calif.: The Scientific Press, 1990).
10. Charles Handy, *Age of Unreason* (Cambridge, Mass.: Harvard Business School Press, 1993).

Principle 4: Put Money in Perspective

1. Special thanks to Diana Chan, Founder and Principal of Chan CPA & Company of Los Gatos, CA and Ken Kam, CEO, Marketocracy and the Masters 100 Mutual Fund of Los Altos, CA for providing tools, templates, and advice on budgeting and financial planning.

Principle 5: Make People a Priority

1. John Cook, *The Book of Positive Quotations* (Minneapolis: Fairview Press, 1993).
2. "Getting Hired," chart in Kemba J. Dunham, "The Jungle," *Wall Street Journal*, July 10, 2001, B8.
3. Sherrie Gong Taguchi, "Getting a Great Job in a Weak Market," "Ten Creative Places to Find the Hidden Jobs," and "Keeping Up Your Job Search Momentum (When It's in Overtime)," (*http://www.WetFeet.com*, 2001–2003).
4. For more about expanding your network, see Karen O. Dowd, "Creative Job Search Strategies," *BusinessWeek Careers How to Get a Job Guide*, 1985; "Contacts: How to Make Them, How to Use Them," *BusinessWeek Careers How to Get a Job Guide*, 1986; and Karen O. Dowd, "Job Search Strategies for Executives," *BusinessWeek Guide to Careers*, 1987.

5. For more on the important subject of career development for minorities, see David Thomas and Monica Higgins, "Mentoring and the Boundaryless Career," in Michael B. Arthur and Denise M. Rousseau, eds., *The Boundaryless Career* (Oxford: Oxford University Press, 1996).

6. Richard N. Bolles, *What Color Is Your Parachute?* (Berkeley: Ten Speed Press, 1994).

7. Kathy E. Kram, "A Relational Approach to Career Development," in Arthur and Rousseau, *The Boundaryless Career.* For additional insights into dual-career issues from an organizational perspective see Karen O. Dowd, "Dual Career Assistance Programs," *Journal of Career Planning and Employment,* winter 1987.

8. Sherrie Gong Taguchi, *Hiring the Best and the Brightest* (New York: American Management Association, 2001), pp. 241–264. Discussion on best practices from Bertelsmann, Goldman Sachs, Hewlett-Packard, and McKinsey and Co. and other executives on what companies are doing to develop and keep top talent and how employees can initiate continuous learning and development for themselves.

Principle 6: Plan Ahead—Now!

1. *The Book of Positive Quotations* (Minneapolis: Fairview Press, 1993).

2. Adapted from Karen O. Dowd and Peter E. Veruki, "How to Take Control of Your Job Offers. Are You Ready to Accept?" *Careers and the College Graduate* (*BusinessWeek Guide to Careers,* 1987). See also: K. Dowd, R. Morrow, N. Kessler, E. Polak, and E. Smallman, *Career Management Manuals* (Darden Graduate School of Business, University of Virginia, 1985–1994).

3. Adapted from an exercise conducted at Saint Mary's College, Notre Dame, Indiana, by Dr. Kathleen Rice, and from Beverly Anderson, "How Do You Decide?" Cooperative Extension Service Bulletin, Michigan State University.

Principle 7: Enjoy Your Life and Sustain Your Career

1. Ideas of renowned architect Bill McDonough, as described in Susan Susanka with Kira Obolensky, *The Not So Big House* (Newtown, Conn.: The Taunton Press, 1998), 182.
2. Kevin W. McCarthy, *The On-Purpose Person* (Colorado Springs, Colo.: Pinon Books, 1992).
3. Karen O. Dowd, "Career Concerns of Tenure-Track Faculty," unpublished dissertation, University of Virginia, 1993.
4. See Sherrie Taguchi, *Hiring the Best and the Brightest* (New York: American Management Association, 2001), pp. 243 and 251, for organizational culture questions that can be adapted and researched for career exploration and a job search.
5. The Empower Group, New York, proprietary client research study in which "managing change" was one of eight competencies deemed essential by employers of college graduates.
6. Adapted from activity conducted by Suzanne Brigham at Saint Mary's College, Notre Dame, Indiana. Appears in Suzanne de Janasz, Karen O. Dowd, and Beth Z. Schneider, *Interpersonal Skills in Organizations* (Burr Ridge, Ill.: McGraw-Hill/Higher Education, 2002).
7. Nancy E. Bell and Barry M. Staw, "People as Sculptors versus Sculpture: The Roles of Personality and Personal Control in Organizations," in Michael B. Arthur, Douglas T. Hall, and Barbara S. Lawrence, eds., *Handbook of Career Theory* (Cambridge, England: Cambridge University Press, 1989).
8. Karl E. Weick and Lisa R. Berlinger, "Career Improvisation in Self-Designing Organizations," in Arthur, Hall, and Lawrence, 1989.

Principle 8: Give Yourself a Break

1. Michael B. Arthur and Denise M. Rousseau, *The Boundaryless Career* (Oxford: Oxford University Press, 1996).
2. Adapted from Sherrie Gong Taguchi, various sources: executive development work and employee career coaching while at

Bank of America, Dole Packaged Foods, and Mervyn's Department Stores, 1983—1995.

3. Expanded from Sherrie Gong Taguchi, "Reality Bytes" work life skills seminars, Stanford Graduate School of Business, 1997, and research for speech, "Managing Your Career for a Lifetime and Is Now the Time for an MBA?," including original concept: Maslow's Hierarchy of Needs and Their Career Metaphors, Professional Business Women of California Conference, Santa Clara, Calif., 2001.

Principle 9: Just Do It

1. Based on career management seminars, Sherrie Gong Taguchi, Stanford University Graduate School of Business and Karen O. Dowd, Darden Graduate School of Business, University of Virginia. Adapted for book by S. Taguchi, 2001.

2. A concept and MBA course developed and taught by Professor Jeffrey Pfeffer, Stanford Business School, Palo Alto, California.

3. Expanded from various works including, "A Guide to Researching Industries, Companies, and Functions," B. Scott, U. Kremer, F. Noble, and S. Taguchi, *Stanford Graduate School of Business*, 1995–2001. Two excellent sources are Sherrie Taguchi, *Hiring the Best and the Brightest* (full cite Principle 5 above), "Leveraging the Internet for Your Job Search and Top 30 Web Sites," pp. 230– 249, and "Top Pick Web Sites for MBAs and A-List Talent," *www.Wetfeet.com.*

4. Another excellent resource for researching functions and industries is C. Randall Powell, *Career Planning Today* (Dubuque Kendall-Hunt Publishing Co., 2000).

5. Expanded from S. Taguchi presentation in collaboration with Harvard Business School: "Recruiting Trends, Themes, and Best/Worst Practices," International Placement Directors Conference, Paris, France 2001; Student Guidebooks 1995—2001, Stanford Graduate School of Business, MBA Career Management

Center, with Uta Kremer, Fran Noble, Charlotte Carter, Becky Scott, and Liliane Baxter.

6. Based on Philip Kotler's 5-P Framework used for corporate marketing strategy. Philip Kotler, *A Framework for Marketing Management,* 2d ed., Prentice Hall College Division. Adapted to career context by Sherrie Gong Taguchi. First introduced in speech "Marketing Yourself Using the 5 Ps for Job Searches," University of California, Berkeley, 1984. Updated in "Reality Bytes," a work life skills series of workshops, "Managing Your Career Inside and Outside the Organization," Stanford School of Business, 1997.

7. Originally appeared in Sherrie Gong Taguchi, "Winning Résumés and Repositioning Yourself in the Marketplace," presentation, Stanford University Asian Staff Forum, 2001.

8. Expanded from Sherrie Gong Taguchi, "When It's Your Turn to Ask Questions," and "Eleven Executives Discuss What They Are Looking For When They Interview Candidates," research and a feature article on favorite interviewing questions and approaches representing companies such as General Mills, Del Monte Foods, Bain & Co., Booz, Allen, and Hamilton, and the San Mateo City Library. *www.WetFeet.com,* 2001.

9. Adapted from an original concept from the Career Action Center, Cupertino, California. Values card sort self-assessment tool is used by organizations for effective teamwork and dealing with conflict in work groups and by individuals in their career exploration and career changing, 1995.

10. For additional information, see Sherrie Gong Taguchi, "Acing Your Interviews," "Finding a Great Job in a Weak Job Market," "Seven Tips for Smarter Compensation Negotiation," and other articles on *www.WetFeet.com.*

11. Sherrie Gong Taguchi, *Hiring the Best and the Brightest* (New York: AMACOM, 2001), "15 Extraordinary Executives Share Their Interviewing Lessons Learned," pp. 54–76.

12. An excellent resource is Sherrie Gong Taguchi, *Hiring the Best and the Brightest,* AMACOM Books, 2001, New York, pp. 91–106. Particularly refer to sections: "Foundational Knowledge: What is Total Compensation," "A Macro View: External Considerations,"

"A Micro View: Internal Considerations," "Down to Business: Elements of the Negotiation," "Compensation Resources and Experts." Also see Karen O. Dowd and Denise Skinner, "Salary Negotiation for Women MBAs," Crimson and Brown Publications, Cambridge, Mass., 1998.

13. Based on various work by S. Taguchi, including hands-on experience as hiring manager and head of recruiting in industry and presentation: "Understanding Your Values and Negotiating Your Best Compensation Package" seminar for the Stanford Graduate School of Business Alumni Women's Conference, 1997.

14. The 7-S framework is McKinsey's model for strategy development in companies. Thomas J. Peters and Robert H. Waterman, Jr., *In Search of Excellence* (New York: Warner Books, 1982).

Principle 10: Own Your Career

1. Framework developed by Sherrie Gong Taguchi used for new hire orientations and coaching executives to integrate effectively into a new company. (Bank of America, Dole Packaged Foods, and Mervyn's Department Stores, 1983 – 1995.) Another excellent resource is "Getting Set for Success—New Hire Orientations and the First 90 Days," *HR Magazine*, Society of Human Resource Management, The Employment Management Report, May/June 2002.

2. Sylvia Ann Hewlett, *Baby Hunger: The New Battle for Motherhood* (New York: Hyperion, 2002).

3. Expanded from various works by S. Taguchi: speeches for the Professional Business Women of California Conference, contributions to *The San Francisco Chronicle*'s "Workers Dozen" career advice columns, and "Keeping Top Talent in Good and Tough Times . . . 7Cs Retention Strategies" (National Association of Colleges of Employers, Fall Journal, 2001), a study on what companies can do to keep their employees motivated and what individuals can do for themselves to keep developing.

Index